Mastering Excel VBA Programming

A Hands-On Guide to Automating Excel and Building Custom Solutions with VBA and Macros

Nathan George

Mastering Excel VBA Programming: A Hands-On Guide to Automating Excel and Building Custom Solutions with VBA and Macros

Copyright © 2025 by Nathan George

All rights reserved. The right of Nathan George to be identified as the author of this work has been asserted by him in accordance with the Copyright, Designs and Patents Act, 1988. It is illegal to copy, distribute, or create derivative works from this book in whole or in part or to contribute to the copying, distribution, or creating of derivative works of this book.

Disclaimer: Every effort has been made in the preparation of this book to ensure the accuracy of the information presented. However, the information in this book is sold without warranty, either express or implied. Neither the author nor publishers will be held liable for any damages caused or alleged to have been caused directly or indirectly by this book or from the use of the programs accompanying it.

Published 2025.

Published by GTech Publishing.

ISBN: 978-1-915476-14-2

https://www.excelbytes.com

Contents

Introduction 19
    Who Is This Book For? 20
    How to Use This Book 20
    Assumptions 21
    Sample Files and Source Code 21

Chapter 1: Introduction to VBA 22
    What You Can Do With VBA 23
    What to Consider Before Using VBA 25
    The Difference Between Excel Macros and VBA 26

Chapter 2: Recording and Running Macros 27
    Displaying the Developer Tab... 28
    Where to Store Macros and VBA Code 30
        Storing Code in the Personal Macro Workbook 31
        Storing Code in a Macro-Enabled Workbook 32
        Storing Code in a Workbook Template.. 32
            Saving a Workbook as a Template 33
            Creating A Workbook from a Template 34
    Starting the Macro Recorder... 35

Contents

Relative versus Absolute Reference Macros 36
Example: Recording a Macro 37
    Running the Macro 40
    Viewing and Saving the Macro 41
Assigning a Macro to a Button on the Ribbon 44
    Step1: Create a New Custom Tab and Group 44
    Step 2: Assign a Macro Command to the New Group 45
Assigning a Macro to a Button on the Quick Access Toolbar 47
Assigning a Macro to an Image 48
Assigning a Macro to a Button on the Worksheet 49
    Formatting Form Controls 51
Macro Security 51
    Trust Center Macro Settings 52
    Trusted Locations 54
    Adding a Trusted Location 56

Chapter 3: Understanding The Visual Basic Editor 59

Visual Basic Editor Overview 60
The Project Explorer Window 63
    Inserting a New Module 64
    Renaming a Module 65
    Removing a Module 65
    Importing and Exporting VBA Objects 66
Using the Code Window 67
    Opening a Code Window 67
    Resizing a Code Window 68
    Arranging Multiple Code Windows 69
    The Object Box 69

The Procedures/Events Box	70
Splitting the Code Window	70
Switching Between Code Windows	71
Full Module View and Procedure View	71
Entering a Procedure in the Code Window	72

Other Code Navigation Features 74
- Finding Text 74
- Replacing Text 76
- Finding Items with the Object Browser 77
- Viewing a Called Procedure 78
- Using Bookmarks 78

Documenting and Formatting Code 80
- Indenting 80
- Adding Comments 81
- Using the Line-Continuation Character 82

Customizing the VBA Environment 83

Customizing the Toolbar 89

Chapter 4: VBA Essentials 92

Variables and Data Types 93
- Variable Data Types 93
- Variable Naming Guidelines 94
  - Variable Naming Rules 94
  - Conventions for Naming Variables 95
- Declaring Variables 95
- Using Option Explicit 97
- Assigning Values to Variables 100
- Scope of Variables 102
  - Local Variables 102

| Module Variables 102

| Public Variables 103

| Lifetime of a Variable 103

| Using Static Variables 104

| Using String Variables 105

| Using Date Variables 105

| Using Constants 106

| Operators in VBA 108

| Arithmetic Operators 108

| Concatenation 108

| Comparison Operators 109

| Logical Operators 109

| Operator Precedence 110

| Parentheses and Operator Precedence 111

| Built-In VBA Functions 112

| The MsgBox Function 112

| Displaying a Simple Message Box 113

| Getting a Response from Users 115

| Using vbNewLine or vbCrLf 118

| The InputBox Function 118

| Other Useful Built-in VBA Functions 120

Chapter 5: Using Arrays 124

Declaring Arrays 125

Changing Array Bounds 126

Using LBound and UBound 127

Populating an Array 127

Multidimensional Arrays 129

Dynamic Arrays 132

Declaring Dynamic Arrays 132
Preserving the Contents of Dynamic Arrays 133
Using the Array Function 135
Scope of Arrays 136

Chapter 6: Working with Procedures 137

General Procedures 138
Procedure Naming Rules 139
Sub Procedures 139
Running a Sub Procedure 140
From Excel's Interface 140
In the Visual Basic Editor 141
From Another Procedure 141
Function Procedures 143
Calling a Function Procedure 144
Overview of Event Procedures 147

Chapter 7: Controlling Program Flow 148

If...Then...Else 149
Select Case 151
Do...Loop 152
Breaking an Endless Loop 154
For...Next 155
For Each...Next 158
Looping Through Collections 158
Looping Through an Array 161

Chapter 8: Debugging 162

Overview of Debugging 163

Contents

Debugging Tools in VBA 164
Break Mode 165
    Setting a Breakpoint 166
    Displaying the Margin Indicator 168
    Stepping Through Code Execution 169
Using the Immediate Window 170
    Using the Debug.Print Statement 172
Using the Locals Window 174
Using the Watch Window... 175
    Watch Expressions 176
    Adding a Watch Expression 176
    Editing or Deleting a Watch Expression 178
The Call Stack 179

Chapter 9: Handling Runtime Errors 181

Understanding Runtime Errors 182
On Error Statement 184
Resume Options 186
The Err Object 188
Inline Error Handling 190
Passing Back Errors 191
The Raise Method 191

Chapter 10: Introducing Excel Objects 194

Overview of Objects 195
    Object Properties, Methods, and Events 196
    Advantages of Objects 196
    Object Library References 197

The Excel Object Model 198
The Hierarchy of Objects.. 198
Navigating the Object Hierarchy... 200
Setting Properties and Calling Methods 202
Setting Object Properties 203
Calling Object Methods 203
Using the With Statement with Objects 206
Using Object Variables 207
Triggering Object Events 207
Using the Object Browser.. 208
Using Auto List Members with Objects 210

The Application Object 212
Using Worksheet Functions from VBA 212
Working with the Active Object... 213

Chapter 11: Working with Workbooks 215
The Workbook Object... 216
Opening a Workbook... 216
Adding a New Workbook 217
Referencing a Workbook 217
Saving a Workbook 218
Closing a Workbook 219

Workbook Events 220
Adding Code to Workbook Events... 221
Order of Workbook Events 222
Open Event 223
Activate and Deactivate Events 225
BeforeClose Event 226
BeforePrint Event 226

NewSheet Event.. 227

Chapter 12: Working with Worksheets 228

The Worksheet Object 229

Adding a New Worksheet 230
Naming a Worksheet 231
Activating a Worksheet 232
Deleting a Worksheet 233

Worksheet Events 233

Activate and Deactivate Events 234
Calculate Event 235
Change Event 235

Practice: Working With Worksheets 237

Chapter 13: Working with Range Objects 240

Returning a Range Object 241

Referencing a Range at Design Time 241
Cells Property 242
Rows and Columns Properties 242
Range Property 243
Resizing and Repositioning a Range 244
Selection Property 244
CurrentRegion Property 245
Offset Property 246
Resize Property 247
Range Selection versus Direct Referencing 249
Practice: Returning a Range Object 251

Using a Range Object 255

Formatting a Range 256

Using a Preformatted Template File 258
Overview of Formula Referencing 258
　A1 Reference versus R1C1 Reference 259
　Absolute versus Relative Referencing 259
　Using A1 Referencing Style 260
　Using the R1C1 Referencing Style 261
Entering Values and Formulas 262
　Value Property 262
　Formula2 Property 263
　Formula2R1C1 Property 263
　Address Property 264
　AutoFill Method 266
Practice: Working with a Range Object 268
Defining Named Ranges 271
　The Scope of Named Ranges 271
　Defining a Name Manually 272
　Defining a Name Programmatically 273

Chapter 14: UserForms 276

Introduction to UserForms 277
　Examining an Input Box Example 277
Inserting a new UserForm 280
　Running a UserForm 281
　　Running a UserForm From the Visual Basic Editor 281
　　Displaying a UserForm Programmatically 281
　Closing a UserForm 282
The Properties Window 283
　Setting UserForm Properties 284
UserForm Controls 286

Contents

The Control Toolbox 286
Adding Controls to a UserForm 289
Setting Control Properties 290
    Setting Control Properties at Design Time 291
        Control Naming Rules and Conventions 292
        Naming Controls 292
    Setting Control Properties at Runtime 293
        Using a With statement to Set Control Properties 293
    Returning Control Properties At Runtime 294
Arranging Controls on a UserForm 294
    Selecting Multiple Controls 294
    Aligning, Sizing, and Positioning Controls 295
    Changing the Tab Order 297
    Assigning Accelerator Keys 298
Basic Controls in the Toolbox 299
    Label 300
    TextBox 302
    CommandButton 303
    ComboBox 304
    ListBox 306
    OptionButton 307
    Frame 309

Practice: Creating a Dialog Box 310

Understanding UserForm Events 314
Common UserForm Events 314
Initializing Controls at Runtime 316

Understanding Control Events 317
Adding Code to Control Event Procedures 318
Changing the Name of a Control 319

Contents

Practice: Adding Events to a UserForm 320
    Providing Access to the UserForm in Excel 322
        Creating a Macro to Open the UserForm 323
        Assigning a Shortcut Key 323
        Creating a Button in the Quick Access Toolbar 325
    Testing the UserForm 327
Practice: Room Booking Form 329
    Inserting a new UserForm 330
    Adding Controls to the UserForm 330
    Entering Code to Initialize the UserForm 331
    Adding Event Procedures to the Controls 333
    Designing the Worksheet to Store the Data 336
    Providing Access to the UserForm 337
    Testing the UserForm 339
    Adding Data Validation 341
    Testing the Data Validation Routine 344

Chapter 15: Using Built-In Dialog Boxes 345

GetOpenFilename 346
GetSaveAsFilename 350
The FileDialog Object 352
Displaying Ribbon Dialog Boxes 356

Chapter 16: Working with Excel Form Controls 359

Introduction to Form Controls 360
    Naming a Form Control 360
    Preparing the Data List 361
List Box Example 363
Combo Box Example 367

xiii

Spin Button Example 370

Option Button Example 374

Chapter 17: Accessing External Data with ADO 380

Where to Store Data 381

Storing Data in Excel 381

Excel Versus Relational Databases 382

Working with Data 383

Manually Importing External Data 383

Using ActiveX Data Objects (ADO) 384

Overview of ADO 384

Overview of OLE DB 385

Data Consumers 386

Service Components 387

Data Providers 387

The ADO Object Model 387

The Connection Object 388

The Recordset Object 389

Setting a Reference to the ADO Library 389

Retrieving Data from a Data Source 391

Creating a Connection 391

Declaring a Connection Object 392

Setting Connection Properties 392

Opening the Connection 393

Creating a Recordset 394

Closing the Recordset and Connection 395

Transferring records to a Worksheet 395

Retrieving Microsoft Access Data with a Recordset 396

Returning Field Headers 398

Contents

Additional Recordset Properties 400
    CursorType Property 400
    LockType Property 401

Accessing Data in Recordsets 402
    Navigating Records 403
        Using Move Methods 403
        BOF and EOF Properties 405
        Looping Through All Records 406
    Filtering Records 407
        Removing a Filter 407
    Practice: Navigating a Recordset on a UserForm 408
        Step1: Create a new UserForm 409
        Step 2: Add controls to the UserForm 409
        Step 3: Enter the Code to Load the Data 410
        Step 4: Testing the UserForm 415

Building a Query 416
    Overview of SQL 416
    Selecting Records with SQL 417
        Using SELECT 418
        Using the WHERE Clause 418
        Using Logical Operators with the WHERE Clause 419
        Using the ORDER BY Clause 420
    Opening a Recordset with an SQL Query 420

Handling Data Access Errors 423

Retrieving SQL Server Data 425

Chapter 18: Creating Charts 428

Chart Basics 429
    Changing Your Default Chart Type 429

Contents

Manually Creating a Chart 430
Creating a Chart Programmatically from Scratch 439
    Using the AddChart2 method 439
    Using Direct Referencing 441
    Identifying Chart Styles 442
    Referencing a new Chart Object 443
    Referencing an Existing Chart 444
    Setting Individual Chart Characteristics 444
        Specifying the Size and Position of a Chart 445
        Applying a Chart Layout 445
        Using the SetElement Method 445
        Editing the Chat Title 447
        Individually Adding Axis Titles 447
        Formatting the Plot Area 448
    Putting It All Together 448

Chapter 19: Creating PivotTables 451

PivotTable Basics 452
    Preparing Your Data 452
Creating a PivotTable Manually 453
Creating a PivotTable Programmatically 458
    Using the CreatePivotTable Method 458
    Adding Fields to PivotTable Areas 460
        Specifying Column and Row Fields 460
        Specifying Data Fields 461
        Putting It All Together 462
    Formatting a PivotTable 463
        Applying PivotTable Styles 464
        Removing Grand Totals 465

Removing Subtotals 465
Replacing Blank Values 466
Putting It All Together 466
Grouping PivotTable Data 468
Example: Grouping Data by Date 470

Chapter 20: User-Defined Functions and Add-ins 472

Working with User-Defined Functions 473
Where to store the UDF 473
Creating a UDF 474
Adding a Description to a UDF 478
Entering a UDF with the Insert Function dialog box 481
Creating Excel Add-Ins 483
Overview of Add-ins 483
Converting a Workbook to an Add-in 484
Converting a UDF to an Add-in 486

More Help 493

Appendix: Code Window General Use Keys 494

Index 496

About the Author 503

Other Books by Author 504

Contents

Introduction

Welcome to *Mastering Excel VBA Programming*. As you're probably aware, Visual Basic for Applications (VBA) is a programming language that enables you to automate any action that you can perform manually in Excel. But it doesn't stop there. VBA allows you to extend Excel's functionality and create solutions you can't create with Excel's standard features.

Whether you regularly format a set of reports, perform data-crunching calculations, or create automated solutions to support other Excel users, you've come to the right place in picking up this book. With VBA, you can write code that allows Excel users to perform complex tasks with the click of a button. Users do not have to go through repetitive and time-consuming processes each time, which can significantly increase productivity. VBA allows you to automate tasks so they are executed consistently each time, reducing the risk of errors that manual actions can introduce.

This book will give you all the information you need to quickly get up and running with Excel programming. After reading this book, you will know the essentials of the VBA language and how to use Excel objects to create and manipulate workbooks, worksheets, and ranges. You will learn how to programmatically retrieve data from external databases like Microsoft Access and SQL Server for use in Excel. You will be able to create applications with UserForms to streamline user input and other user interactions. This book will show you how to create custom functions and deploy them to users as Excel add-ins.

Who Is This Book For?

Mastering Excel VBA Programming is for you if you already have basic skills in Excel and want to learn how to use VBA programming to extend what you can do with Excel. This book does not assume you have any programming experience. We start with programming basics before progressing to programming Excel objects.

This book does not cover Office Scripts, which is a way to automate Excel using the TypeScript language. Office Scripts is still quite limited compared to VBA, and the Automate tab (Office Scripts) is not available to all versions of Excel. For example, Office Scripts is currently not available in general release to the personal or family desktop versions of Microsoft 365.

As the title implies, this book focuses on using VBA to automate Excel and extend its functionality. It is not a general-purpose Excel book. Hence, this book assumes you're already familiar with the standard features of Excel. If you need a general-purpose Excel book, check out my *Mastering Excel 365* book.

How to Use This Book

Mastering Excel VBA Programming can be used as a step-by-step training manual or a reference guide where you can skip to a particular topic. If you're new to VBA, I recommend reading the chapters sequentially, as some topics covered are based on the skills or knowledge you'll acquire in earlier chapters. If you're already familiar with Excel macros, you can skip to the chapters covering VBA programming.

Assumptions

The software assumptions made when writing this book are that you already have Excel installed on your computer and that you're working on a Windows 10 or 11 platform. If you're running Excel on a Mac, substitute any Windows keyboard commands mentioned in the book for the Mac equivalent.

Sample Files and Source Code

All code examples and sample data in the book are available online. You can download the files from the following location:

https://www.excelbytes.com/mastering-excel-vba-download/

Notes:

- Type the URL in your Internet browser's address bar and press Enter to display the download page. If you encounter an error, double-check that you have correctly entered all characters in the URL.

- The files have been zipped into one download. Windows 10 or 11 comes with a built-in feature to unzip files. If your OS does not have this feature, you'll need to get software like WinZip or WinRAR to unzip the file.

- Microsoft's default security settings disable macros in all files downloaded online. To use the macro-enabled workbooks containing the source code for this book, create a Trusted Location on your computer to store the files. See **Adding a Trusted Location** in Chapter 2 of this book.

- If you experience any problems downloading these files, please contact me at **support@excelbytes.com** and include the title of this book in your email. The practice files will be emailed directly to you.

Chapter 1

Introduction to VBA

In this chapter:

- What you can do with VBA.
- Things to consider before using VBA – pros and cons.
- The difference between macros and VBA.

Visual Basic for Applications (VBA) is a programming language developed by Microsoft that allows you to extend the functionality of some Microsoft 356 applications. VBA has been around for a long time, but it's still the best language for programming Excel. If you are unable to solve a problem with the built-in features in Excel, you can write VBA code to build a custom solution.

VBA was derived from the Visual Basic programming language. Visual Basic is known for its natural language attributes compared to other languages like C++ or C#. If you're familiar with Visual Basic, you will be at home with VBA. If you are new to programming, VBA is a good place to start your programming career. VBA's natural language syntax can make learning core programming constructs like loops and conditional statements easier.

Chapter 1: Introduction to VBA

This chapter covers some essential background information and how VBA can fit into your overall scheme of creating solutions with Excel.

What You Can Do With VBA

Automate Tasks You Perform Often

Suppose you need to prepare a weekly report that involves a lot of formatting, styling, and calculations. You could use VBA to automate the process for faster and more consistent results. Almost any formatting or editing change done manually can be done in VBA.

Automate Repetitive Tasks

You can use VBA to automate tasks that are repetitive and tedious. For example, suppose you have to clean up imported data, generate a report, and repeat the process for several worksheets. You can record a macro while carrying out the task for the first worksheet, refine the code in the VBA editor, and then use that macro to automatically process the other worksheets.

Create Custom Excel Functions

Creating custom functions in VBA might be more efficient if you often create complex and convoluted formulas. Built-in Excel functions are essentially predefined formulas. Custom functions (also called user-defined functions) can perform specific calculations or tasks not available with Excel's built-in functions. Once you become proficient in VBA, you'll find it easier to solve complex calculations with code than using Excel's built-in functions.

Programmatically Manipulate Workbooks and Worksheets

VBA enables you to create, delete, rename, and manipulate worksheets and workbooks. Suppose you receive a worksheet regularly with data for one year that needs to be split into 12 worksheets before performing other formatting tasks to create monthly reports. You could write a VBA procedure to automatically create and name the twelve worksheets, copy & paste the requisite data into each, and perform additional formatting tasks. This can save you a lot of time while ensuring the process is standardized across the worksheets.

Generate Charts and Summaries

VBA enables you to generate dynamic reports by pulling data from various sources, performing calculations, and presenting the formatted results. You can automate the creation, modification, and formatting of PivotTables to summarize data. You can create, modify, and format charts dynamically using VBA, making it easier to represent your data visually.

Automate Data Import and Export

You can use ActiveX Data Objects (ADO) to programmatically connect to an external data source like Microsoft Access and SQL Server to import data. You can use ADO to manipulate and transform recordsets before using them in your worksheet. For example, suppose you have a worksheet that depends on dynamic data from an external database. Instead of having to refresh the data manually each time, you can use VBA to connect to the database and automatically refresh the data so that users always have the latest data in Excel.

Interaction with Users

VBA provides UserForms and other tools that allow you to create custom dialog boxes, input boxes, and forms to obtain user input, display messages, and interact with users.

Integration with Other Applications

VBA allows you to automate other Microsoft 365 applications from Excel. For example, you could write a routine that creates a new Microsoft Word document, transfers data from Excel into the document, and then formats the document. You can use VBA in cases where manually performing the process would be too time-consuming.

Create Custom Add-ins

Add-ins provide additional commands and features that extend the functionality of Excel. Excel comes with some add-ins that you can enable. VBA enables you to create your own custom add-ins that you can use to provide custom features to users.

What to Consider Before Using VBA

- **Is VBA the best approach?**

    VBA gives you more power and flexibility regarding the solutions you can create, but it may not necessarily be the best approach. Sometimes, it may be easier to achieve your aims using other methods. The important question to ask is whether there is an easier way. Before you start a VBA project, consider the built-in tools in Excel and what you can achieve with standard features like formulas and functions.

    For example, if you have a repetitive formatting or layout task, can you perform the task once and then use the copy-and-paste commands to repeat it? Or maybe you can create a template document with the correct format, which you can reuse.

    Excel is a powerful application that is constantly being improved. Many tasks that required programming a few years ago can now be performed with built-in features. The solution that you need may be achievable using built-in features. Take some time to learn more about the features in Excel before creating a VBA solution.

- **Programming proficiency requires time and practice.**

    Unlike some other Excel features, programming is not something you can learn and instantly use proficiently in an ongoing project. It takes time and experience to become proficient in any programming language. If you have no prior programming experience, VBA is not something you can learn as needed to complete ongoing work. Programming can produce unpredictable results for a beginner, leading to frustration and delays in your project.

    Before starting a VBA project in a production setting, ensure you have gained some experience in the language. Don't turn to a VBA solution at the eleventh hour unless you're comfortable with the programming language. If you have a deadline to meet, you might be better off using standard methods, even if they are repetitive and time-consuming.

- **VBA code adds maintenance and security overheads.**

    VBA code needs to be documented and updated with any Excel updates that might affect the code's functionality. Also, a macro-enabled workbook requires different security considerations and Trust Centre settings.

The Difference Between Excel Macros and VBA

An Excel macro is a recorded set of instructions stored as VBA code. You can run macros directly from Excel's interface to perform tasks. The difference between Excel macros and VBA programming can be fuzzy because macros are stored as VBA Sub procedures, but not all VBA procedures are macros. For example, you can create Function procedures and Event Procedures in VBA that are not traditionally seen as macros.

You don't necessarily need VBA programming skills to record and run simple Excel macros. However, you need to be familiar with the VBA programming language to write the macro directly in the Visual Basic Editor or to edit a recorded macro. Occasionally, creating macros will involve editing the generated code to change how the macro behaves or fix errors. VBA gives you more flexibility and power to control Excel than the macro recorder. In this book, as much as possible, the term *macro* refers to Sub procedures created with the macro recorder, while *VBA code* refers to the code written manually.

Chapter 2

Recording and Running Macros

In this chapter:

- Discovering where to store macros and VBA code.
- Recording a macro using the macro recorder.
- Testing and running a recorded macro.
- Viewing the source code and saving a recorded macro.
- Assigning a macro to a custom button on Excel's ribbon.
- Assigning a macro to a command on the Quick Access Toolbar.
- Assigning a macro to an object in the worksheet area.
- Understanding the Trust Center settings for macro security.
- Understanding how Trusted Locations work in Microsoft 365, and adding a new Trusted Location.

In this chapter, you'll learn how to record your first macro, where macros can be stored, and how to examine the VBA code generated by Excel in the Visual Basic Editor. There are multiple ways you can create macros in Excel. The most accessible method is to use Excel's macro recorder to record your actions as you perform various tasks in the worksheet. With this method, you don't need to manually write any code.

Displaying the Developer Tab

Before we start programming Excel, you need to display the **Developer** tab on your Excel ribbon (if it's not already displayed). A default installation of Excel does not add the Developer tab. The Developer tab makes accessing commands related to creating macros and writing VBA code easier.

Figure 2-1: The Developer tab.

If you don't have the Developer tab on your ribbon, follow the steps below to add it to the ribbon:

1. Right-click anywhere on the ribbon (below the buttons) and select **Customize the Ribbon**. Excel opens the **Customize the Ribbon** pane in the Excel Options dialog box.

Chapter 2: Recording and Running Macros

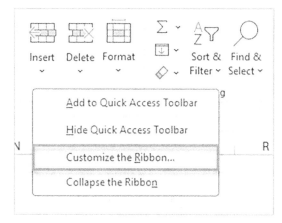

Figure 2-2: Customizing the ribbon.

Note You can also open the **Excel Options** dialog box by selecting **File > Options > Customize Ribbon**.

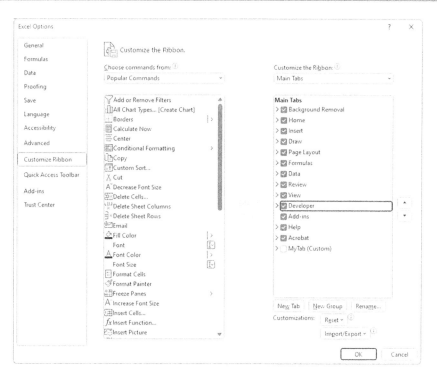

Figure 2-3: Customizing the ribbon in Excel Options.

29

2. On the right side of the Customize Ribbon pane, ensure **Main Tabs** is selected in the dropdown list. Select the **Developer** check box and then click **OK**.

Where to Store Macros and VBA Code

Before creating a macro or writing a VBA procedure, you must decide where to store the code. For security reasons, Excel does not allow code to be saved in a standard Excel workbook (xlsx). Thus, you can only store code in Excel file types designated to handle VBA code.

The table below provides a breakdown of where you can store macros and for what reasons:

Where to store code	Description
Personal Macro Workbook	By default, the PERSONAL.XLSB file is opened (in hidden mode) whenever Excel opens. This workbook allows you to create and store macros anytime without converting your current workbook to a macro-enabled workbook. As the workbook is always open, its macros are always available for use in other workbooks on the computer.
	This is the recommended location to store macros used in different workbooks on the computer.
Excel Macro-Enabled Workbook (xlsm)	If you want to store code in a standalone workbook, it must be saved as a Macro-Enabled Workbook (xlsm).
	Store code in a macro-enabled workbook if you aim to use it only in one workbook or if you intend to distribute the application to other users.

Excel Macro-Enabled Template (xltm)	A macro-enabled template allows you to combine the power of Excel templates and VBA in one solution. Suppose you regularly create a worksheet that requires extensive formatting. You can pre-design the template with all the necessary formatting and only add code for other actions to be automated.
	When you create a workbook from the template, the new macro-enabled workbook will include all the formatting and code in the template.

Storing Code in the Personal Macro Workbook

The **Personal Macro Workbook** is a hidden workbook that is available to all workbooks on the computer. It is named **PERSONAL.XLSB** and stored in the following location:

`C:\Users\[Username]\AppData\Roaming\Microsoft\Excel\XLSTART`

The Personal Macro Workbook can be a central repository for all VBA code on the computer, which makes it easier to manage your macros in one place. Another benefit of the Personal Macro Workbook is that you don't have to convert every workbook in which you want to run a macro into a macro-enabled workbook.

When you open any Excel workbook, Excel also opens the Personal Macro Workbook in the background in hidden mode. This ensures any code stored in the hidden workbook is ready and available for use in other workbooks.

When recording a macro, you choose where to save it, its name, and shortcut keys to assign. When assigning shortcut keys to run the macro, you can assign the Ctrl key plus a letter from A to Z or the Ctrl+Shift keys plus a letter from A to Z. For example, Ctrl+M or Ctrl+Shift+M.

There are some shortcut keys you can't assign, for instance, Ctrl+ (any number) or Ctrl+ (a punctuation mark). Avoid using known Windows shortcut keys like Ctrl+C or Ctrl+V (i.e., the shortcut keys for copy and paste).

To view the Personal Macro Workbook, do the following:

1. On the **View** tab, in the **Window** group, select **Unhide**.
2. In the **Unhide** dialog box, choose PERSONAL.XLSB and click **OK**.

To hide the Personal Macro Workbook again, do the following:

1. Ensure PERSONAL.XLSB is the active workbook.
2. On the **View** tab, in the **Window** group, select the **Hide** button.

Storing Code in a Macro-Enabled Workbook

It is sometimes best to store your macros or VBA procedures in a standalone workbook rather than the Personal Macro Workbook. Any code stored in a macro-enabled workbook is not readily available to other Excel workbooks on the PC.

You can store macros in a macro-enabled workbook for the following reasons:

- The code is specific to that workbook.
- You have a large project with many procedures. Organizing the code in a separate workbook explicitly created for that project would be best in such a scenario.
- You want to distribute the application to people using other computers.

It depends on how you want to organize your code. Storing your code in a separate workbook is a good idea for specific large projects. The Personal Macro Workbook should be reserved for macros that are often used in different workbooks on the computer.

Storing Code in a Workbook Template

You can store your code in an Excel template file called an **Excel Macro-Enabled Template (*.xltm)**. When you create a workbook from a template, the new workbook is based on the template and will include any code stored in the template. The template is

Chapter 2: Recording and Running Macros

not linked to the new workbook. Thus, when you modify code in an Excel template, the changes are not reflected in workbooks previously created from the template.

A template file can be used to save time for tasks performed regularly. It enables you to combine the power of Excel templates and macros in one solution. For example, suppose you want to automate the process of creating a weekly data report that includes a lot of formatting and other actions that can be automated with code. You can create a template that contains all the required formatting, including code that performs other actions. Whenever users need to produce the report, they create a new workbook based on the template.

Saving a Workbook as a Template

Follow the steps below to save a workbook as a template file:

1. If you're saving a workbook as a template for the first time, start by setting the default personal templates location in **Excel Options**:

    i. On the ribbon, select **File** > **Options**.

    ii. Select the **Save** tab.

    iii. Under **Save workbooks**, in the **Default personal templates location** box, enter the folder path where you want to store your templates.

    > **Note** There is a folder named **Custom Office Templates** in the **Documents** folder in Windows that is used as a general location for Office template files. You can select this folder.

    iv. Select **OK**.

    Once the default template location is set, all custom templates saved to that folder will appear under the **Personal** category on the **New** pane in Excel (**File** > **New**).

2. Open the workbook you want to save as a template.

3. Select **File** > **Export**.
4. Under **Export**, select **Change File Type**.
5. Under **Workbook File Types**, double-click **Save as Another File Type**.

   Excel displays the **Save As** dialog box.
6. In the **File name** box, enter the name you want for the template.
7. In the **Save as type** box, select **Excel Macro-Enabled template (*.xltm)**.
8. Select **Save**, and then close the template.

Creating A Workbook from a Template

Follow the steps below to create a workbook from a template:

1. Select **File** > **New**.
2. Select **Personal**.

   Any template saved to your default template location will be listed here.
3. Double-click the template you want to use.

   Excel creates a new workbook that is based on the selected template.

Chapter 2: Recording and Running Macros

Starting the Macro Recorder

There are three ways you can start the macro recorder in Excel:

- **From the Status bar**

    Click the **Record Macro** button on Excel's status bar (bottom left of the window, next to the Ready indicator). The **Record Macro** button on the status bar is convenient as it allows you to start and stop the macro recorder without switching tabs on the ribbon.

    Figure 2-4: The Record Macro button on the status bar.

- **From the Developer tab**

    On the **Developer** tab, click the **Record Macro** command button.

- **From the View tab**

    On the **View** tab, select **Macros > Record Macro**.

Relative versus Absolute Reference Macros

Excel cell references are relative by default unless manually defined as absolute. Conversely, macros use absolute references by default unless you enable the relative reference option. A relative cell reference is dependent on the position of the current cell, so it changes when copied to other cells. Conversely, absolute cell references do not change when copied to other cells. For example, the cell reference $A$3 means the row and column have been set to absolute. With absolute cell referencing, the macro recorder will store specific cell references as part of the code instructions.

For instance, suppose you record a macro that enters a value in cell A1 in one worksheet. When you run that macro in another worksheet, it will always enter the value in cell A1 regardless of the current active cell. If you want the macro to perform actions relative to the active cell, you must enable **Use Relative References** before recording the macro.

To enable relative references, select **Developer > Code > Use Relative References** on the Excel ribbon.

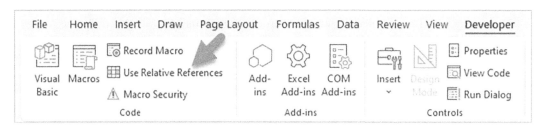

Figure 2-5: Enabling relative references in macros.

Example: Recording a Macro

> **Note** The solution for this example is stored in **Ch2_Solution.xlsm** in the practice files for this chapter.

The following example records a macro that carries out the following tasks:

- Enters the text "My Company Name".
- Increases the font to 14 points.
- Bolds the text.
- Merges four adjacent cells in the same row and centers the text.

We will examine the VBA code generated by the macro recorder after recording it.

Follow the steps below to record the macro:

1. Create a new Excel workbook. Excel creates a worksheet called Sheet1 by default.

2. On the ribbon, select **Developer > Code > Use Relative References** to enable relative references for the macro.

   This option enables you to run the macro anywhere in the worksheet. The difference between absolute and relative reference macros is explained in the section above.

3. On the **Developer** tab, in the **Code** group, select **Record Macro**.

   Excel opens the Record Macro dialog box.

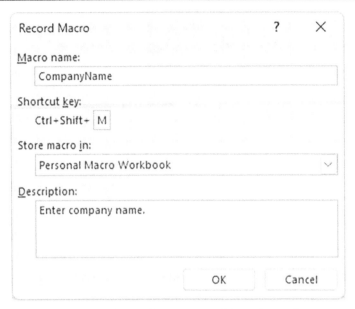

Figure 2-6: Specifying the name and location of a macro.

4. In the **Macro Name** box, enter the name of the macro. For this example, enter *CompanyName*.

   Note that a macro name must begin with a letter and cannot have spaces. You can use capitalization to separate words.

5. For the **Shortcut key**, hold down the Shift key and press M.

   Excel enters Ctrl+Shift+M for the shortcut key. You can use other key combinations, but avoid popular Windows shortcut keys.

   The shortcut key is optional. But if you assign one, you can use it as an alternative way to run the macro.

6. In the **Store macro in** box, select **Personal Macro Workbook**. This option ensures that the macro is saved in the global PERSONAL.XLSB workbook and not the current workbook.

7. In the **Description** box, you can enter a brief description of the macro.

   The description is optional, but if you're creating many macros, entering a description for each macro makes maintaining them easier.

8. Click **OK** to close the Record Macro dialog box and start the macro recorder.

   A small square button on the left of the status bar indicates that the macro recorder is running.

   The following steps involve performing the Excel tasks being recorded.

9. On the ribbon, select the **Home** tab, and then select cell **A1**.

10. Type *"My Company Name"* in cell A1 and click **Enter** (this is a checkmark in the set of buttons next to the formula bar).

11. Change the font size to 14 and bold the text.

12. Select range A1:A4. On the **Home** tab, in the **Alignment** group, select **Merge & Center**.

13. Stop the macro recorder. On the status bar, click the **Stop Recording** button (a square button).

Figure 2-7: Stopping the macro recorder.

With that, your macro recording has been completed. Next, we'll run the macro.

Running the Macro

After recording a macro, you need to test it by running it from the Macro dialog box.

1. Open the worksheet you used for the previous example (if it's not open).

2. Click the **New sheet** button at the bottom of the window to create a new sheet.

3. Select cell A1 (or anywhere on the sheet where you want to insert the text).

4. On the **Developer** tab, in the **Code** group, select the **Macros** button.

   Excel opens the **Macro** dialog box, which lists all available macros.

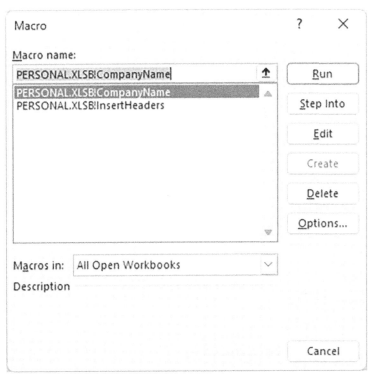

Figure 2-8: Running a macro using the Macro dialog box.

5. In the **Macros in** box, ensure **All Open Workbooks** is selected.

6. Select the macro in the list box and click the **Run** button. For this example, select *PERSONAL.XLSB!CompanyName*.

   The macro enters "My Company Name" in the selected cell with the text size set to 14 and bolded. The macro merges four cells in the selected row and centers the text.

   Note that the *PERSONAL.XLSB* prefix indicates that the macro was saved in the Personal Macro Workbook.

Tip: If you assigned a keyboard shortcut to the macro, for example, Ctrl+Shift+M, you could press those keys to automatically run the macro without opening the Macro dialog box.

It is best to test a macro in a new worksheet (or a different range in the current worksheet) to see if it replicates your actions when recording it.

If you run the macro in a worksheet with existing data, there is a risk that the macro will overwrite your existing data or formatting. Always test the macro in a new worksheet to ensure you don't mistakenly overwrite data. Only run the macro against production data when you're happy with it. For instance, you may create a macro that adds formatting to existing data. In such cases, ensure you test the macro first against test copies of the data before running it against your production data.

Viewing and Saving the Macro

Follow the steps below to view the source code created by the macro recorder:

1. On the Excel ribbon, select **Developer** > **Code** > **Visual Basic**.

   Excel displays the Visual Basic Editor.

2. In the **Project Explorer** (on the window's left pane), expand the project named **VBAProject(PERSONAL.XLSB)**.

3. In the **Modules** folder, double-click **Module1** to display it in the Code window.

   If you have more than one module under Modules, and the *CompanyName* macro is not in Module1, open the last module in the Modules folder (this should be the one with the highest suffix number).

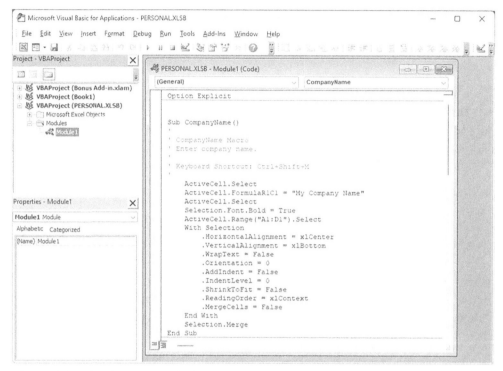

Figure 2-9: Viewing a recorded macro in the Visual Basic Editor.

You can make minor changes to the code in the Code window, for example, changing values assigned to cells in the macro.

> **Note** The Visual Basic Editor is covered in detail in Chapter 3.

4. Save the macro by selecting **File > Save PERSONAL.XLSB** (or click the **Save** button on the toolbar represented by a blue disk icon).

Subsequent chapters in this book cover VBA in detail, giving you all the knowledge required to edit generated macros or write them from scratch.

Saving Your Macro in an Excel Macro-Enabled Workbook

If you recorded the macro in a standard Excel workbook, Excel turns off AutoSave and prompts you to save the file as an Excel Macro-Enabled Workbook when attempting to close it.

Follow the steps below to save a workbook as an Excel Macro-Enabled Workbook:

1. Select **File** > **Save As** (Excel displays this option instead of **Save a Copy** when AutoSave is off).

2. In the **Save As** pane, select the folder where you want to save the file, and then choose **Excel Macro-Enabled Workbook (*.xlsm)** as the file type.

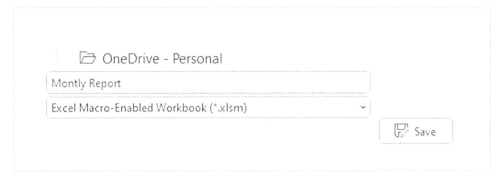

Figure 2-10: Saving a recorded macro as a macro-enabled workbook.

3. Select **Save**.

Assigning a Macro to a Button on the Ribbon

If you need to run a macro often, assigning it to a command button on Excel's ribbon would be a good idea instead of running it from the Macros dialog box each time. You must create a new custom group for your macro button, as you can't add a custom button to one of the default groups in Excel. You can either create a new custom group in one of the default tabs or create a new custom tab in which you add your custom group and button.

Step1: Create a New Custom Tab and Group

You may want to create a new tab for your custom group and button to keep the ribbon organized.

Follow the steps below to create a new tab and then add a macro command button to it:

1. Right-click anywhere on the Excel ribbon below the tabs, and select **Customize the Ribbon** from the shortcut menu. Excel displays the **Excel Options** dialog box.

2. On the right of the Excel Options dialog box, click the **New Tab** button (at the bottom of the Main Tabs box). Inside the tab, you must create at least one group before adding a command button from the left side of the dialog box.

3. To name the tab, select the **New Tab (Custom)** item and click the **Rename** button. Enter your preferred tab name in the **Rename** dialog box. For this exercise, enter the name *MyTab* and then click **OK**.

4. You can use the arrow buttons to the right of the Main Tabs box to move your new tab item up or down the list, depending on where you want to place it.

5. To create a new **custom group**, select the tab where you want to create the group. This could be one of the default tabs or a new custom tab. Click **New Group** (at the bottom of the dialog box). Excel creates a new group in the currently selected tab.

6. To create a name for the group, select the **New Group (Custom)** item and click the **Rename** button. Enter your preferred name in the **Rename** dialog box, for example, *MyMacros*.

7. Click **OK**.

You now have a custom group in which you can add your macro command buttons.

Step 2: Assign a Macro Command to the New Group

Follow the steps below to add a macro command button to the new custom group:

1. Select your custom group in the **Main Tabs** list box.

2. Click the dropdown list box named **Choose commands from** (on the left of the dialog box) and select **Macros** from the dropdown list. The box on the left lists the macros created in all open workbooks, including the PERSONAL.XLSB workbook.

3. Select the macro name you want to add to your custom group in the list box on the left.

4. Click the **Add** button to add the macro command to the new custom group in the list box on the right.

> **Note** If you accidentally add the wrong command, select it in the list box on the right and click the **Remove** button.

5. Click **OK** on the Excel Options dialog box to confirm the change.

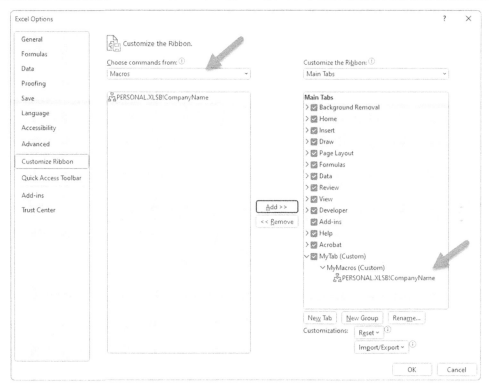

Figure 2-11: Assigning a macro to a custom button on the ribbon.

After adding the macro, the macro's name appears on a button with a generic icon (a program diagram chart). When you click the button, Excel runs the macro.

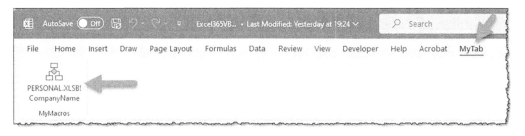

Figure 2-12: A custom button on the ribbon.

Assigning a Macro to a Button on the Quick Access Toolbar

You can also add a macro button to the Quick Access Toolbar if you have it displayed and use it regularly.

Follow the steps below to add a custom macro button to the Quick Access Toolbar:

1. Click the dropdown arrow at the end of the Quick Access Toolbar.

2. On the dropdown menu, select **More Commands**.

    Excel displays the **Customize the Quick Access Toolbar** pane in Excel Options.

3. Select **Macros** from the dropdown list named **Choose commands from**.

    The resultant list box displays all macros created in the current workbook and those saved in the PERSONAL.XLSB workbook.

4. In the list box on the left, select the macro you want to add to the Quick Access Toolbar and click the **Add** button to add it to the list on the right.

    Note If you accidentally add the wrong command, select it in the list box on the right side of the dialog box and click the **Remove** button.

5. Click **OK**.

Excel displays your macro button as a generic macro icon on the Quick Access Toolbar. To run the macro, click the button.

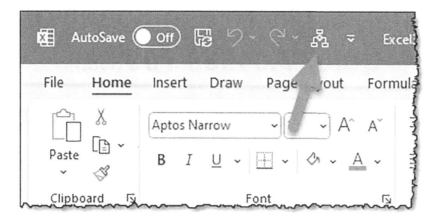

Figure 2-13: Assigning a macro to the Quick Access Toolbar.

Assigning a Macro to an Image

You can assign macros to images in your worksheet, including Pictures, Shapes, and Icons that you can insert from the **Illustrations** group on the **Insert** tab. You can also assign macros to images you have drawn using tools on the **Draw** tab.

To assign a macro to an image, do the following:

1. Insert the image in the worksheet area. For example, an icon from **Insert** > **Illustrations** > **Icons**.
2. Right-click the icon and select **Assign Macro**.
3. In the **Assign Macro** dialog box, select the macro name from the **Macro name** list box.
4. Click **OK**.

When you hover over the icon, the mouse pointer changes to a hand with a pointing index finger, indicating that you can click the icon to run the macro.

Assigning a Macro to a Button on the Worksheet

You can add an Excel **Form Control** from the Developer tab in your worksheet, which you can use to execute macros. The **Button** control is like a button on a form to which you can assign a macro. The macro runs and performs actions in the worksheet when a user clicks the button.

To add a Button to your worksheet, do the following:

1. On the ribbon, select **Developer > Controls > Insert**.

2. Under **Form Controls**, select the **Button** control.

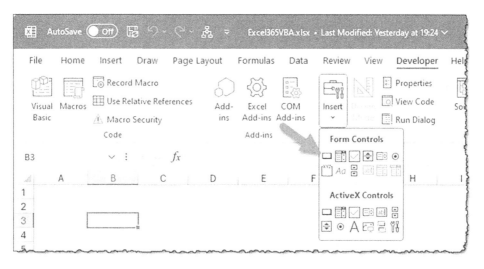

Figure 2-14: Inserting a Button in a worksheet.

3. In the worksheet area, draw the button with your mouse.

    When you release the left mouse button, Excel displays the **Assign Macro** dialog box.

4. Select the macro you want to assign to the button from the Macro name box and click **OK**.

For this example, we'll use the macro recorded earlier in this chapter: ***PERSONAL.XLSB!CompanyName***.

5. To edit the button's caption, right-click the button and select **Edit Text**, then enter the caption you want for the button.

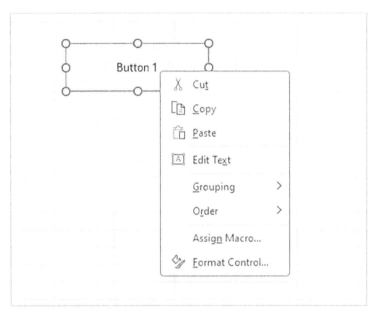

Figure 2-15: Editing the caption on a Form button.

6. Click anywhere in the worksheet area to exit design mode. Excel deselects the button.

7. Click the button to test it.

   If everything works correctly, Excel should run the macro, which adds, formats, and centers a piece of text to the selected cell.

Note When you right-click the button, the worksheet goes into design mode, and the button becomes inactive. To reactivate the button, click anywhere else in the worksheet. Excel deselects the button, and it responds to clicks again.

Formatting Form Controls

To format the button and change other properties, for example, the font or caption, right-click the button and select **Format Control**. Excel opens the **Format Control** dialog box, where you can change several control properties. When you're done, click **OK** on the Format Control dialog box. Click any cell in your worksheet to exit design mode.

Macro Security

Excel uses an authentication system called Authenticode to digitally sign macro projects or add-ins created with VBA. The macros you create locally on your computer are automatically authenticated. Thus, when you run them on your computer, Excel does not display a security alert.

For macros from an external source, the developer can acquire a certificate issued by a reputable authority or a trusted publisher. In such cases, Excel will run the macro if it can verify that it is from a trusted source.

Suppose Excel cannot verify the digital signature of a macro from an external source because it perhaps doesn't have one. A security alert is displayed in the message bar (below the Excel ribbon). This alert allows you to enable or ignore the macro. You can click the **Enable Content** button to run the macro if you trust the source and are sure that the macro poses no security threat to your computer.

If you try to save a macro in a standard Excel workbook (XLSX file), Excel will display a message saying the file can't be saved as a standard Excel workbook and must be saved as a macro-enabled workbook.

Figure 2-16: You can't save VBA code in a standard Excel workbook.

To save the file as a macro-enabled workbook, go to **File > Save As** and select **Excel Macro-Enabled Workbook (*.xlsm)** as the file type.

Trust Center Macro Settings

Microsoft 365 security and privacy settings are located in the **Trust Center**. The Macro Settings tab of the Trust Center contains the macro security settings for your computer. Macro security is essential to protect your computer against the threat of malicious code that can be inserted in Microsoft 365 macros.

You can access the **Macro Settings** in the Trust Center in the following ways:

- On the **Developer** tab, in the **Code** group, select **Macro Security**. Excel opens the **Macro Settings** pane of the Trust Center dialog box.

- Another way to open Macro Settings is to select **File > Options > Trust Center > Trust Centre Settings > Macro Settings**.

Chapter 2: Recording and Running Macros

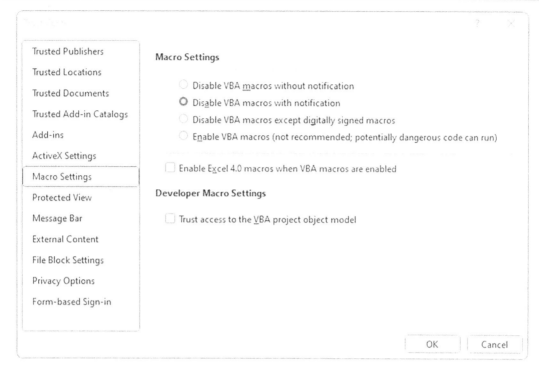

Figure 2-17: Macro settings in the Trust Center.

By default, Excel disables all macros from external sources. It displays a security alert on the message bar, which allows you to enable or ignore macros. This setting is the default when you install Excel. However, there are other security options you can select.

You can select one of the following options in Macro Settings:

- **Disable VBA macros without notification**: This option automatically disables macros on your computer. This setting means no macros will run on your computer, and you'll not get a security alert giving you the option to run the macro. This option is useful for shared computers, for instance, where you don't want anyone using the computer to run macros.

- **Disable VBA macros with notification**: This option is the default. All macros from external sources are disabled, with a security alert on the message bar. With this option, you have to specifically choose to enable the macro before it can run.

- **Disable VBA macros except digitally signed macros**: This option disables all macros apart from the digitally signed macros from publishers you have added to your Trusted Publishers in the Trust Center. With this setting, a digitally signed macro from a publisher you've not trusted yet will generate an alert, allowing you to add them to your trusted publishers.

- **Enable VBA macros (not recommended; potentially dangerous code can run):** This option enables all macros without any notifications or security alerts, even macros that are not digitally signed or authenticated. As the title indicates, this option is not recommended because you can inadvertently run malicious code that corrupts your data or damages your computer.

- **Enable Excel 4.0 macros when VBA macros are enabled**: Excel 4.0 (XLM) macros are disabled without notification by default. Select this checkbox if you want the settings above for VBA macros to also apply to Excel 4.0 (XLM) macros.

- **Trust access to the VBA project object model**: By default, Excel blocks programmatic access to the VBA object model from an automation client to prevent unauthorized programs from building harmful code. This option is for code that automates and manipulates the VBA object model. The user running the code must grant automation clients access to the VBA object model. This setting is per-user and per-application. To grant access, select the check box.

Trusted Locations

The **Trusted Locations** tab of the Trust Center dialog box enables you to add, remove, or modify trusted locations. If you have macro-enabled workbooks from a trusted external source that you need to run on your computer without alerts, place them in a trusted location on your computer. In doing so, Excel knows the workbooks are safe and will not display security alerts when you open them.

Chapter 2: Recording and Running Macros

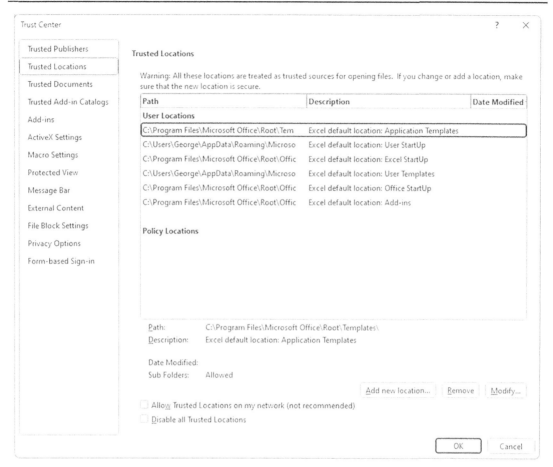

Figure 2-18: Creating a trusted location.

You can use the following options to change Trusted Locations settings:

- **Add new location**: To add a new trusted location, click the **Add new location** button on the **Trusted Locations** tab. In the **Microsoft Office Trusted Location** dialog box, click **Browse** and navigate to the folder you want to add to the list of trusted locations. Select the folder and click **OK** twice.

   Excel adds a new Trusted Location to your computer. In this folder, you can store any macro-enabled file from a trusted external source.

- **Allow trusted locations on my network (not recommended):** Select this option if you want to add folders on your network to your trusted locations. As

55

indicated by the title, this is not recommended, as you can't entirely trust the safety of external locations. However, if you're working on a shared network drive that you trust and is the only way to collaborate with others, this may be an option for sharing macro-enabled files. Only use it as a last option.

- **Disable all trusted locations**: Select this option if you want to immediately disable all trusted locations. With this option enabled, macros in your trusted locations will not run. Only the macros digitally signed and recognized as trustworthy by Excel will run on the computer.

Note The macro-enabled worksheets you create locally on your computer do not need to be stored in a trusted location to run on your computer. They're automatically digitally authenticated by Excel.

Adding a Trusted Location

When you try to open a macro-enabled workbook from an external source, Excel displays a security banner. This alert allows you to enable the macro or use the workbook with the macro disabled. If you trust the source and are sure that the macro poses no security threat to your computer, you can enable macros by selecting the **Enable Content** button in the banner.

Another way to enable macros in Excel workbooks from external sources is to create a new trusted location on your PC and add the workbooks to the associated folder. A trusted location should be on the local PC. The default setting of Microsoft 365 is to not trust locations on a network drive.

To get Excel to trust some files automatically, do the following:

1. Create a folder on your computer and add any Excel macro-enabled workbooks you want to trust.
2. On the Excel ribbon, select **File** > **Options** to open Excel Options.
3. In **Excel Options**, select **Trust Center** > **Trust Center Settings** to open the Trust Center dialog box.

Chapter 2: Recording and Running Macros

4. In the **Trust Center** dialog box, select **Trusted Locations** > **Add new location**.

5. In the **Microsoft Office Trusted Location** dialog box, click **Browse** and select the folder you created in step 1.

6. You can optionally add a short description in the **Description** box to mark the location as user-created.

7. To trust subfolders in the folder, select **Subfolders Of This Location Are Also Trusted**.

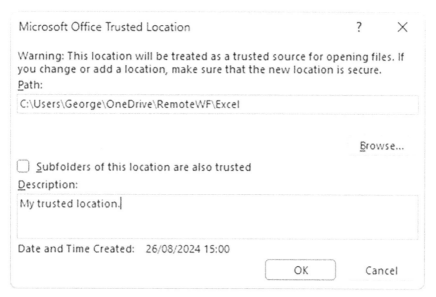

Figure 2-19: Adding a trusted location.

8. Click **OK** to add the folder as a trusted location in Excel.

9. In **File Explorer**, add the macro-enabled workbooks you want to trust to the trusted folder.

Excel will no longer display security messages for those files.

⚠ **Important**: Ensure the folder selected as your trusted location contains only files you want Excel to trust. Do not select a folder used by the operating system.

For example, when you download a file from the internet, the operating system automatically stores the file in the Downloads folder by default. Hence, you do not want to make the Downloads folder a trusted location. Likewise, do not set the C drive (and other system directories) as trusted locations. You should have complete control of what goes in the trusted location.

Chapter 3

Understanding The Visual Basic Editor

In this chapter:

- Becoming familiar with the Visual Basic Editor.
- Using the Project Explorer window to insert and rename modules.
- Importing and exporting VBA objects.
- Familiarizing yourself with the Code window.
- Entering a new procedure in the Code window.
- Discovering additional code navigation features.
- Documenting and formatting code.
- Customizing the VBA environment.
- Customizing menus and toolbars.

Microsoft 365 applications that were part of the old Microsoft Office suite, like Access, Excel, PowerPoint, and Publisher, share a common development environment, the Visual Basic Editor. This consistency enables you to use the knowledge gained in one application across the whole suite. You can accomplish common programming tasks like inserting modules and procedures, setting design-time properties, building forms, and debugging code in your solution.

Visual Basic Editor Overview

The Visual Basic Editor has its own menu and command buttons and has a separate window from the host application. This separate window enables you to run code in one window and watch the results in Excel in a different window. You can only open the Visual Basic Editor from the host application.

To open the Visual Basic Editor in Excel, select the **Developer** tab, and in the **Code** group, select the **Visual Basic** button.

> **Tip:** A quick way to open the Visual Basic Editor is to press Alt+F11 when Excel is active. In the Visual Basic Editor, press Alt+F11 to return to Excel or click the **Close** button on the toolbar.

The image below shows the Visual Basic Editor and some key features. At first glance, the Visual Basic Editor may look quite busy, but it quickly becomes familiar with use. The Visual Basic Editor is made up of several windows that are highly customizable. You can rearrange, hide, or dock windows in different parts of the development environment. When you start using the Visual Basic Editor, the two most important windows are the Project Explorer and the Code window.

Chapter 3: Understanding The Visual Basic Editor

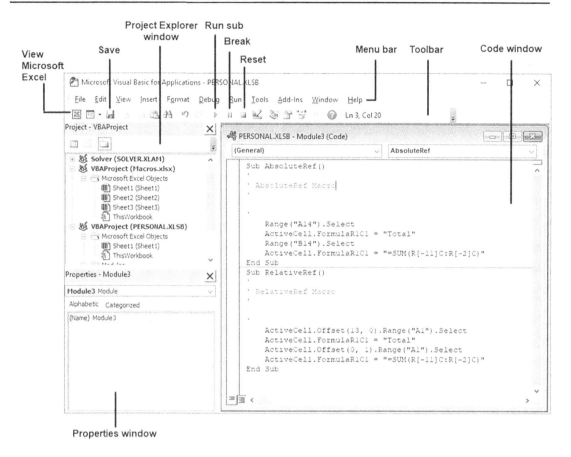

Figure 3-1: The Visual Basic Editor.

Menu bar

The menu bar for the Visual Basic Editor works just like the menu bar of other applications you've encountered. It contains commands to carry out various tasks within the editor. Many of the menu commands also have shortcut keys for them.

Toolbar

Under the menu bar, you have the Standard toolbar, which contains command buttons that make it easy to access many features with one click. You can customize the toolbars by adding buttons, repositioning buttons, or displaying other toolbars.

61

Project Explorer

The Project Explorer window displays a collapsible tree showing all the workbooks currently open in Excel and their associated code modules. You can double-click items on the list to expand or collapse them.

If you can't see the Project Explorer window, select **View** >**Project Explorer** on the menu bar (or press Ctrl+R to display the window).

You can hide the Project Explorer window by clicking the close button in its title bar. You can also right-click anywhere in the Project Explorer window and select **Hide** on the shortcut menu.

A project comprises all the code, UserForms, and other objects associated with a particular workbook.

Code window

The Code window contains the recorded or manually written code. Every object displayed in the Project Explorer window has an associated Code window. To view the Code window for an object, double-click the object in the Project Explorer window. For example, to display the Code window for Sheet1, double-click Sheet1 in the Project Explorer window, and its Code window will be displayed on the right. The Code window will be empty if you haven't added any code.

The macros you create are stored in modules that are given names in the format *Module1*, *Module2*, *Module3*, and so on. You can view them in the code window by double-clicking the module name in the Project Explorer window.

Properties window

A property is a characteristic of an object, such as a name, caption, or color. You can use the Properties window to set properties at design time. For example, the properties window allows you to rename a module named *Module1* or *Module2* to a more descriptive name. See the section on creating modules below for more details.

Chapter 3: Understanding The Visual Basic Editor

The Project Explorer Window

The Project Explorer window displays all the elements of a project. The elements in a project include Excel objects, forms, modules, and class modules. To display the Project Explorer window, select **View >Project Explorer** on the menu bar (or press Ctrl+R). You can also display the Project Explorer window by selecting the Project Explorer icon on the toolbar.

Each open Excel workbook and add-in is displayed as a project, which includes the hidden Personal Macro Workbook, PERSONAL.XLSB. A project is a collection of objects arranged in a tree format. To expand a project, click the plus sign (+) at the left of its name in the Project Explorer window. To collapse a project, click the minus sign (-) to the left of its name. You can also double-click the name of an item to expand it.

If a project is password-protected, Excel prompts you for the password when you double-click its name. You'll be unable to view or modify any part of a password-protected project if you don't have the password.

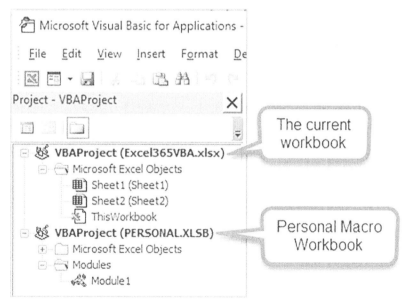

Figure 3-2: The Project Explorer.

The figure above lists two open VBA projects in the Project Explorer window. The first project is the current workbook, which is named *Excel365VBA.xlsx*. The second VBA project is the Personal Macro Workbook named *PERSONAL.XLSB*. Note that no macros are saved in the project for the current workbook, so there is no **Modules** folder.

To insert a new element in a project, right-click the project and select **Insert** on the shortcut menu. Then select the item you want to insert.

There are three basic objects in a VBA project:

- **Microsoft Excel Objects**

    The Excel objects section of the Project Explorer consists of modules for each sheet in the workbook and one for the workbook itself. The code written for a worksheet, like event procedures, are placed in the corresponding *Sheet* element. Workbook events are placed in the workbook element called *ThisWorkbook*.

- **Forms**

    Excel enables you to design UserForms for your VBA application, which you can use to interact with users. For example, you can create a data input form or a dialog box that provides information.

- **Standard Modules and Class Modules**

    Standard modules are a container for recorded macros and the procedures you write. Excel automatically creates a module to store a recorded macro. You can use an existing module to store your code or create a new one. Class modules differ from standard modules because they enable you to define objects. Class modules are outside the scope of this book.

Inserting a New Module

To create a new module, do the following:

1. Create a new workbook (or open an existing workbook).
2. Select **Developer** > **Visual Basic** to open the Visual Basic Editor.
3. In the Project Explorer window, select **VBAProject (PERSONAL.XLSB)** or the name of the project to which you want to add the code.

4. Right-click the project's name and select **Insert** > **Module** from the shortcut menu. You can also use **Insert** > **Module** on the menu bar to add a new module.

The Visual Basic Editor adds a new module to the project and gives it a default name in the format *ModuleN*. To rename the module, follow the steps below.

Renaming a Module

Renaming modules from the default name given by the Visual Basic Editor is not always necessary. Procedure names are what matter when it comes to executing code. However, if you have many modules in one project, organizing them with meaningful names makes it easier to maintain the code.

To rename a module, do the following:

1. In the Project Explorer window, select the module you want to rename. For example, Module1.

2. In the Properties window, change the **Name** property to the new name (overwriting the previous name) and press enter.

    Note that the name must start with a letter and cannot have spaces. If you want to separate two words, use capitalization.

Removing a Module

Occasionally, you may need to remove a VBA module you no longer need from a project. To remove a module, do the following:

1. Right-click the module and select **Remove [module name]** on the shortcut menu. For example, if the module's name is Module1. You would select **Remove Module1**.

    Alternatively, you can use **File** > **Remove [module name]** on the menu bar to remove the module.

2. Excel displays a prompt asking if you want to export the code in the module before removing it. Select **No** to delete the module without exporting it, or select **Yes** to export the code as a .bas file.

If you select **Yes** at the prompt, Excel displays a dialog box, enabling you to save the code in a text file with a .bas file extension (BASIC source code file).

Importing and Exporting VBA Objects

You can export objects in a VBA project as a separate file. Likewise, you can import objects into a VBA project. Exporting and importing is important if you reuse code or objects, like a UserForm, from different projects. You can also export VBA project objects to share with co-workers.

Follow the steps below to export an object:

1. Select the object you want to export in the Project Explorer window.
2. On the menu bar, select **File > Export File** (or select Ctrl+E).

   Excel displays a dialog box asking you for the file name. Enter the file name.
3. Select the folder where you want to save the file, enter the file name in the **File name** box, and select **Save**.

Note that when you export a VBA object, it's not removed from the project. To remove an object from a project, you must use **File > Remove [object name]**. The file created by the export can usually be opened as a text file using Notepad. So, you can use a text editor to open and view the contents of the export regardless of its file extension.

To import an object into a VBA project, do the following:

1. Select the project's name in the Project Explorer window.
2. On the menu bar, select **File > Import File** (or select Ctrl+M).

   Excel displays a dialog box asking you for the file name.
3. Navigate to the folder that contains the file you want to import, choose the file, and select the **Open** button.

> **Note** Only import VBA project objects from trustworthy sources, as you do not want to introduce malicious code into your project.

Using the Code Window

You use the Code window to create and edit your VBA code or the code generated by the macro recorder. The VBA development environment enables you to have several code windows open simultaneously. If you are working on several projects, you can open several windows simultaneously and switch between code windows.

Opening a Code Window

When you double-click a module or an object that can store code, Excel opens its Code window. You can minimize, maximize, resize, hide, or rearrange code windows. When working in a particular module, you might find it easier to maximize the Code window for that module to remove distractions.

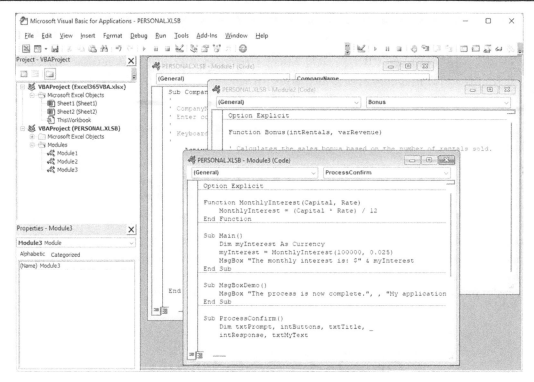

Figure 3-3: Working with many Code windows.

Resizing a Code Window

To maximize the code window, select the maximize button on the top-right of its title bar (the square box next to the X). You can also double-click the title bar to maximize it.

To minimize the code window, select the **Minimize** button on its title bar. To restore the Code window to its original size, click the **Restore** button (the Restore button replaces the Minimize button when the code window is minimized).

When the code window is maximized, the title bar is not visible. Thus, to resize a maximized Code window, use the Minimize, Restore, or Close buttons on the top-right of the development environment, just under the title bar of the Visual Basic Editor.

Chapter 3: Understanding The Visual Basic Editor

Arranging Multiple Code Windows

Occasionally, you may want to arrange code windows so you can view code in different code windows simultaneously. The **Windows** menu option on the toolbar enables you to tile code windows horizontally, vertically, or in a cascading order.

The Object Box

The **Object** box displays the name of the selected object. Use the arrow to the right of the dropdown list to select an object on a UserForm. For modules, only **General** is available.

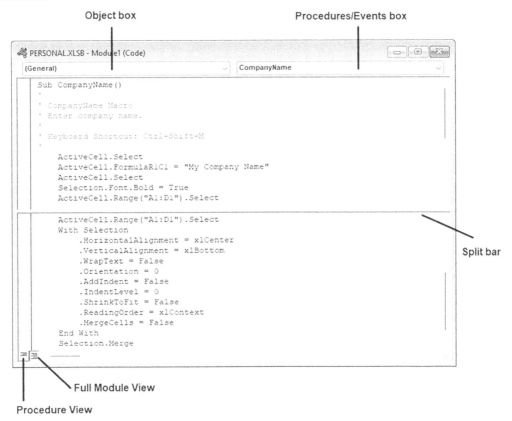

Figure 3-4: Understanding different aspects of the Code window.

69

The Procedures/Events Box

The **Procedure** box displays the name of the procedure with the focus. Use the arrow to the right of the box to go to a specific procedure. For objects, this list shows the event procedures for the object displayed in the **Object** box.

Splitting the Code Window

You can split the code window horizontally to view different code segments of a module simultaneously. Each pane can be scrolled independently - horizontally and vertically. The **Object** and **Procedure** boxes refer to the pane with the focus, and any code changes are reflected immediately in both panes.

The following illustration shows the split bar on the right side of the Code window.

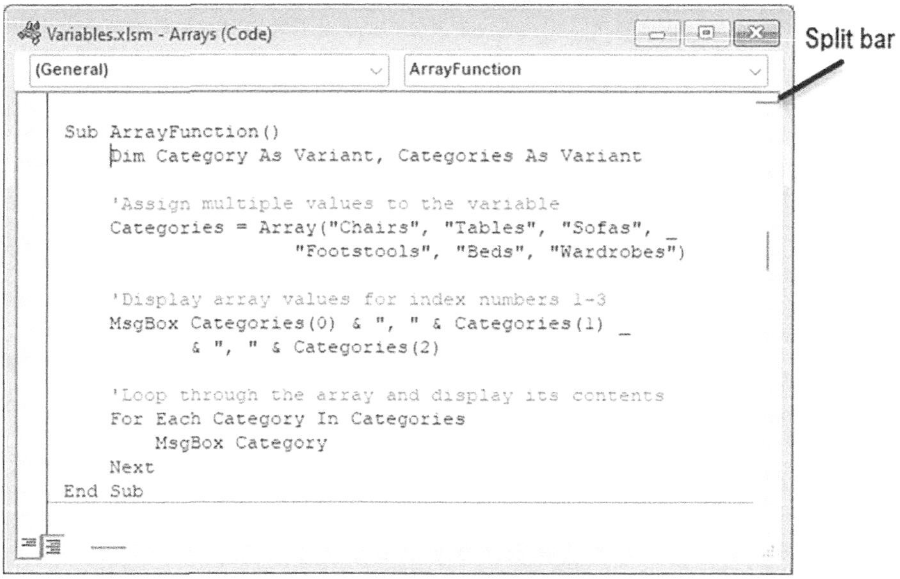

Figure 3-5: Splitting a Code window.

To split the Code window into panes, do one of the following:

- On the menu bar, select **Window** > **Split**.
- Drag down the **split bar** at the top of the vertical scroll bar (on the right of the Code window).

To remove a split from the Code window, do one of the following:

- On the menu bar, select **Window** > **Split** to cancel the selection.
- Double-click the split bar.
- Drag the split bar to the top or bottom of the Code window.

Switching Between Code Windows

You can use the Ctrl+F6 keyboard shortcut to quickly switch between Code windows. You can cycle through all open Code windows by repeatedly selecting Ctrl+F6. To cycle through the Code windows in reverse order, select Ctrl+Shift+F6.

Full Module View and Procedure View

If you have several procedures in one module and want to display only one at a time, select the **Procedure View** icon (on the bottom left of the Code window). In Procedure View, you can switch between different procedures by selecting the procedure name in the **Procedures** box. The **Full Module View** icon (default) displays all code in the module.

Entering a Procedure in the Code Window

This section provides quick steps on how to enter and run Sub procedures. Procedures are covered in more detail in Chapter 6.

Note This book uses the terms *Sub procedure*, *procedure*, and *routine* interchangeably. In programming, the word procedure is generally used to describe an automated task. In VBA, a procedure can be a Sub, Function, or Event procedure, which are also sometimes called *routines*. There are important differences between Sub, Function, and Event procedures, as detailed later in this book. For now, don't let the terminology confuse you. They all refer to a block of code used to automate a task.

There are two ways you can enter a procedure in a module:

- Type the opening and closing statements directly in the Code window (recommended).

    -or-

- Use the **Insert > Procedure** menu command to enter the opening and closing statements.

Follow the steps below to enter a new procedure in the Visual Basic Editor:

1. **Insert a new module in the project.**

    In the Project Explorer window, select the VBAProject where you want to create the procedure. The project could be an Excel Macro-Enabled Workbook (XLSM file) or the Personal Macro Workbook - VBAProject (PERSONAL.XLSB).

    Insert a new module by following the steps covered under **Inserting a New Module** in this chapter.

    Double-click the module in the Project Explorer window to open its Code window.

2. **Enter the start and end statements for the procedure.**

   To enter a Sub procedure, type the **Sub** keyword followed by a space, and then the name of the procedure followed by parentheses. Press **Enter** on your keyboard to let the Visual Basic Editor automatically enter the end statement - **End Sub**.

   The code below shows a Sub procedure named Greetings:

   ```
   Sub Greetings()

   End Sub
   ```

   To enter a Function procedure, use the **Function** keyword instead of **Sub**. The closing statement for a Function procedure is **End Function**.

   The code example below shows a Function procedure named CalcInterest:

   ```
   Function CalcInterest()

   End Function
   ```

3. **Write your code.**

   Enter your code between the opening and end statements of the procedure, as shown below.

   ```
   Sub Greetings()
       MsgBox "Hello world!"
   End Sub
   ```

   To indent a line of code, press Tab. To outdent a line of code, place the cursor before the first character in the line and press Shift+Tab or the Backspace key.

4. **Save your procedure.**

   Once done, save your code by selecting **File** > **Save** on the menu bar. Alternatively, you can click the **Save** button on the toolbar (blue disk icon).

5. **Run your code.**

   Test your code to ensure it is working. Use one of the following methods to run a procedure without arguments in the Visual Basic Editor.

- Place the cursor inside the procedure and select the **Run Sub/UserForm** button (the green right-pointing triangle icon on the toolbar).

    -or-

- Press F5.

    -or-

- On the menu bar, select **Run > Run Sub/UserForm**.

> **Note** See **Chapter 5: Working with Procedures** for a detailed coverage of procedures and their different execution methods.

Other Code Navigation Features

This section covers other features in VBA that are used for navigating through code. When you have a lot of code in your application, navigating and finding specific items can be difficult. Fortunately, VBA has an array of tools that make it easier to manage your project. You can use the Object and Procedure boxes in the Code window to find procedures within your module. The Object Browser allows you to browse objects in your application and identify the location of procedures and variables. The **Find** dialog box lets you search for text in a procedure, module, or project.

Finding Text

Use the **Find** command on the **Edit** menu to search for specific text. You can search for the text in the current procedure, module, project, or selected text. The Find dialog box also gives you other options, like finding whole words only or matching the case of the search term.

The following image shows the Find dialog box:

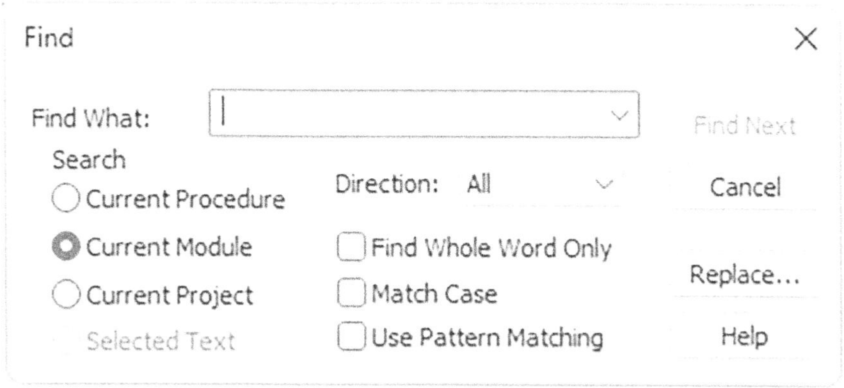

Figure 3-6: Finding text.

Follow the steps below to find text:

1. On the Visual Basic Editor menu, select **Edit > Find**.
2. In the Find What box, enter your search term.
3. Under **Search**, choose one option from **Current Procedure**, **Current Module**, **Current Project**, or **Selected Text**.
4. Set other search options if necessary.
5. Click **Find Next** to find the next occurrence of the text.

Replacing Text

You may occasionally need to replace text, for instance, the name of a variable used in several places in your code. Use the **Replace** dialog box to find and replace text.

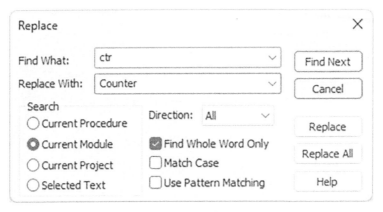

Figure 3-7: Finding and replacing text.

Follow the steps below to replace text:

1. On the Visual Basic Editor menu, select **Edit** > **Replace**.
2. In the **Find What** box, enter your search term.
3. In the **Replace With** box, type the replacement text.
4. Under **Search**, choose one of the options.
5. Set other search options, for example, **Find Whole Word Only**, to search for whole words.
6. Select **Find Next** to find the next occurrence of the text. This step checks that the search term finds the right text before performing any replacement operation.
7. Select **Replace** to replace the text one at a time or **Replace All** to replace all occurrences.

Chapter 3: Understanding The Visual Basic Editor

Finding Items with the Object Browser

You can use the **Object Browser** to display the procedures, module-level variables, and module-level constants available in a module. This tool gives you a top-level view of project objects and where certain procedures, variables, and constants have been placed.

The following image shows the Object Browser displaying the members of the *Arrays* module.

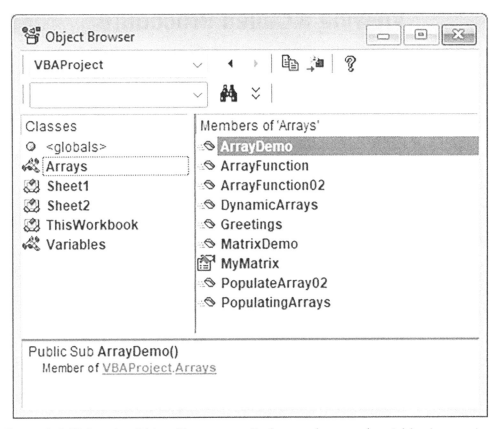

Figure 3-8: Using the Object Browser to find procedures and variables in a project.

To find a procedure using the Object Browser, do the following:

1. On the Standard toolbar, click the **Object Browser** button (or select **View > Object Browser** on the menu bar).

77

2. In the **Project/Library** dropdown list box, select the project containing the procedure you want to view.

3. Select the module under **Classes**.

4. Right-click the procedure name in the **Members** box and select **View Definition** to open the procedure in the Code window.

Viewing a Called Procedure

You can quickly navigate to a called procedure in your code using Shift+F2. This feature is useful if you have a lot of code and many procedures in your project.

To view a called procedure in your code, do the following:

1. In the calling procedure, place the cursor within the called procedure's name and select Shift+F2.

2. Select Ctrl+Shift+F2 to return to the calling procedure.

Note The Visual Basic Editor maintains a history of the last eight accessed or edited lines. So, you can use the **View > Last Position** menu command to quickly navigate to the previous location in your code.

Using Bookmarks

Another feature that comes in handy when you have a lot of code to navigate is using Bookmarks, which are placeholders in the Code window. You can mark points in the Code window you want to access quickly.

Chapter 3: Understanding The Visual Basic Editor

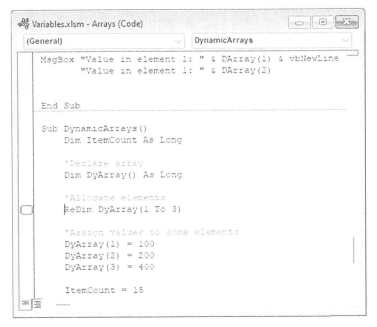

Figure 3-9: Using bookmarks in the Code window.

To set a bookmark, do the following:

1. Place the cursor on the line of code you want to bookmark.
2. On the menu, select **Edit** > **Bookmarks** > **Toggle Bookmark**.

To clear a bookmark, do the following:

1. Place the cursor on the bookmarked line.
2. On the menu, select **Edit** > **Bookmarks** > **Toggle Bookmark**.

To jump to a bookmark:

- On the Edit menu, select **Bookmarks** > **Next Bookmark** (to go forward) or **Bookmarks** > **Previous Bookmark** (to go backward).

To clear all bookmarks:

- On the menu, select **Edit** > **Bookmarks** > **Clear All Bookmarks**.

Documenting and Formatting Code

This section covers editing features in VBA that make your code easier to read. These features include indenting code, breaking up long lines of code, and adding comments to code.

Indenting

Proper use of indenting enables your code to be more readable. Use indents to differentiate parts of code like looping blocks and conditional branches.

Indenting

To indent a line of code, position the cursor before the first character in the line and do one of the following:

- Press the Tab key.
- Select **Edit > Indent** on the menu.
- Select the **Indent** button on the **Edit** toolbar.

To indent a code block, select the whole block and use one of the methods above.

Outdenting

To outdent a line of code, position the cursor before the first character in the line and do one of the following:

- Press Shift+Tab or the Backspace key.
- Select **Edit > Outdent** on the menu.
- Select the **Outdent** button on the **Edit** toolbar.

To outdent a block of code, select the whole block and use one of the methods above.

The example below shows indented code:

```
Select Case Score
     Case 70 To 100
           Result = "Merit"
     Case 50 To 69
           Result = "Credit"
     Case 40 To 49
           Result = "Pass"
     Case Is < 40
           Result = "Fail"
     Case Else
           Result = "Undetermined"
End Select
```

Adding Comments

Before you start writing code in a procedure, you may want to include a brief description of what the procedure does, the date it was created, and your name (if you're working in a shared environment). Adding comments is part of the documentation process and helps with code maintenance. It should be standard practice in a production setting.

To add comments to your code, type an apostrophe at the beginning of each line of text you want to enter as a comment. VBA ignores these lines during code execution.

By default, comments are identified in the Code window as green text, which enables you to tell the difference between comments and executable code.

> **Tip:** When testing code, you can use an apostrophe to comment out code that you don't want to run. For instance, you may want to test how the code executes without a particular line of code. Instead of deleting the line, you can add an apostrophe in front of it like this:
>
> ```
> 'Selection.Columns.AutoFit
> ```
>
> You can also use the **Comment Block** and **Uncomment Block** button on the **Edit** toolbar to comment or uncomment several lines of code.

Using the Line-Continuation Character

When writing code, you may occasionally create lengthy statements that require horizontal scrolling in the Code window. This doesn't affect program execution but can make the code more difficult to read. In such cases, you could break a long statement into several lines. Use the line-continuation character, the underscore (_), to break up a single line of code into several lines.

To break a line of code in two, place the cursor in the position where you want to break the line and press the Spacebar key (to insert a space) and then an underscore (_), as shown in the following example code:

```
MsgBox Categories(0) & ", " & Categories(1) _
       & ", " & Categories(2)
```

> **Note** You can't use the line-continuation character within a text string. Also, comments cannot be added after a line-continuation character on the same line.

Customizing the VBA Environment

The Visual Basic Editor includes an Options dialog box that lets you set options that affect its environment. For example, you can set options to determine which windows are docked (attached to the edge of the Visual Basic Editor) and which ones you want to be floating. You can also set options to change the font type, size, color, and background in the Code window.

To customize the Visual Basic Editor, select **Tools** > **Options**.

Excel displays the Options dialog box.

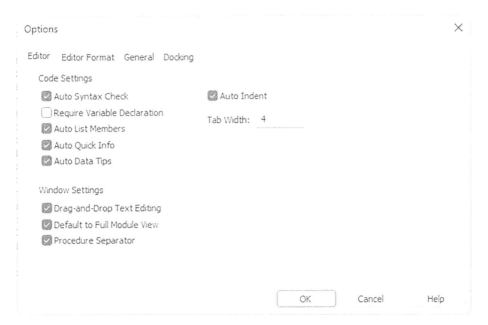

Figure 3-10: The Editor tab in the Options dialog box.

The following section describes the various tabs and the settings you can change:

Editor tab

- **Auto Syntax Check**: This setting determines whether VBA automatically checks the syntax as you're typing the code in the Code window. If the Visual Basic Editor discovers an error, it will display a dialog box with some information about the error. When this option is turned off, the Visual Basic Editor will flag syntax errors in red. If you're new to VBA, it is important to select this option.

- **Require Variable Declaration**: This option determines whether variables need to be explicitly declared before they can be used in modules. When you select this option, VBA adds the **Option Explicit** statement to the Declarations section of each new module. The change only applies to new modules, and existing code is unaffected. Option Explicit is discussed in more detail in Chapter 4.

- **Auto List Members**: As you type in the Code window, this feature provides IntelliSense help when a property, method, or object name is required to complete the statement. This feature provides a list of options to logically complete the statement.

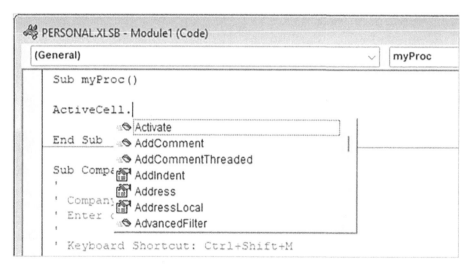

Figure 3-11: Using Auto List Members, i.e., VBA's IntelliSense.

- **Auto Quick Info**: This option displays information about functions and their arguments as you enter them in the Code window. This feature is similar to the pop-up tip in Excel, which lists the arguments and their order as you enter a function.

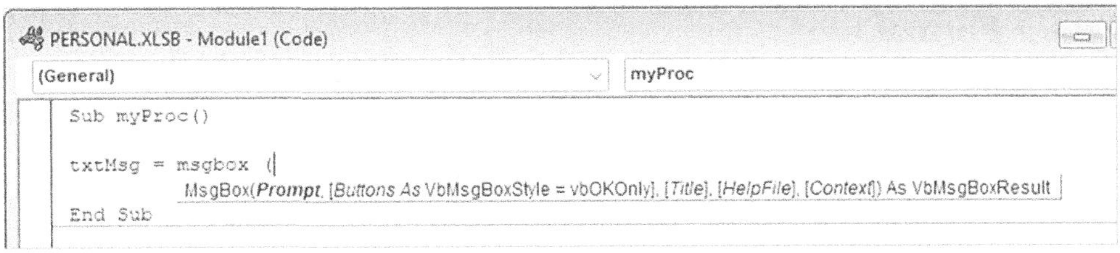

Chapter 3: Understanding The Visual Basic Editor

```
Sub myProc()

txtMsg = msgbox (
          MsgBox(Prompt, [Buttons As VbMsgBoxStyle = vbOKOnly], [Title], [HelpFile], [Context]) As VbMsgBoxResult
End Sub
```

Figure 3-12: Using Auto Quick Info.

- **Auto Data Tips**: This option is only available in break mode while debugging your application. It displays the value of a variable when you hover your mouse pointer over it.

- **Auto Indent**: Ensures that when you indent any line of code, subsequent lines are started at the same level of indent. This feature makes code easier to read. Use the tab key to indent code rather than the spacebar.

- **Tab Width**: Determines the number of spaces for each tab. This number can range from 1 to 32. For most instances, the default of 4 is okay.

- **Drag-And-Drop Editing**: You can drag and drop code segments within the same window or from the Code window into other windows like the Immediate or Watch windows. The Code window does not allow you to drag and drop code selections if this option is cleared.

- **Default to Full Module View**: Full Module View lets you see all the procedures in the Code window as a single scrollable list. When this option is cleared, the Code window only displays one procedure at a time.

- **Procedure Separator**: This setting displays a separation line at the end of each procedure in the Code window, making it easier to read the code.

Editor Format tab

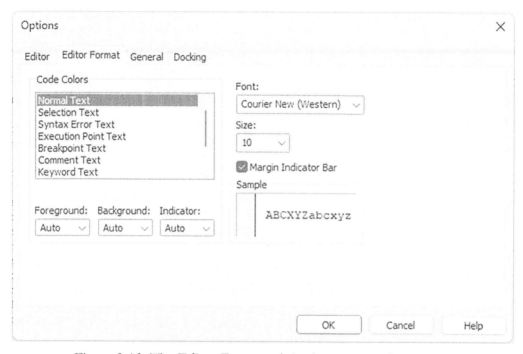

Figure 3-13: The Editor Format tab in the Options dialog box.

On this tab, you can select a text option under **Code Colors** and change various properties for the option, including the Font, Size, Background, Foreground, and Indicator. The Sample box previews the selected text option and how it would look in the Code window.

For example, if you prefer your Code window to have white text against a black background, select Normal Text and change the Foreground and Background to the preferred colors. If you like the default colors of the Code window, you don't need to make any changes here.

General tab

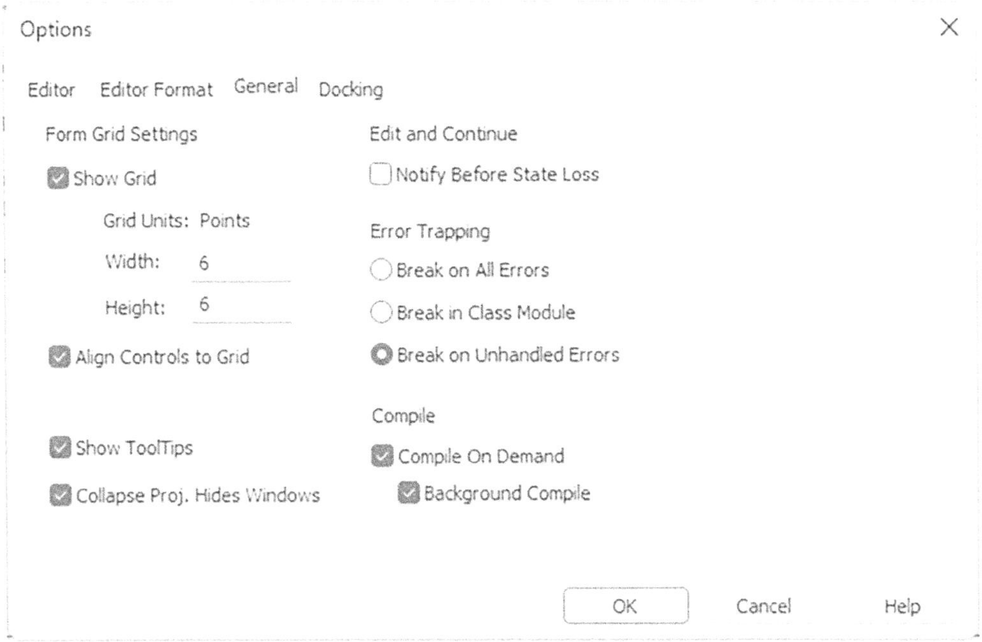

Figure 3-14: The General tab in the Options dialog box.

The General tab has several options for different aspects of the project, including form settings, error handling, and compile settings. You do not need to change the default settings here if you're new to VBA. However, you should know what changes you can make here to customize the Visual Basic Editor for specific requirements. For example, when testing a project, you may temporarily enable **Break on all Errors** to check when certain errors are triggered, even when handled.

Docking tab

Figure 3-15: Docking windows in the Visual Basic Editor.

The **Docking** tab allows you to select which windows you want to be dockable in the Visual Basic Editor. If you want a window to be floating, you can clear its selection here. A docked window is when it is anchored to one edge of the Visual Basic Editor. The default settings have most of the windows set as dockable, apart from Object Browser. For most users, the default options here work just fine.

To undock a window in the Visual Basic Editor, click its title bar, drag it from its current docked location, and then release the mouse.

To dock a window, click its title bar and move it close to (or over) one of the edges of the Visual Basic Editor. When the window is over a docking location, a transparent rectangle appears. Release the mouse to dock the window to that location.

Customizing the Toolbar

Most commands you need when using the Visual Basic Editor can be found on the **Standard** toolbar. However, additional toolbars for specific tasks contain commands geared to that task. For example, the **Debug** toolbar comes in handy when debugging your code. There is also a **UserForm** toolbar that makes it easier to access commands related to designing UserForms.

Adding Additional Toolbars

To display other toolbars, right-click anywhere on the Visual Basic Editor toolbar area and select **Customize**.

The Visual Basic Editor displays the **Customize** dialog box (shown below).

Figure 3-16: Use the **Customize** dialog box to show/hide toolbars.

The **Customize** dialog box has three tabs:

- **Toolbars**: Allows you to select which toolbars to display.
- **Commands**: You can drag and add commands from different categories to any of the displayed toolbars.
- **Options**: Provides additional settings. For example, you can display larger icons on the toolbar or select specific menu animations.

Edit Menu Bars and Toolbars

Follow the steps below to rearrange items on menu bars and toolbars:

1. Right-click anywhere on the Visual Basic Editor toolbar and select **Customize** on the shortcut menu.
2. In the **Customize** dialog box, on the **Commands** tab, click **Rearrange Commands**.
3. In the **Rearrange Commands** dialog box, select the menu bar or toolbar you want to rearrange.

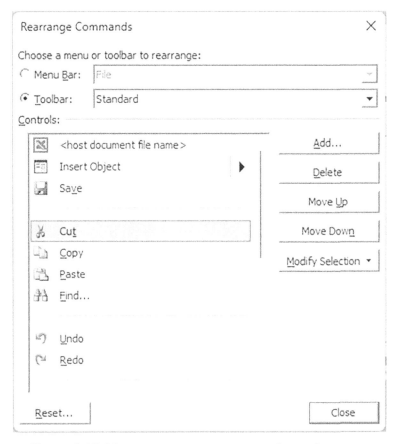

Figure 3-17: You can rearrange commands on the menu.

4. In the **Controls** box, select the item you want to reposition and click **Move Up** or **Move Down** to change its position on the selected menu bar or toolbar.

5. Add or remove items on the selected menu bar or toolbar by clicking the **Add** or **Delete** buttons.

Chapter 4

VBA Essentials

In this chapter:

- Using variables and constants.
- Understanding the data types in VBA.
- Using operators in VBA.
- Using the MsgBox and InputBox functions to interact with users.
- Overview of other useful built-in VBA functions.

This chapter will cover the essentials to begin writing VBA code statements. As you start using VBA, you'll often use variables, operators like the assignment operator, and the MsgBox function, even for basic lines of code. After reading this chapter, you will be armed with the prerequisites to learn the other more exciting VBA language features.

Variables and Data Types

Variables are used to store and manipulate data in your code. Think of a variable as a named memory location where you can temporarily hold data while your program runs. Once created, you can use the name to refer to that memory location for the rest of the program. You can store, update, and retrieve data from the variable in your code. When the program ends, the values are removed from memory.

Variable Data Types

There are different types of variables for the different types of data they hold, also referred to as data types. The table below lists the common VBA data types with their storage size and range:

Data type	Storage size	Range
String (Variable length)	10 bytes + string length	0 to approximately 2 billion characters.
String (fixed length)	Length of string	1 to approximately 64K characters.
Byte	1 byte	0 to 255
Integer	2 bytes	-32,768 to 32,767
Long	4 bytes	-2,147,483,648 to 2,147,483,647
Single	4 bytes	-3.40E38 to -1.40E-45 for negative values 1.40E-45 to 3.40E38 for positive values
Double	8 bytes	-1.79769313486231E308 to -4.94065645841247E-324 for negative values 4.94065645841247E-324 to 1.79769313486232E308 for positive values
Boolean	2 bytes	True or False

Variant	Varies	Any kind of data.
Object	4 bytes	Holds a generic object reference.
Currency	8 bytes	922,337,203,685,477.5808 to 922,337,203,685,477.5807
Date	8 bytes	1/1/0100 to 12/31/9999

Variable Naming Guidelines

VBA has certain rules and conventions when naming variables, procedures, constants, and arguments in a module. Rules are mandatory for the code to run. Conversely, naming conventions are recommendations that make your code easier to read and maintain.

Variable Naming Rules

There are certain naming VBA rules you must follow for naming variables:

- The first character must be a letter.
- Only use alphanumeric characters, as well as the underscore character.
- Use unique variable names within the same scope.
- VBA is not case-sensitive. Thus, you can't use the same name for two variables even if the cases differ. For example, *UserName* is the same name as *username* or *USERNAME*. However, VBA preserves any capitalization used during variable declaration.
- You can't use spaces in variable names. To separate words, use a combination of uppercase and lowercase characters.
- Variable names cannot exceed 255 characters. Of course, you would not want to make a variable name anywhere near that long.

Conventions for Naming Variables

If you're using more than one word to name a variable, capitalize the first letter of each word to differentiate words in the variable name. This naming convention is known as **Pascal case**, a variation of **Camel case**. For instance, use *CustomerName* instead of *Customername*.

One benefit of using Pascal case is that it makes it easier to tell if you mistyped a variable name. After declaration, whenever you type the variable name in your procedure, VBA's automatic syntax checking will convert it to its proper case. You'll know a variable has been mistyped if VBA's automatic syntax checking does not correct the case when you type the variable in all lowercase. Mistyped variables can lead to bugs that can be difficult to find if **Option Explicit** is not enabled.

Note Visual Basic once had a popular naming convention called Systems Hungarian, where a three-letter prefix is added to a variable name to represent its data type. For example, *intCount* instead of *Count*. The prefix lets you know the data type of a variable wherever it is used in your code.

Systems Hungarian has largely fallen out of favor as type-checking has improved in modern compilers. Adding prefixes to variable names may also make code less readable. However, naming conventions are recommendations and not rules. They are used as a matter of style. Use a style that works best for you, but be consistent.

Declaring Variables

Variable declarations are non-executable code statements that name variables and specify their data type. Declare variables to tell VBA the variables you'll use later. You can declare variables either implicitly or explicitly in VBA.

Implicit variable declaration

Implicit variable declaration means you can type a variable name and assign a value to it anywhere in your code without first declaring it. The variable is implicitly declared when it is first used. Variables that are not explicitly declared can cause errors that are difficult to debug. Therefore, implicitly declared variables are not recommended even though you can theoretically use them in VBA.

Explicit variable declaration

To explicitly declare a variable in VBA, use a **Dim** statement followed by the name of your variable and its data type. Dim is short for dimension.

The following code declares three variables using the Dim statement:

```
Dim UserName As String
Dim MyNumber As Long
Dim UserMsg As Variant
```

Declare a variable inside a procedure to create a local variable or place it in the **Declarations** section of a module to create a module-level variable. We'll cover the scope of variables later in this chapter.

You can declare multiple variables in one statement. You must specify the data type individually for each variable if you want to give them a data type. Use a comma to separate the variables.

The following statement declares three variables of the Long data type:

```
Dim Count As Long, Periods As Long, Num As Long
```

VBA uses the **Variant** data type by default if you don't specify a data type when declaring a variable. In the following statement, *InterestRate* and *CustName* are assigned the **Variant** data type by default, while Period is declared as a Long data type:

```
Dim InterestRate, CustName, Period As Long
```

> **Note** Unlike some other programming languages, VBA doesn't allow you to declare a set of variables to all be of the same data type with only one **As** keyword. You must explicitly specify the data type of each variable.

Explicit variable declaration allows you to use VBA's IntelliSense feature when using variables. After typing the first two letters of a variable name, select Ctrl+Spacebar to complete the name entry or display a list of auto-complete options (if there are several names starting with those letters). The Visual Basic Editor will display a list from which you can select the variable name you want.

Also, whenever an explicitly declared variable is used, VBA automatically converts its name to match the case in the declaration statement. This feature lets you quickly determine whether your entry is correct, which is particularly useful when working with long variable names.

Using Option Explicit

VBA allows you to use undeclared (implicit) variables, meaning you can just create a name anywhere in your procedure and assign a value to it. Besides small lines of demo code, implicit variable declaration is not recommended. For any substantial work or work done in a production environment, always declare your variables.

To ensure that all variables used in a module are explicitly declared, add the **Option Explicit** statement to the top of the module before the first procedure. This area is called the **Declarations** section.

Enter this statement once at the top of the module:

```
Option Explicit
```

This statement ensures all variables are declared before use in all procedures in the module. VBA generates a syntax error whenever it detects an undeclared variable.

Mastering Excel VBA Programming

Figure 4-1: The Declarations section.

You can go a step further and enable the **Require Variable Declaration** option under **Code Settings** in the Visual Basic Editor **Options** dialog box.

To enforce variable declaration for all subsequent modules, do the following:

1. On the Visual Basic Editor toolbar, select **Tools** > **Options** to open the **Options** dialog box.
2. On the **Editor** tab, select **Require Variable Declaration** and select **OK**.

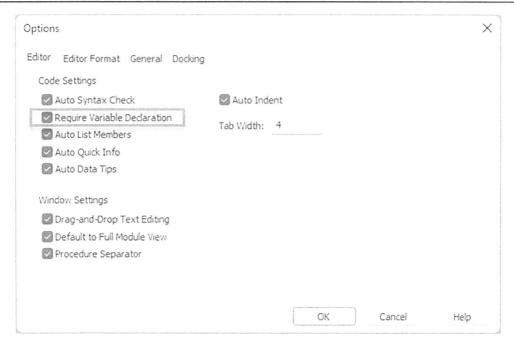

Figure 4-2: Enabling explicit variable declaration in VBA Options.

When you select **Require Variable Declaration**, all new modules automatically have an **Option Explicit** statement inserted in the Declarations section.

Option Explicit prevents errors caused by mistyped variable names. Without Option Explicit, you can type any variable name and assign a value to it at any point in your code.

Implicit variable declarations may make writing code faster, but they can also introduce errors that are difficult to identify. For example, you could mistype a variable name you've previously used by one letter, but VBA's automatic syntax checking feature will not flag the name as an error. The misspelled variable name could lead to unexpected results when running your program, but VBA sees the code as valid. Ensure Option Explicit is enabled at the top of your modules to avoid errors caused by mistyped variables.

Assigning Values to Variables

To assign a value to a variable, you need to use an assignment statement. An assignment statement assigns the value or result of an expression to a variable or an object. If you've created formulas in Excel before, you'll be familiar with the concept of expressions. In Excel, to insert a formula in a cell, you precede the formula with an equal sign (=). In VBA, you use an equal sign to assign values to variables.

Below is an example of how you assign a value to a variable:

```
'Dimensioning the variable.
Dim Heading As String

'Assign a value to the variable.
Heading = "Figures for 2015 to 2025"
```

This statement assigns the text "Figures for 2014 to 2024" to an area in memory named Heading. Once assigned, you can use this variable name to refer to that piece of text in memory for the rest of the procedure. The example below assigns a value from the current worksheet to a variable:

```
MyNumber = Range("A1").Value
```

This statement assigns the value in cell A1 in the current worksheet to MyNumber. Once assigned, you can use this variable name to refer to that number in memory for the rest of the procedure.

You can also assign the result of an expression to a variable like this:

```
Total = Num1 + Num2
```

In this case, the values in two variables are added, and the sum is passed to a third variable called Total.

Unlike mathematical calculations, where the answer ends up on the right of the statement, in programming, an assignment goes from right to left. Hence, the answer of an evaluation will end up in the leftmost variable before the equal sign.

Just remember that the equal sign has two roles in VBA. It can be used as an assignment operator and a comparison operator.

Examples of variable declaration, assignment, and then use:

```
Sub Assignment()
    'Declare variables
    Dim Counter As Long
    Dim Rate As Variant
    Dim Amount As Double
    Dim Status As Boolean
    Dim UserName As String
    Dim StartDate As Date

    'Assign values to the variables
    Counter = 0
    Counter = Counter + 1
    Rate = 0.025
    Amount = 3482.67
    Status = False
    UserName = "Bob Johnson"
    StartDate = #1/1/2025#

    'Display the values in a message box
    MsgBox Counter & vbNewLine & _
        Rate & vbNewLine & _
        Amount & vbNewLine & _
        Status & vbNewLine & _
        UserName & vbNewLine & _
        StartDate
End Sub
```

Note VBA has an assignment keyword called **Let**. However, it is optional and usually omitted from assignment statements. Using a **Let** statement is redundant and only used as a matter of style. The code below assigns a value to a variable using the **Let** keyword.

```
Let MyNumber = 100
```

Scope of Variables

The scope of a variable determines its visibility. The scope level you declare for a variable depends on the procedures that need to have access to that variable. VBA has three scope levels: local, module, and public.

Local Variables

Local variables can only be used within the procedure they have been declared. The variables are initialized when the procedure starts. That means they always start from zero (0) or Null each time the procedure is run. Declare variables to be used locally with a **Dim** statement.

Example:

```
Dim MsgText As String
```

The **Static** statement is also used to declare local variables in some instances. See more on static variables below.

Module Variables

If you want a variable to be accessible from every procedure in a module, declare the variable using the **Private** or **Dim** statement in the module's **Declarations** section. Using Private or Dim means the variable will only be available to procedures within the module and not the entire application. Variables declared at the module level are initialized to zero (0) or Null when the application starts. Module-level variables maintain their values while the program is being run. They may be set and reset from different procedures in the module.

Note that at the module level, the **Dim** statement is equivalent to the **Private** statement, as variables are private within their declared scope by default. However, you can use the Private statement to make your code easier to understand.

Example of module variables:

```
Dim UserName As String
Private InterestRate As Double
```

Public Variables

Public variables are available to the entire application. To make a variable available to the entire application (rather than just a module or procedure), declare the variable with the **Public** statement in the **Declarations** section of any module or UserForm. You can't declare a Public variable within a procedure, as VBA generates a compile error when you try to run the code. Variables declared within procedures are always Private.

Example of a public variable:

```
Public ApplicationName As String
```

Lifetime of a Variable

The lifetime of a variable determines how long its value is stored in memory as the application runs. Module-level, public, and static variables have their values stored in memory for as long as the application runs.

Except for static variables, local variables in a procedure have a lifetime only within that procedure. When the procedure stops, the variables are removed from memory. Whenever a procedure is executed, all local variables are initialized to zero (0) or Null. Numeric variables are initialized to zero (0), while string variables are initialized to Null.

Using Static Variables

To preserve the value of a local variable even when the procedure has stopped running, use the **Static** statement instead of the **Dim** statement to declare the variable. Variables declared with a Static statement retain their values for the lifetime of the application.

You use static variables when you need to call a procedure multiple times from another procedure, and you want a variable inside the called procedure to retain its last value between calls instead of reinitializing each time to zero (0) or Null.

The procedure below keeps a count of how many times it has been executed and displays the number in a message box:

```
Sub StaticVariable()
   Static Counter As Long
   Counter = Counter + 1
   MsgBox "This procedure has been called " & Counter & " times."
End Sub
```

Each time you run the procedure by clicking the **Run** command, it increments the counter in the displayed message. VBA does not reset the *Counter* variable after the procedure ends. The variable is only reset to 0 when you select the **Reset** button on the toolbar or close and reopen the workbook.

Note that a module-level variable can produce the same results as the example above. However, all procedures within the module would have access to the variable and can potentially change its value. Thus, if you want a variable to be local to a procedure yet retain its value between procedure calls, use the **Static** statement to declare the variable.

You can manually reset all variables stored in memory by selecting the **Reset** button on the Visual Basic Editor toolbar (the blue square icon on the standard toolbar).

The following table summarizes the scope of variables and where to declare them:

Level	Scope	Declaring the variable
Local variables	Procedure only	Use **Dim** or **Static** within a procedure.
Module variables	Module only	Use **Dim** or **Private** in the Declarations section of the module.

| Public variables | All procedures in all modules | Use **Public** in the Declarations section of any module in the application. |

Using String Variables

VBA has two types of string variables: Fixed-length and variable-length strings. The maximum number of characters a fixed-length string can hold is approximately 65,400 characters, while variable-length strings can theoretically hold up to 2 billion characters.

When declaring a string with the Dim statement, you can specify whether it's a fixed-length or a variable-length string. A variable-length string is sufficient for most scenarios, as you don't have to worry about its capacity when assigning values to it. You can use fixed-length strings to restrict the number of characters stored or conserve memory space (RAM). For example, you can use a fixed-length string for a name variable you anticipate will never exceed 50 characters.

```
'Fixed length string of 50 characters
Dim CustName As String * 50

'Variable length string
Dim MsgText As String
```

Using Date Variables

You can store dates in string variables to use in your code, but you cannot perform automatic date calculations using string variables. On the other hand, you can use a **Date** data type, which allows you to store dates and perform date calculations.

Note that dates must be stored in Date data type variables in a US date format.

For example:
- *#January 14, 2025#*
- *#01/14/2025#* (i.e., mm/dd/yyyy)

However, VBA displays dates using the short date format of your region. For instance, if the date format for your region is dd/mm/yyyy (like in the UK), you need to enter the date as #01/14/2025# in a Date variable. Whenever the value of that variable is displayed, VBA will display the date as 14/01/2025.

Generally, you want to choose the data type that takes the least memory resources (RAM) but can handle all the data you want to store in the variable in all circumstances.

```
Dim StartDate As Date
Const ContractStartDate As Date = #1/1/2025#
Const StartTime = #09:00:00#
```

Using Constants

Constants are similar to variables in that they are named locations in memory used to store values to be used in an application. However, constants contain values that do not change during the execution of a program, hence the name - *constant*. Constants can have the same data types as variables.

Using a constant instead of repeatedly typing the same value throughout your code is good practice. Duplication of values could introduce errors and maintenance issues down the line. For example, suppose a value used in several parts of your code in different modules needs to be changed. Manually changing the values could introduce errors. If the value was assigned to a constant, it only needs to be changed in one place. Examples of constants are business rules, constraints, interest rates, number of months, and your company's name.

To declare a constant, use the **Const** statement as shown in the examples below:

```
'Constants are Private by default
Const Period As Long = 12

'Declaring a Public constant
Public Const AppName As String = "Highland Furniture LTD"

'Declaring a Private constant
Private Const ContractMonths As Long = 6
```

```
'Declaring multiple constants on the same line
Const MyStr = "Hello", InterestRate As Double = 5.75
```

Constants are private by default. However, you can declare constants with the **Public** statement in the Declarations section of a module to make them available to all objects in your application. Constants declared in a procedure are always private and cannot be made public.

Constants also have a scope similar to variables. Note the following points on how to determine the scope of your constants during declaration:

- **Local**: Declare a constant inside a procedure if you want it to be available only within the procedure.

- **Module-level**: To make a constant available to all procedures in a module, declare it in the module's Declarations section.

- **Public**: To make a constant available to all modules in an application, declare it using the **Public** keyword in the Declarations section of any module in the application.

As constants do not change after being declared, if you try to change the value of a constant at runtime, VBA generates an error.

Tip: To distinguish between constants and variables, you can use all uppercase letters to name constants. The uppercase letters help to remind you that you can't change constants in the code after declaration.

Operators in VBA

The operators in VBA work in a similar way to Excel operators. So, if you're familiar with Excel operators, the operators in VBA will be second nature to you. The one slight difference is the modulus operator. To carry out mod calculations in Excel, you use the MOD function instead of an operator. In VBA, you use the Mod operator just like any of the other operators.

Arithmetic Operators

The following arithmetic operators perform basic mathematical calculations in VBA, such as addition, subtraction, multiplication, and division:

Operator	Meaning
+ (plus sign)	Addition
– (minus sign)	Subtraction or Negation
* (asterisk)	Multiplication
/ (forward slash)	Normal division
^ (caret)	Exponentiation
\ (backslash)	Divide two numbers and return an integer result.
Mod (modulus)	Divide two numbers and return only the remainder.

Concatenation

Operator	Meaning
& (ampersand)	Used to combine two string expressions.

Comparison Operators

Comparison operators allow you to compare two values and return a logical value, True or False.

Operator	Meaning
=	Equal to
>	Greater than
<	Less than
>=	Greater than or equal to
<=	Less than or equal to
<>	Not equal to
Is	For comparing two object reference variables

Logical Operators

Logical operators compare Boolean expressions and return True or False. The And, Or, and Xor operators take two operands, while the Not operator takes only one operand. Logical operators evaluate conditional expressions to determine whether something is true or false.

Operator	Description
And	Returns True if both expressions are true. Otherwise, it returns False.
Or	Returns True if any part is True. Otherwise, it returns False.
Not	Performs a logical negation on an expression. It reverses True and False.
Xor	Performs a logical exclusion on two expressions. Returns True if one expression is True. Otherwise, it returns False.

> **Note** There are other logical operators in VBA, but you'll rarely need to use more than the operators listed above in your programming career.

Operator Precedence

If you combine several operators in a single statement, VBA performs the operations in the following order:

Order	Operator	Description
1	-	Negation (as in -1)
2	%	Percentage
3	^	Exponentiation
4	* and /	Multiplication and floating-point division
5	+ and -	Addition and subtraction
6	&	String concatenation
7	=, < >, <=, >=, <>	All comparison operators

At a basic level, just remember that multiplication and division are performed before addition and subtraction. If a statement contains operators with the same precedence, for example, multiplication and division, VBA evaluates the operators from left to right.

Parentheses and Operator Precedence

You can change the order of evaluation by enclosing parts of your statement in parentheses (). The part of the statement in parentheses will be calculated first.

For example, the following calculation produces 75 because VBA calculates multiplication before addition. VBA multiplies 7 by 10 first before adding 5 to the result.

5+7*10

Answer = 75

In contrast, if we enclose 5+7 in parentheses, VBA will calculate 5 + 7 first before multiplying the result by 10 to produce 120.

(5+7)*10

Answer = 120

In another example, we want to add 20% to 300. Due to the parentheses around the second part of the statement, VBA carries out the addition first before the multiplication to produce 360.

300 * (1 + 0.2)

Answer = 360

Use parentheses whenever possible to ensure that your calculations produce the right results. Using parentheses also makes it easier to read your code because it breaks longer statements into smaller units.

Built-In VBA Functions

VBA provides a number of built-in functions that you can use in your code to perform different types of calculations and other actions without needing to reinvent the wheel. Note that built-in VBA functions are different from worksheet functions, although some of them perform the same calculations. The built-in VBA functions are used in code, while worksheet functions are used to perform actions on worksheets, even when invoked from VBA. For more details about calling worksheet functions in code, see Chapter 10.

The MsgBox Function

User interaction is an important part of any application with a user interface. VBA has several tools you can use to enable users to interact with your application. The message box is an essential tool you'll often use in VBA, not just for communicating with users but for testing and debugging your application during development.

Use the **MsgBox** function when you want to display a message to the user or ask a question that requires a response with a button click at runtime.

The **MsgBox** function can be used in two ways:

- **To display a simple message.**

    You display a simple message to the user and do not want to capture a response.

- **To display a message and get a response from the user.**

    You display a message to the user and capture their response as a return value, which is used to make decisions in your application.

Syntax:

MsgBox (*prompt*, [*buttons*,] [*title*,] [*helpfile, context*])

The table below describes the arguments for the MsgBox function. Only the *prompt* argument is required. The other arguments are optional.

Argument	Description
prompt	The text that is displayed to the user in the message box. The text can be a maximum of 1024 characters. You can break up the lines by using the **vbNewLine** constant if the text needs to be in multiple lines.
buttons	A number specifying the number and type of buttons to display. If omitted, it defaults to 0, which shows only the OK button.
title	The text shown in the title bar of the dialog box. If omitted, the name of the application will be displayed in the title bar.
helpfile	This text string identifies the Help file that provides context-sensitive help for the dialog box. If *helpfile* is provided, the *context* argument must also be provided. This argument is only required if you're providing context-sensitive help.
context	The number assigned to the appropriate Help topic. If *context* is provided, the *helpfile* argument must also be provided.

Displaying a Simple Message Box

If you don't need a response from the user, don't put parentheses around the arguments of the MsgBox function. The example below enters the *Prompt* and *Title* arguments but omits the *Button* argument. When you omit a positional argument, you must include the corresponding comma delimiter.

```
MsgBox "The process is now complete.", , "Highland Furniture"
```

The code above will display the following message box:

Figure 4-3: A simple message box.

In the example below, a simple message box displays the sum to the user and doesn't return a result. The only argument used is *prompt*. The prompt must be enclosed in quotes as it is a text string. The ampersand (&) concatenates the text in quotes with a number variable to make up the prompt.

```
Sub SumNumbers()
    Dim NumSum As Long
    NumSum = 1 + 2
    MsgBox "The sum is: " & NumSum
End Sub
```

While the message box is displayed, code execution is paused until the user clicks OK to dismiss it.

Figure 4-4: Concatenating text in a message box.

Getting a Response from Users

To capture the user's response when they click a button, you need to use parentheses around the MsgBox function arguments. A message box with more than just the OK button requires additional code to determine the clicked button. To specify the icon and buttons to display on the message box, use the constants listed below for the *buttons* argument.

VBA constants for the *buttons* argument of the MsgBox function:

Constant	Value	Description
vbOKOnly	0	Displays the OK button only.
vbOKCancel	1	Displays the OK and Cancel buttons.
vbAbortRetryIgnore	2	Displays the Abort, Retry, and Ignore buttons.
vbYesNoCancel	3	Displays the Yes, No, and Cancel buttons.
vbYesNo	4	Displays the Yes and No buttons.
vbRetryCancel	5	Displays the Retry and Cancel buttons.
vbCritical	16	Displays the Critical Message icon.
vbQuestion	32	Displays the Warning Query icon.
vbExclamation	48	Displays the Warning Message icon.
vbInformation	64	Displays the Information Message icon.
vbDefaultButton1	0	The first button has the focus.
vbDefaultButton2	256	The second button has the focus.
vbDefaultButton3	512	The third button has the focus.
vbDefaultButton4	768	The fourth button has the focus.

To use more than one of these constants as an argument, add them up with the plus operator (+). For example, to display a message box with **Yes** and **No** buttons, a critical icon, and the **No** button as the default, use the following combination:

```
vbYesNo + vbCritical + vbDefaultButton2
```

The default button is the button with the focus when the message box is displayed. When the user presses Enter on their keyboard, the button with the focus is selected.

The return value of a message box is the value returned when the user clicks a button on the dialog box. There are VBA constants for the return values (shown in the table below). Suppose the user selected **Cancel** in the message box. Instead of checking whether the return value is 2, you would check whether it is **vbCancel**. Using the constants rather than numbers makes the code easier to write and read.

VBA constants for the MsgBox return value:

Constant	Value	Button clicked
vbOK	1	OK
vbCancel	2	Cancel
vbAbort	3	Abort
vbRetry	4	Retry
vbIgnore	5	Ignore
vbYes	6	Yes
vbNo	7	No

In the following code example, the procedure displays a critical error message in a message box with **Yes** and **No** buttons. The **No** button is set as the default response. The values for the arguments are assigned to variables to make the code easier to read. The value the MsgBox function returns depends on which button the user clicks.

This time, the MsgBox function arguments are enclosed in parentheses, as we want to return a value.

```
Sub ProcessConfirm()
    Dim Response As Long
    Dim Buttons As Long
    Dim Prompt As String
    Dim MsgText As String
    Dim MsgTitle As String
```

```
        Prompt = "Excel identified an issue. "
        Prompt = Prompt + "Do you want to proceed?"
        Buttons = vbYesNo + vbCritical + vbDefaultButton2
        MsgTitle = "MsgBox Demo"
        
        'Display message.
        Response = MsgBox(Prompt, Buttons, MsgTitle)
        If Response = vbYes Then    'User clicked Yes.
            MsgText = "Yes"    'Perform this action.
            MsgBox "Your answer was Yes"
        Else    'User clicked No.
            MsgText = "No"     'Perform this action.
            MsgBox "Your answer was No."
        End If
End Sub
```

The code above displays the following message box:

Figure 4-5: A message box that returns a value.

When the message is displayed, the code is paused until the user clicks **Yes** or **No**.

The line of code that follows then checks the value of the response. If the response is vbYes (meaning the user selected Yes), the first part of the If block is executed. If the response is not vbYes, the Else block is executed (because it means the user selected No).

Using vbNewLine or vbCrLf

You can use the vbNewLine constant (or the vbCrLf constant) to break a message box prompt into multiple lines. vbNewLine is similar to using a carriage return character and a linefeed character, i.e., Chr(13) + Chr(10) in Windows. vbCrLf works as a carriage return + linefeed on Windows and Mac computers.

The following example uses vbNewLine to break the message box prompt into two lines:

```
MsgBox "The interest rate is: " & Rate & vbNewLine & _
       "The capital is: " & Amount
```

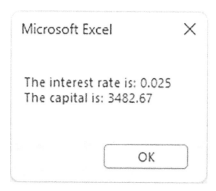

Figure 4-6: Breaking text into multiple lines in a message box.

> **Note** For a comprehensive list of built-in VBA functions, search for "Functions (Visual Basic for Applications)" using your favorite internet browser.

The InputBox Function

The MsgBox function only allows the user to click a button. To capture simple text input from users at runtime, use the **InputBox** function. The InputBox function displays a dialog box containing a text box that allows users to enter text at runtime. It allows you to get user input that can't be achieved with a simple button click.

Syntax:

InputBox(prompt, [title], [default], [xpos], [ypos], [helpfile, context])

The table below describes the arguments for the InputBox function. Only the *prompt* argument is required. The other arguments are optional.

Argument	Description
prompt	The text that is displayed in the dialog box. The message can be a maximum of 1024 characters. If the prompt is more than one line, you can break up the lines using **vbNewLine**.
title	The caption that is shown in the title bar of the input box. If omitted, "Microsoft Excel" is displayed in the title bar.
default	A default value in the text box when the input box is initially displayed. If you omit this argument, the text box is left blank.
xpos	The horizontal distance from the screen's left edge to the dialog box's left edge. The dialog box will be centered horizontally if this argument is omitted.
ypos	The vertical distance from the screen's top edge to the dialog box's top edge. If this argument is omitted, the dialog box will be displayed at approximately a third of the way down the screen.
helpfile	The context-sensitive Help file to use for the dialog box. If *helpfile* is provided, you must also provide the *context* argument.
context	A number that the Help file author assigned as the context number. If you provide *context*, you must also provide the *helpfile* argument.

The InputBox function displays a dialog box with a textbox and waits for the user to enter text or select a button. If the user selects **OK**, the input box returns a string containing the contents of the text box.

The example below calculates the interest on an amount and interest rate provided by the user. The first input box statement prompts the user to enter the amount, and the value is assigned to a variable named *Amount*. The second input box statement prompts the user to enter the interest rate, which is then assigned to the *Rate* variable. The routine calculates and displays the result to the user in a message box.

```
Sub InputBoxDemo()
    Dim MsgText As String, Title As String, Rate, Amount
    
    Title = "Calculate Interest"
    
    'Get amount from user
    MsgText = "Enter the amount (e.g. 10000):"
    Amount = InputBox(MsgText, Title)
    
    'Get IR from user
    MsgText = "Enter the interest rate e.g 5.5):"
    Rate = InputBox(MsgText, Title)
    
    'Calculate interest if values are numeric
    If IsNumeric(Amount) And IsNumeric(Rate) Then
        MsgBox "The interest is: " & Amount * (Rate / 100)
    Else
        MsgBox "Please enter numeric values."
    End If
End Sub
```

Tip: One way to keep your input box statement neat and easier to read is to first assign the values for the arguments to variables. Then, use the variables as the arguments for the function.

Note Use the input box for basic user input. For more complex user interactions involving multiple input values, use a UserForm. UserForms are covered in Chapter 14.

Other Useful Built-in VBA Functions

There are a multitude of built-in VBA functions for different types of calculations. Many of them are for specialized tasks that you may never use. However, others are quite useful, and you may use them often in your applications. These built-in functions can save you time from having to write code from scratch to perform a particular action. The list below describes some of the more useful functions.

Function	Description
Array	Creates and returns an array of Variant values based on the arguments provided.
CCur	Converts a number to currency.
CurDir	Returns the current directory on the computer.
Date	Use this function to return the current system date.
DateAdd	Adds a time interval to a date.
DateDiff	Returns the difference between two dates. You can have a multitude of intervals, including years, months, days, and weeks.
DateSerial	Combines different date parts into a date.
Day	Returns the day from the specified date value.
Format	Returns a formatted expression based on the specified named or user-defined format expression.
FormatCurrency	Formats a number to your local currency based on the specified arguments.
FormatDateTime	Returns a formatted date or time based on the specified named format provided.
FormatPercent	Formats a number to a percentage by multiplying it by 100 and adding a trailing percentage character (%).
InputBox	Displays a dialog box prompting a user to input text.
InStr	Returns a number specifying the starting position of one string within another.
IsArray	Returns True if the specified argument is an array; otherwise, it returns False.
IsDate	Returns True if the specified argument is a valid date or time; otherwise, it returns False.

IsEmpty	Returns True if a variable has not been initialized with a value. This is different from a null value.
IsError	Returns True if an expression returns an error value. Use for scenarios where an expression can potentially return an error.
IsMissing	Used to test whether an optional argument was passed to a procedure when called. Returns True if the optional argument is missing.
IsNull	Used to check whether an expression contains no valid data, i.e., a Null value. This is different from an empty string ("") or an uninitialized variable, which is Empty.
IsNumeric	Returns True if an expression is a number or can be evaluated as one.
LBound	Returns the lowest index number of an array.
LCase	Converts a string to all lowercase letters.
Left	Returns a string that contains a number of characters from the left side of a string based on the specified length.
Len	Returns a number representing the number of characters in a string.
Trim, LTrim, and RTrim	Trim removes leading and trailing spaces from a string. LTrim removes only leading spaces, while RTrim removes only trailing spaces.
Mid	Returns a string containing a specified number of characters from the middle of a string.
Month	Returns a number between 1 and 12 representing the month part of the specified date.
MsgBox	Used to display a message box to users. You can also capture user input through button clicks to make decisions in your application.
Now	Returns the current date and time based on your computer's operating system date and time.
Replace	Use this function to find and replace text within a string.
Right	Returns a string containing a number of characters from the right side of a string based on the specified length.

Split	Splits a string into an array of strings using a delimiter that is part of the string.
String	Returns a repeating character based on the specified length.
Timer	Returns the number of seconds that have passed since midnight. Use to calculate elapsed time.
TimeSerial	Returns the time based on the specified values for the hour, minute, and second arguments.
TypeName	Returns a string that provides information on the data type of the specified variable.
UBound	Returns the largest index number of an array.
UCase	Converts a string to all uppercase letters.
Weekday	Returns a number representing the day of the week based on the date provided.
Year	Returns the year portion of the specified date value.

Note For more details on a particular function, type the function name in the Code window, place the cursor within the text, and press F1.

Chapter 5

Using Arrays

In this chapter:

- Declaring arrays.
- Populating arrays with values.
- Using the LBound and UBound functions to determine the limits of an array.
- Working with multidimensional arrays.
- Understanding dynamic arrays.
- Using the Array function to create an array.

Arrays allow you to store a group of values of a similar data type under one name and use an index number to tell them apart. For example, you can declare an array of 6 elements to hold numbers. Suppose you named the array called Quantity. You can refer to the first element of the array as Quantity(0), the second as Quantity(1), the third as Quantity(2), and so on. Arrays are useful for storing a temporary list of values to be used in your application. Once the application ends, the values are discarded.

Declaring Arrays

An array can be imagined as a single row of data, as illustrated below:

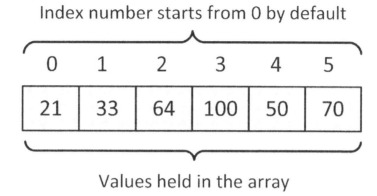

Figure 5-1: A one-dimensional array with six elements.

There are two types of arrays in VBA:

- A fixed-size array, which always remains the same size.
- A dynamic array that can change in size at runtime.

All the elements in an array are of the same data type. You can declare an array using any of the data types discussed under **Variables and Data Types** in Chapter 4.

In VBA, you must explicitly declare arrays before you can use them, even if **Option Explicit** is not enabled. This strict rule differs from variables that can be declared implicitly. Arrays have upper and lower bounds, with the individual elements in sequential order within those bounds. By default, the lower bound of an array starts from zero (0), and the upper bound cannot exceed the range of the Long data type (2,147,483,647).

To declare a fixed-size array, use the **Dim** statement followed by the name of the array and the upper bound index number in parentheses, as shown below:

```
'A 15 element array
Dim Counter(14) As Long

'A 20 element array
Dim SubTotals(19) As Double
```

The upper bound of the 15-element array declared above is 14, as the index numbers run from 0 to 14. Likewise, the upper bound of the 20-element array is 19 as the elements count from 0 to 19.

> **Note** VBA allocates memory space for each element in an array when the application initializes, so avoid declaring an array larger than necessary.

Changing Array Bounds

Using the default lower bound of 0 can sometimes be confusing as we usually don't count from 0 in other situations. It can be easy to forget that an array's index number starts from 0 when specifying the number of elements required. Thus, a clearer way to declare an array is to specify the lower and upper bound index numbers, allowing you to specify a different lower bound index number.

To specify a different lower bound number, define it explicitly with the **To** keyword, as shown in the examples below:

```
'A 15 element array
Dim Counter(1 To 15) As Long

'A 20 element array
Dim SubTotals(1 To 20) As Double
```

In the array declaration statements above, the upper bound index numbers are the required number of elements, making this code easier to understand.

Another way to simplify array declarations in your code is to change the default lower bound index number from 0 to 1. To do this, include the following statement in the **Declarations** section of your module:

```
Option Base 1
```

This statement ensures VBA uses 1 as the lower bound for arrays that declare only the upper bound number.

With an **Option Base 1** statement present, the following array declarations are identical, both having 15 elements:

```
Dim Counter(15) As Long
```

```
Dim Counter(1 To 15) As Long
```

Using LBound and UBound

You can use the built-in **LBound** function to return the lower bound index number of an array. Similarly, the **UBound** function returns the upper bound index number. Both functions take in just one argument, the name of the array.

For the array example declared below, `LBound(Counter)` returns 1, and `UBound(Counter)` returns 15.

```
Dim Counter(1 To 15) As Long
```

Populating an Array

You can assign values to an array in different ways. The procedure below assigns values to individual elements of an array. A **For...Next** loop then loops through the values of the populated array and displays each value in a message box:

```vba
Sub PopulatingArrays()
    Dim i As Long
    
    'An array of 6 elements
    Dim Categories(5) As String
    
    'Populate the array with values
    Categories(0) = "Chairs"
    Categories(1) = "Tables"
    Categories(2) = "Sofas"
    Categories(3) = "Footstools"
    Categories(4) = "Beds"
    Categories(5) = "Wardrobes"
    
    'Loop through the array and display the values
    For i = 0 To 5
        MsgBox Categories(i) & " is in element " & i
    Next i
End Sub
```

You can also populate an array with a looping construct like a **For...Next** loop. The code below declares an array with 5 elements. A loop populates the array using a statement that multiplies the index number of each element by 100. A second loop then goes through the array and assigns the values to a string variable, *MsgText*, before displaying it to the user with a message box.

```vba
Sub UsingArrayBounds()
    Dim i As Long
    Dim MsgText As String
    Dim Nums(1 To 5) As Long
    
    'Populate the array
    For i = LBound(Nums) To UBound(Nums)
        Nums(i) = i * 100
    Next i
    
    For i = LBound(Nums) To UBound(Nums)
        MsgText = MsgText & Nums(i) & vbNewLine
    Next i
    MsgBox "Items in array:" & vbNewLine & MsgText
End Sub
```

Note VBA looping constructs are covered in Chapter 7.

Multidimensional Arrays

So far, we have created one-dimensional arrays. If we imagine a one-dimensional array as a single row of values, a two-dimensional has many rows and columns. A three-dimensional array is made up of multiple two-dimensional arrays. VBA allows you to create arrays up to 60 dimensions, although you rarely need that much! An array of more than two or three dimensions can get complex fast. If you need more than three dimensions, it may indicate that using an array is not the best approach for creating a solution for the problem.

A two-dimensional array lets you track several related values in multiple rows. For example, you can store several values for a chart's x and y coordinates in a two-dimensional array.

A two-dimensional array consists of multiple rows and columns, as illustrated below.

Dim Scores(4, 5) as Long

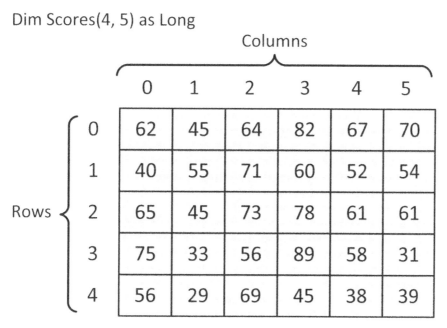

Figure 5-2: A two-dimensional array.

In a two-dimensional array, specify the upper bound row index before the upper bound column index in the parentheses. The following example declares an array of 30 elements:

```
Dim Scores(4, 5) As Long
```

You can also declare both dimensions with explicit lower bounds, as shown in the code example below:

```
Dim Scores(1 To 5, 1 To 6) As Long
```

To access an element in this array, specify the index numbers for the row and column in your assignment statement.

The following code example populates the first row of a two-dimensional array and displays the values in a message box:

```
Sub TwoDArray()
    Dim Scores(1 To 5, 1 To 6) As Long
    Dim i As Long, MsgTxt As String
    
    'Populate the first row of the array
    Scores(1, 1) = 62
    Scores(1, 2) = 45
    Scores(1, 3) = 64
    Scores(1, 4) = 82
    Scores(1, 5) = 67
    Scores(1, 6) = 70
    
    'assign the values to a variable
    For i = 1 To 6
        MsgTxt = MsgTxt & Scores(1, i) & ", "
    Next i
    
    'Display the numbers without the trailing comma
    MsgBox Left(MsgTxt, Len(MsgTxt) - 2)
End Sub
```

The above code displays the following message box:

Figure 5-3: The values in the first row of a 2D array.

To create a three-dimensional array, imagine it as a cube or multiple instances of a two-dimensional array stacked together in a cube format. Visualizing arrays that are more than three dimensions is more challenging.

The example below declares a three-dimensional array with 1500 elements:

```
Dim Cube(1 To 10, 1 To 10, 1 To 15) As Long
```

The total number of elements in the array above is the product of the three dimensions (10 x 10 x 15), or 1500.

> **Note** Exercise caution when adding additional dimensions to an array, as it can significantly increase the total storage requirements for the array. The number of dimensions is particularly important when using Variants, as they demand more storage memory than other data types.

Dynamic Arrays

In certain scenarios, the size of an array can change at runtime, especially for programs with different decision paths. For such instances, you may not know the size an array could grow to when declaring it. You can use a dynamic array for scenarios like this, as it can be resized when necessary. After declaring a dynamic array, you can add new elements as required instead of specifying the array's size when initially writing the code.

Declaring Dynamic Arrays

To declare a dynamic array, give it an empty dimension list, as shown in the example below:

```
Dim DyArray() As Long
```

After declaring the array, you can allocate the number of elements as needed with a **ReDim** statement. The **ReDim** statement can be used multiple times to change the array's size. The example code below allocates the number of elements for the array based on the variable *ItemCount*.

```
ItemCount = 15
ReDim DyArray(1 To ItemCount)
```

In the code above, the value currently in *ItemCount* becomes the array's upper bound. Notice that you can also use the **To** keyword within a ReDim statement to specify the lower and upper bounds.

A **ReDim** statement can only be used in a procedure. Unlike other declaration statements like **Dim** or **Static**, ReDim is an executable statement. ReDim makes the application perform an action at run time. Each ReDim statement can change the number of elements for each dimension, including the lower and upper bounds. But you can't change the number of dimensions in the array.

The code below declares a dynamic array in the Declarations section of the module:

```
Dim MyMatrix() As Long
```

Inside a procedure, we can then allocate space for the array, as demonstrated in the following example code:

```
Sub MatrixDemo()
   ReDim MyMatrix(9, 19)
End Sub
```

The ReDim statement above creates a two-dimensional array made up of 10 rows and 20 columns for a total of 200 elements. Alternatively, you can use variables (that are set at run time) to set the bounds of a dynamic array, as shown in the following example:

```
ReDim MyMatrix(X, Y)
```

Preserving the Contents of Dynamic Arrays

Whenever you use **ReDim** on an array, its current values are lost as VBA resets all the elements to their default initial values. This reset can be useful when preparing the array for new data or reducing its size. However, there are scenarios where you want to modify the array's size without losing its current data. You can do this by using ReDim along with the **Preserve** keyword.

The first ReDim statement in the example below creates 5 elements for the array. The second ReDim statement increases the size of the array to 10 elements without deleting the existing data by using the **Preserve** keyword.

```
'Erases all existing data.
ReDim DArray(1 To 5)

'Preserves existing data.
ReDim Preserve DArray(1 To 10)
```

When using the Preserve keyword in a multidimensional array, you can only change the upper bound of the last dimension. If you attempt to change any of the other dimensions or the starting index of the last dimension, VBA generates a runtime error.

The procedure below declares and resizes a dynamic array while preserving the existing data:

```
Sub DynamicArrays()
    Dim ItemCount As Long
    
    'Declare array
    Dim DyArray() As Long
    
    'Allocate elements
    ReDim DyArray(1 To 3)
    
    'Assign values to elements
    DyArray(1) = 100
    DyArray(2) = 200
    DyArray(3) = 400
    
    ItemCount = 15
    
    're-dimension array but preserve existing data
    ReDim Preserve DyArray(1 To ItemCount)
    
    'Assign value to a new element
    DyArray(4) = 800
    
    MsgBox "Value in element 1: " & DyArray(1) & vbNewLine & _
        "Value in element 2: " & DyArray(2) & vbNewLine & _
        "Value in element 3: " & DyArray(3) & vbNewLine & _
        "Value in element 4: " & DyArray(4)
End Sub
```

The example code above does the following:

➤ Declares a dynamic array named *DyArray* of data type Long.

➤ Allocates memory for it using ReDim with a size of 3 elements.

➤ Assigns 100, 200, and 400 to the three elements, respectively.

➤ Resizes the array to 15 elements using the *ItemCount* variable while preserving existing data.

➤ Adds 800 to element 4, which is a new element derived from the resize action.

➤ Displays a message box showing the four values stored in the array.

Using the Array Function

The built-in **Array** function in VBA allows you to assign several values to one variable of the **Variant** data type. You can access the individual values in the variable in the same way you would access values in an array.

Syntax:

Array(*arglist*)

The *arglist* argument can be one or more values separated by commas. If arguments are omitted, a zero-length array is created.

Generally, arrays in VBA are declared with the name followed by parentheses containing an index number specifying the elements of the array. When using the **Array** function, the variable containing the array must be declared as a Variant, not an array.

> **Note** A Variant variable can contain an array even when it is not declared as an array. A Variant containing an array has characteristics different from those of an array declared as a Variant, but the elements are accessed in a similar way.

In the following example, the first statement creates two variant variables: *Category* and *Categories*. The second statement uses the **Array** function to assign an array of six values to Categories. The next statement accesses the values in the array using their index numbers and displays the values in a message box. The last block of code loops through the Categories array using a For Each loop and displaying each value with a message box.

```
Sub ArrayFunction()
    Dim Category As Variant, Categories As Variant

    'Assign multiple values to the variable
    Categories = Array("Chairs", "Tables", "Sofas", _
                       "Footstools", "Beds", "Wardrobes")

    'Display array values for index numbers 1-3
    MsgBox Categories(0) & ", " & Categories(1) _
         & ", " & Categories(2)

    'Loop through the array and display its contents
    For Each Category In Categories
```

```
        MsgBox Category
    Next
End Sub
```

The **Array** function is useful when the number of values assigned to the array is unknown at design time. You can assign one or several values to the variable at run time.

 Note For more details on how to use a **For Each...Next** loop, see Chapter 7.

Scope of Arrays

To define the scope of your array, use the same methods for scoping variables. For example, to create a public array, use **Public** instead of **Dim** in the Declarations section of a module.

```
Public Counters (1 To 15) As Long
Public Totals (1 To 20) As Double
```

Tip: Before using arrays in Excel, determine whether you can perform the same task using a worksheet range to store the data. Using a worksheet to store and retrieve lookup values in VBA is more efficient than using arrays.

Arrays come in handy for scenarios where you need to create a quick temporary list at runtime, but they are not extensively used in Excel or Access VBA because of the existence of worksheets and tables, respectively. Chapter 13 covers accessing and using values in a worksheet range in code.

Chapter 6

Working with Procedures

In this chapter:

- Knowing the difference between general procedures and event procedures.
- Understanding the rules for naming procedures.
- Working with Sub procedures and Function procedures.
- Understanding the various ways of executing Sub procedures.
- Understanding the different ways of calling Function procedures.
- An overview of Event procedures.

A procedure is a set of code instructions that tells your application how to perform a specific task. Use procedures to organize your code in a module and break them into more manageable units. Excel's macro recorder generates macros as procedures, but you can enter them manually in the Code window.

There are two main types of procedures in VBA:

1. **General procedures**: Sub procedures and Function procedures.

2. **Event procedures**: Used in Excel objects like workbooks, worksheets, and UserForms.

General Procedures

There are two types of general procedures: **Sub** procedures and **Function** procedures. A Sub procedure runs a code segment to perform a series of actions without returning a value. A Function procedure runs a piece of code and returns a value, similar to the built-in functions in Excel. Unlike an event procedure that is executed automatically when the associated event happens, you must explicitly invoke a general procedure to execute it.

Generally, a VBA module can hold three types of code:

- **Declarations**: You can declare variables or constants in a module (usually at the top) that you want to be available for use in all procedures inside the module. These are usually referred to as global variables.

- **Sub procedure**: A code segment that performs a series of actions when executed but doesn't return a value. All recorded macros are saved as Sub procedures, but you can create Sub procedures manually in the Code window.

- **Function procedure**: A code segment that performs actions and returns a single value or an array, similar to the built-in functions in Excel that return a value. Function procedures must be created manually in the Code window.

You can store a mix of all three types of code in a module. The type of procedure you create will depend on the outcome you seek. If you intend to create several procedures for the same application, you can organize related code into separate modules with names, making it easier to maintain the code.

Note Property procedures are a type of procedure you can use in VBA to work with custom properties. This type of procedure is seldom used in VBA unless you're creating custom class modules, which is outside the scope of this book.

Procedure Naming Rules

The naming rules for procedures in VBA are similar to those of variables covered in Chapter 4.

The naming rules are revisited in the list below:

- The first character must be a letter.
- You can only use alphanumeric characters. You can't use characters like @, &, #, !, $, ^, *, or %.
- You can't use spaces between procedure names. Use capitalization to separate words.
- A procedure name cannot be more than 255 characters (but you certainly don't want to use anywhere near that length).
- You must use a unique name within the same scope.
- To make code more readable, you ideally want a procedure's name to describe its purpose. One method is to combine a verb and a noun. For example, AddData, PrintValues, CalculateTotal, or SortData.

Sub Procedures

A Sub procedure starts with the **Sub** keyword and ends with the **End Sub** statement. The Sub procedure in the example below is named **AddNumbers**. The procedure adds two numbers and displays the result to the user in a dialog box before running the **End Sub** statement to end execution.

```
Sub AddNumbers()
  Dim MySum As Long
  MySum = 1 + 2
  MsgBox "The sum is: " & MySum
End Sub
```

A Sub procedure can have zero or more arguments that are passed to it when called from another procedure. If your Sub procedure has arguments, list them in parentheses after the name in the declaration. If there are several arguments, separate them with a comma.

The code example below shows a Sub procedure with two arguments:

```
Sub SquareMeter(Length, Width)
    Dim SqM As Single
    SqM = Length * Width
    MsgBox "The square meter is: " & SqM
End Sub
```

In the example above, the *SquareMeter* Sub procedure has two arguments used inside it to calculate the square meter. The result is then displayed in a message box.

You can use the **Exit Sub** statement to immediately exit a Sub procedure at any point. This statement is useful for scenarios where you want program execution to end when a certain condition is met before the end of the procedure. Execution ends in the Sub procedure and returns to the calling procedure (if it was called from another procedure). You can place several instances of **Exit Sub** in a Sub procedure.

Running a Sub Procedure

> **Note** In this book, the terms *run, call, execute,* or *invoke* are used interchangeably for procedure calls.

Where you can run a Sub procedure depends on whether it has arguments.

From Excel's Interface

You can only run Sub procedures without arguments directly from Excel's interface. To run a Sub procedure (or macro) from Excel's interface, do one of the following:

- Assign it to a custom button on Excel's ribbon.

- Assign it as a command on the Quick Access Toolbar.
- Assign it to a button or image in the worksheet area.
- Run it from the **Macros** dialog box (**Developer > Code > Macros**).

The methods above are covered in detail in Chapter 2: Recording and Running Macros.

In the Visual Basic Editor

You can run a Sub procedure directly in the Visual Basic Editor, which you often need to do when testing your code. If the Sub procedure requires arguments, you must call it from another procedure and pass in the arguments. For example, you can create a temporary calling procedure in the Code window to test a Sub procedure with arguments.

To run a Sub procedure with no arguments in the Code window, do the following:

1. Place the cursor inside the Sub procedure you want to run (between the Sub and End Sub statements).
2. Use one of the following methods:
   - Click the **Run Sub/UserForm** button (the green right-pointing triangle icon on the toolbar).
   - Press F5.
   - On the menu, select **Run > Run Sub/UserForm**.

From Another Procedure

You can call a Sub procedure from another procedure. In a large application, one way to organize code is to have a main Sub procedure from which other procedures containing the details are called. This structure ensures related actions are grouped, and execution returns to the main procedure after performing individual actions. Ensure your code is structured this way instead of branching off in multiple random directions, which is also known as "spaghetti code."

A Sub procedure with arguments must be called from another procedure so that you can provide the arguments. To call a Sub procedure from another procedure, type the procedure's name, including any required arguments. The **Call** keyword is required if your calling statement has arguments enclosed in parentheses. Using **Call** is optional for all other cases.

The example below has three Sub procedures: *CarPrice*, *CarCalc*, and *Main*. CarPrice has no arguments, while CarCalc has two arguments. CarPrice and CarCalc are called inside Main.

CarPrice simply displays the price of the car in a dialog box.

```
Sub CarPrice()
    MsgBox "The car price is: " & "$20,800"
End Sub
```

The CarCalc example (below) checks whether 20% of the user's monthly income is less than the monthly payment for the car, at an interest rate of 2.5%, over 36 months. Essentially, it checks whether the user can afford the car.

```
Sub CarCalc(price, income)
    If (income / 12) * 0.2 < (price * 1.025) / 36 Then
        MsgBox "You cannot afford this car as your income is: " & income
    Else
        MsgBox "This car is affordable as your income is: " & income
    End If
End Sub
```

The Main Sub (below) runs the CarPrice and CarCalc Sub procedures:

```
Sub Main()
    'Call a Sub without arguments
    CarPrice
    
    'Call a Sub with 2 arguments
    CarCalc 20800, 30100
    
    'Call a Sub with 2 arguments enclosed parentheses
    Call CarCalc(25950, 49500)
End Sub
```

The Main procedure above has three executable statements:

- The first statement calls CarPrice, which has no parameters.
- The second statement calls CarCalc without parentheses around the arguments. Hence, it wasn't necessary to use the **Call** keyword.

- The third statement calls CarCalc, and it uses parentheses around the arguments. In this case, the **Call** keyword is required.

Function Procedures

A Function procedure is a set of programming instructions that perform one or more actions before returning a value. Built-in Excel functions like SUM, COUNT, LEN, etc., are similar to Function procedures. Like some built-in Excel functions, some Function procedures can also return several values in an array. You can specify the data type the Function procedure returns in its declaration. For instance, you can declare a function to return a String, Date, or Currency data type.

A Function procedure starts with the **Function** keyword and ends with an **End Function** statement. Function procedures cannot be created with the macro recorder, so they have to be created manually.

The code below is an example of a function with two arguments:

```
Function MyTotal(num1, num2)
   MyTotal = num1 * num2
End Function
```

The above function takes in two numbers as arguments and returns their product. After the work in the function is done, assign the return value to the function's name, informing VBA to return the value and exit the function.

As shown in the code below, you can explicitly specify the function's return type with the **As** keyword. In some scenarios, explicitly declaring the function's return type makes the code more efficient, as the function is not declared as a variant.

```
Function ConvertToCelsius(FahrenheitTemp As Single) As Single
    ' Convert Fahrenheit to Celsius
    ConvertToCelsius = Round((FahrenheitTemp - 32) * (5 / 9), 1)
End Function
```

The above function takes in a temperature reading measured in Fahrenheit, converts it to Celsius, and returns the value rounded to 1 decimal place.

You can use the **Exit Function** statement to immediately exit a Function procedure at any point during execution. Exit Function is useful for scenarios where you want execution to end when a certain condition is met before the end of the function. You can place several instances of Exit Function in different parts of a Function procedure.

Calling a Function Procedure

Unlike Sub procedures that can be executed in a variety of ways, Function procedures can only be executed in two ways:

- Call the Function procedure from another procedure.
- Call the Function procedure directly from a worksheet formula.

Calling a Function from another procedure

A function returns a value, so you have to keep that in mind when you call a function. You must include where the return value goes in your function call statement. For example, you can assign the return value to a variable, a UserForm control, or display it in a message box. Functions are usually called in other procedures to process a request or perform a calculation that returns a value. The result is then used in the calling procedure.

The example below calculates the monthly interest based on the given capital and interest rate. We want to calculate the monthly interest on a capital of $50,000 at an annual interest rate of 5.75%.

We have a Sub procedure named *CalcInterest* and a Function procedure named *MonthlyInterest,* which takes in two arguments, *Capital* and *Rate*, and calculates the monthly interest on the capital.

CalcInterest calls the MonthlyInterest function, passing in the values for its Capital and Rate arguments. The statement returns the result to a local variable named *MyInterest*. The value returned is then displayed in a message box to the user.

The function:

```
Function MonthlyInterest(Capital, Rate)
    MonthlyInterest = (Capital * Rate) / 12
End Function
```

The calling procedure:

```
Sub CalcInterest()
    Dim MyInterest As Currency
    MyInterest = MonthlyInterest(50000, 0.0575)
    MsgBox "The monthly interest is: $" & MyInterest
End Sub
```

Note that a **Call** keyword is not required when returning a value from a function, even when arguments and parentheses are used.

Calling a Function procedure in an Excel formula

When you create Sub procedures in VBA, they become available in Excel as macros. On the other hand, Function procedures become available in Excel as user-defined functions. You can use custom functions in Excel like any other built-in Excel function. Any Function procedure you create in Excel will be available in the **User Defined** category in the **Insert Functions** dialog box.

Click the **Insert Function** button (next to the Excel formula bar) and choose the User Defined category. All functions created in the active workbook, or the Personal Macro Workbook, are listed in the User Defined category.

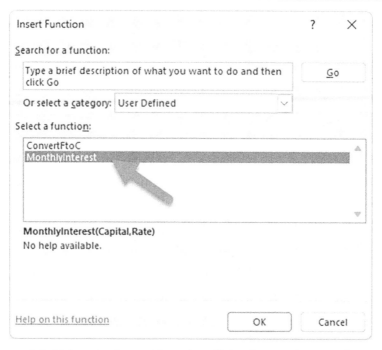

Figure 6-1: Using the Insert Function dialog box to insert a function.

Using the example of the MonthlyInterest function we created previously, we can use the function to perform calculations directly on our worksheet.

	A	B	C	D
1	Capital	Interest Rate	Monthly Interest	
2	$40,000.00	5.75%	$191.67	
3	$50,000.00	5.75%	$239.58	
4	$75,000.00	5.75%	$359.38	
5	$100,000.00	5.75%	$479.17	
6	$250,000.00	5.75%	$1,197.92	
7				
8				

C2 =MonthlyInterest(A2,B2)

Figure 6-2: Using a custom function in Excel.

In the example above, we pass the capital (in cell A2) and interest rate (in cell B2) as arguments in our function, which is the formula in cell C2, =MonthlyInterest(A2,B2).

Overview of Event Procedures

An event procedure is a block of code executed when an event happens to an Excel object. The event can be triggered by a user action or by the system. Several VBA objects like workbooks, worksheets, and UserForms have events that can be triggered automatically in this manner. You can add code to these events that perform various actions based on user actions or system triggers.

For example, a workbook has events like **Open**, **Activate**, **NewSheet**, and **AfterSave**. You can add code to these built-in event procedures that are run when these actions happen to the workbook. For instance, you can enter some code in the **Open** event of a workbook that automatically connects to an external data source. Another example is the **Click** event of a command button on a UserForm. The code that you place in the Click event procedure runs when the button is clicked.

> **Note** Event procedures are covered in Chapter 11: Working with Workbooks, Chapter 12: Working with Worksheets, and Chapter 14: UserForms.

Chapter 7

Controlling Program Flow

In this chapter:

- Making decisions with conditional statements.
- Executing a specific block of code out of several options.
- Understanding looping structures in VBA.
- Iterating through Excel object collections.

A program normally proceeds linearly through statements from top to bottom. For very simple programs, this linear flow would suffice. However, the main power of programming languages is the ability to change the order of code execution and have branches that make decisions using control statements and loops.

Like other programming languages, VBA has control structures that enable you to change the flow of how your code executes. You can write code with control structures that make decisions and repeat actions.

If...Then...Else

Decision structures enable you to test conditions and perform different operations based on the results. For example, you can test for a condition being true or false, for a particular value, or for particular exceptions generated when you run a block of code. If you've used conditional functions like the IF function in Excel before, you would be familiar with the concept of these constructs.

The image below illustrates a decision structure that tests whether a condition is true or false and then performs different actions based on the result.

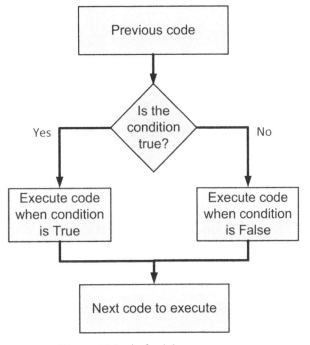

Figure 7-1: A decision structure.

If...Then...Else enables you to create a conditional statement that executes the enclosed code when the condition is met. An **If** statement does not necessarily need to have an **Else** clause.

The code example below tests whether the value in the *Expenses* variable is greater than $10,000. If the test returns True, the application runs the code in the block, which displays a message to the user. If the test returns False, the code in the block is not executed.

```
If Expenses > 10000 Then
   MsgBox "Over Budget! Please reduce expenses."
End If
```

The **Else** clause is optional but can be used if there is another statement to execute if the test returns False.

The code example below tests whether the value in the variable *Expenses* is greater than $10,000. If the result evaluates to True, the next line of code is executed, and the program exits the If block. If the test evaluates to False, the program skips to the **Else** clause and executes that code block before exiting the If block.

```
If Expenses > 10000 Then
   MsgText = "Over Budget"
Else
   MsgText = "Within Budget"
End If
```

Another optional clause to test for multiple conditions is the **ElseIf** clause. Thus, instead of just two code execution paths, you can test for multiple paths, each with its own block of code to be run if the tested condition is met.

In the example below, the **If…Then…Else** statement is extended with a series of **ElseIf** clauses. The **ElseIf** clauses enable you to test for several conditions and run a different block of code, depending on which condition evaluates to True first.

```
Sub Scores()
    Dim Score As Double
    Dim Result As String

    Score = InputBox("Enter score")
        If Score >= 70 Then
            Result = "Merit"
        ElseIf Score >= 50 Then
            Result = "Credit"
        ElseIf Score >= 40 Then
            Result = "Pass"
        Else
            Result = "Fail"
        End If
```

```
        MsgBox "The result is: " & Result
End Sub
```

The routine above enables the user to enter a score in an input box. The **If…Then…Else** block checks the score to determine if it is Merit, Credit, Pass, or Fail. The returned grade is then displayed to the user in a message box.

Select Case

The **Select Case** statement executes one of several code segments based on the value of an expression. Much of what you can do with Select Case can also be performed with an **If… Then… Else** statement. However, Select Case is usually more efficient because the test expression is evaluated only once.

In the example below, the value in *score* is evaluated once and compared against multiple **Case** statements. For this type of problem, a **Select Case** statement is more efficient than **If…Then…Else**, because the test expression is only evaluated once.

The code under the Case statement that passes the test is executed before the program exits the Select Case block. You can use a **Case Else** statement to catch anything not caught by the other Case statements.

```
Sub GetResult()
    Dim Score As Double
    Dim Result As String

    Score = InputBox("Enter score")
    Select Case Score
        Case 70 To 100
            Result = "Merit"
        Case 50 To 69
            Result = "Credit"
        Case 40 To 49
            Result = "Pass"
        Case Is < 40
            Result = "Fail"
        Case Else
            Result = "Undetermined"
    End Select
```

```
    MsgBox "The result is: " & Result
End Sub
```

A **Select Case** statement is easier to read than multiple levels of nested block **If** statements. Use **Select Case** when evaluating a single expression that can return different results. Use block **If** statements when evaluating multiple expressions with logical operators like AND, OR, and NOT, like *Subject* = "Math" AND *Score* >= 70.

These two constructs should cover any scenario where you would use a conditional statement.

Do...Loop

Looping constructs in VBA enable you to execute one or more lines of code repeatedly. This type of construct is called a loop because it gets to the bottom of a block of code and then starts from the top of that block again, like a loop. You can specify the number of iterations or use a particular condition to decide when the loop ends. You can repeat a block of code in that looping structure until a particular condition is true or false, has reached a specified count, or has looped through all elements in a collection.

A **Do...Loop** statement repeats a block of code *while* the condition being tested is true or *until* the condition being tested is true.

There are two types of **Do** loops. Use **Do...While** to repeat a section of code *while* a condition remains true, and use **Do...Until** to repeat a section of code *until* a condition becomes true.

At a basic level, it says:

Repeat this block of code [while/until] the condition being tested is true.

Depending on your specific scenario, you can place the test (or condition) at the top or the bottom of the loop.

Syntax

The condition is at the top of the loop:

```
Do [{While | Until} condition]
      [statements]
[Exit Do]
      [statements]
Loop
```

The condition is at the bottom of the loop:

```
Do
      [statements]
[Exit Do]
      [statements]
Loop [{While | Until} condition]
```

In the example below, the **Do...While** loop continues to run the enclosed code while the user enters a number in the input box. With each iteration, the loop checks that the value in *InputValue* is not empty (indicated with the empty string). The procedure uses the result to either rerun the block of code or exit the loop. The program exits the loop when the user clicks the Cancel button on the input box, meaning *InputValue* will be empty. The result is then displayed to the user in a message box.

```
Sub NumberEntry()
    'Do...While example using an input box
    Dim InputValue As Variant
    Dim Total As Long
    
    InputValue = InputBox("Enter a number or click Cancel to end.")
    Do While InputValue <> ""
        Total = Total + InputValue
        InputValue = InputBox("Enter a number or click Cancel to end.")
    Loop
    MsgBox "The total is: " & Total
End Sub
```

You can place an **Exit Do** statement anywhere in a **Do...Loop** block as an alternative way to exit the loop. An **Exit Do** statement is optional and only used to immediately exit the loop if a certain condition was met before the end of the loop. It ensures no further statements are executed in the loop.

In the following example, the loop is set to run until the *Counter* variable reaches 100. During each loop, a random number between 1 and 10 is generated and assigned to

RandNum. A block **If** statement checks *RandNum*. If its value is 5, the application displays a message to the user and exits the loop with an **Exit Do** statement.

```
Sub Increment()
    Dim Counter As Long
    Dim RandNum As Long

    Counter = 0
    Do
        RandNum = Int((10 * Rnd) + 1)
        If RandNum = 5 Then
            MsgBox "Congratulations! You generated number 5."
            Exit Do    ' Exits loop if MyNumber is 5
        End If
        MsgBox "The generated value is: " & RandNum
        Counter = Counter + 2
    Loop Until Counter = 100
End Sub
```

Breaking an Endless Loop

Occasionally, you'll write code that results in an endless loop due to a logical error. This happens to all programmers so don't panic!

To break an infinite loop in VBA, use one of the following methods:

- Hold down the Esc key for more than a few seconds.
- Select Ctrl+Break (or Ctrl+Pause for keyboards without the Break key).

For...Next

The **For...Next** statement is one of the simpler VBA loops designed to iterate a set number of times specified at the start. If you know how many times you want a section of code to run when writing it, use a For...Next loop that executes the code a specified number of times. A counter variable keeps track of how many times the block of code has iterated.

Syntax:

```
For counter = start To end [Step step]
    [statements]
[Exit For]
    [statements]
Next [counter]
```

In the following example, *ctr* is used as the *counter* variable, and it has been assigned a *start* count of 1 and an *end* count of 100. Therefore, the loop will run 100 times. The **To** keyword is used to define the count range. With each loop, the number in ctr is incremented by 1 until it reaches 100, at which point the loop ends. With each iteration, the value inside ctr is displayed in the **Immediate** window using the **Debug.Print** method.

```
Sub ForNextDemo()
    'Show value of counter in the Immediate window
    Dim ctr As Long
    For ctr = 1 To 100
        Debug.Print ctr
    Next ctr
End Sub
```

Note The **Immediate** window is covered in detail in Chapter 8.

There are variations to the For...Next statement. For example, you can use the **Step** keyword to increase or decrease the counter by the specified value. Suppose we add *Step 2* to the previous example. The loop will skip every even number in the specified range (1 to 100). Hence, it will only run 50 times.

```
For ctr = 1 To 100 Step 2
```

```
        Debug.Print ctr
Next ctr
```

You can also use a For...Next block to loop through an array to populate or access individual elements in an array. In the code example below, the first loop iterates through the 20 elements in *MyArray* and enters a value in each element based on its index number. The second loop accesses each element in the array and displays its contents in the Immediate window using Debug.Print.

```
Sub ForNextArray()
    'Populate an array and display the values
    Dim MyArray(1 To 20) As Long
    Dim i As Long
    For i = 1 To 20
        MyArray(i) = i * 10
    Next
    For i = 1 To 20
        Debug.Print MyArray(i)
    Next
End Sub
```

Just like how the **Exit Do** statement can be used in a **Do...Loop**, you can include one or more **Exit For** statements in a For...Next loop. **Exit For** is optional and used to immediately exit a For...Next loop if a certain condition is met before the set number of iterations.

In the example below, the first For...Next statement populates an array of 10 numbers. The second For...Next statement iterates through the array and displays each number to the user in a dialog box. The message box lets the user select **OK** to see the next number or **Cancel** to exit the program. The **If** block checks the user's answer. If the answer is **vbCancel**, the program runs an **Exit For** statement to exit the loop without finishing any remaining iterations.

```
Sub ExitForDemo()
    Dim MyArray(1 To 10) As Long
    Dim i As Long
    Dim Answer As String
    Dim MsgText As String
    
    MsgText = "Click OK for next number or Cancel to exit"
    
    'Assign values to the array
    For i = 1 To 10
        MyArray(i) = i
```

Chapter 7: Controlling Program Flow

```
        Next

        'Display the values to the user
        For i = 1 To 10
            Answer = MsgBox("Value in element: " & MyArray(i) & _
                vbNewLine & MsgText, vbOKCancel, "Next value")
            If Answer = vbCancel Then
                Exit For
            End If
        Next
End Sub
```

You can also nest For…Next loops to solve more complex problems. For instance, we can use two For…Next loops to populate a two-dimensional array, similar to a range in a worksheet comprising several rows and columns. The example below uses two loops to populate the active worksheet's first ten rows and columns with randomly generated integers between 100 and 2000.

```
Sub RandomFill()
    Dim Col As Long
    Dim Row As Long
    For Col = 1 To 10
        For Row = 1 To 10
            ' Generate a random value between 100 and 2000.
            Cells(Row, Col) = Int((2000 - 100 + 1) * Rnd + 100)
        Next Row
    Next Col
End Sub
```

The result in Excel is shown in the image below:

	A	B	C	D	E	F	G	H	I	J
1	567	1340	471	1984	119	153	494	1930	132	1635
2	819	1811	720	996	388	1673	793	1873	744	688
3	855	540	885	107	817	1589	1190	1986	1416	814
4	1101	1905	390	909	457	1603	754	1696	309	862
5	613	1708	1278	648	1962	732	1104	878	308	1699
6	1204	938	288	1530	1757	957	908	1630	652	878
7	498	1035	489	1794	1205	1155	1189	1980	858	1477
8	249	1562	1416	1662	1486	1627	195	591	1162	1352
9	1802	1687	1058	436	375	1172	1140	431	691	872
10	311	827	448	306	590	487	492	1420	661	1906
11										

Figure 7-2: Populating a worksheet range with a For…Next loop.

For Each...Next

The **For Each...Next** looping construct is used for iterating through collections. This looping construct allows you to loop through a collection of similar objects and perform the same operations on each one. You can use other VBA looping structures to loop through collections, but **For Each...Next** is best suited for looping through objects in a collection. With **For Each...Next**, you do not need to know the number of objects in the collection to loop through it.

Syntax:

```
For Each element In group
    [statements]
[Exit For]
    [statements]
Next [element]
```

The variable used for *element* must be a Variant when iterating through the elements of an array. For collections, *element* can be a Variant variable or an object variable.

Looping Through Collections

The For Each...Next statement is mainly used for iterating through Excel collections like workbooks, worksheets, and ranges. The following code iterates through the **Worksheets** collection of the active workbook and prints the name of each sheet in the Immediate window.

```
Sub ListSheetNames()
    Dim sheet As Worksheet
    For Each sheet In ActiveWorkbook.Worksheets
        Debug.Print sheet.Name
    Next sheet
End Sub
```

In the following example, a For Each...Next statement is used to hide all worksheets in the active workbook apart from the active worksheet. The procedure checks the name of each sheet in the workbook, and if it's different from that of the active sheet, it is hidden.

Note that as we're using an object variable, it is easier to identify properties for the object using VBA's IntelliSense. In this case, the **Visible** property of the Worksheet object is set to hidden.

```
Sub HideWkSheets()
    Dim wks As Worksheet
    For Each wks In ActiveWorkbook.Worksheets
        If wks.Name <> ActiveSheet.Name Then
            wks.Visible = xlSheetHidden
        End If
    Next wks
End Sub
```

The next example is similar to the previous one. However, the procedure makes all sheets in the workbook visible in this case. The procedure unhides any hidden worksheets in the workbook.

```
Sub UnhideWkSheets()
    Dim wks As Worksheet
    For Each wks In ActiveWorkbook.Worksheets
        If wks.Name <> ActiveSheet.Name Then
            wks.Visible = xlSheetVisible
        End If
    Next wks
End Sub
```

Populating a range

The example below loops through the range A1:J10 in the active worksheet and adds a randomly generated value between $1,000 and $2,000 to each cell. The code doesn't need to specify the number of cells in the range at the start of the loop. It iterates through all cell objects in the specified collection: *Range("A1:J10")*.

```
Sub AddRandomValuesToRange()
    Dim cell As Range
    For Each cell In Range("A1:J10")
        'Enter a random value between $1,000 - $2,000.
        cell.Value = CCur((2000 - 1000 + 1) * Rnd + 1000)
    Next
End Sub
```

The result in Excel is shown in the following image:

	A	B	C	D	E	F	G	H	I	J
1	$1,623.17	$1,672.26	$1,998.54	$1,037.97	$1,550.07	$1,054.05	$1,610.94	$1,169.70	$1,495.30	$1,448.31
2	$1,990.51	$1,600.21	$1,752.44	$1,286.16	$1,900.45	$1,848.12	$1,325.67	$1,865.83	$1,512.66	$1,210.16
3	$1,886.88	$1,487.44	$1,985.31	$1,029.03	$1,973.02	$1,850.01	$1,286.90	$1,205.58	$1,443.62	$1,685.73
4	$1,281.42	$1,966.17	$1,183.65	$1,655.49	$1,049.80	$1,876.32	$1,054.62	$1,486.61	$1,472.62	$1,109.60
5	$1,098.86	$1,364.89	$1,054.05	$1,963.78	$1,993.14	$1,574.84	$1,005.08	$1,619.21	$1,748.46	$1,389.25
6	$1,567.97	$1,163.47	$1,669.18	$1,211.89	$1,593.92	$1,853.24	$1,551.28	$1,967.59	$1,374.05	$1,626.46
7	$1,137.02	$1,739.44	$1,716.61	$1,874.73	$1,819.67	$1,665.36	$1,272.40	$1,452.91	$1,591.70	$1,073.85
8	$1,117.52	$1,950.05	$1,253.99	$1,878.98	$1,578.28	$1,198.54	$1,866.52	$1,213.71	$1,308.42	$1,047.43
9	$1,448.12	$1,330.33	$1,621.58	$1,372.16	$1,936.57	$1,733.29	$1,063.97	$1,341.39	$1,383.95	$1,572.21
10	$1,248.34	$1,935.17	$1,417.18	$1,284.09	$1,927.20	$1,706.30	$1,935.89	$1,482.90	$1,321.24	$1,801.02
11										

Figure 7-3: Populating a range with a For…Each loop.

You can also nest **For…Each** blocks to iterate through different levels of collections. The following example loops through all the worksheets in a workbook and adds random values to range A1:D10 in each.

```
Sub AddValuesToSheets()
    Dim wks As Worksheet
    Dim cell As Range

    For Each wks In ActiveWorkbook.Worksheets
       For Each cell In wks.Range("A1:D10")
            'Enter a random value between 500 and 2000.
            cell.Value = CCur((2000 - 1000 + 1) * Rnd + 1000)
       Next
    Next
End Sub
```

Note The **Range** object is covered in Chapter 13.

Looping Through an Array

A For Each…Next loop can also be used for looping through an array already populated with values. The following example has an array of five elements populated with customer names. The control variable *Customer* is a Variant that holds each value in the array for each iteration. The program then displays the value in the Immediate window.

```
Sub ForEachNextArray()
    Dim Customers(1 To 5) As String
    
    'Declare a variant to hold the array element
    Dim Customer As Variant
    
    'Populate the array
    Customers(1) = "Henry"
    Customers(2) = "Catherine"
    Customers(3) = "Darla"
    Customers(4) = "Toby"
    Customers(5) = "Brenda"
    
    For Each Customer In Customers
        Debug.Print Customer
    Next
End Sub
```

Chapter 8

Debugging

In this chapter:

- Understanding the difference between syntax errors and logic errors.
- Setting breakpoints in your code to enter break mode.
- Stepping through code in break mode.
- Using the Immediate window to display information from your code at runtime.
- Using Debug.Print to view information about your application at runtime.
- Monitoring variables and properties with the Locals window.
- Monitoring expressions at runtime with the Watch window.
- Tracing the flow of execution through multiple nested procedures with the Call Stack.

In this chapter, we will cover the tools in the Visual Basic Editor that you can use to debug your code. You'll encounter errors when writing code, even if you are an experienced programmer. Logic errors are especially difficult to find because there is nothing wrong with the code syntactically, but it does not produce the expected results. You'll use the debugging tools primarily for logic errors.

Overview of Debugging

A game-changer in my early programming career was learning to step through code in break mode, observe the program flow, and see what was happening to my variables. If there is one thing you take from this chapter, it should be how to step through your code in break mode and examine what variables are changing and what actions are changing them. Stepping through code will save you time figuring out why a procedure is not producing the expected results.

There are three types of errors in programming:

- **Syntax errors**

    Syntax errors occur when a mistake is made in the syntax. Examples include a keyword entered incorrectly or a construct being used incorrectly, like using an **If** statement without an **End If**. Syntax errors are the easiest to identify, as you won't even be able to run the code until you correct them.

    The Visual Basic Editor has an automatic syntax checking feature (**Auto Syntax Check** in the Visual Basic Editor options) that can detect and correct some syntax errors as you type your code. Those syntax errors generate an error message as soon as you try to leave the line, telling you what the error is and offering some help. Other syntax errors are only detected when you attempt to run the code. At that point, VBA halts code execution and highlights the line that generated the error.

- **Runtime errors**

    A runtime error occurs when a piece of code attempts an operation that is impossible to execute. An example of a runtime error is trying to reference an inaccessible object, like a closed workbook. You can anticipate this type of error and create an error handler to process it, display instructions or help to the user, and gracefully exit the routine. Runtime errors are covered in Chapter 9.

- **Logic errors**

    Logic errors occur when there is nothing wrong with the syntax, but the application does not produce the expected outcome. These errors are difficult to identify because VBA does not generate an error. The code will run normally but simply not produce the expected results. This type of error is caused by a logic error in one or more code statements. Often, the only way to identify the source of the error is to put a breakpoint in your code and step through it line by line to observe the values of your variables and expressions at different points.

Debugging Tools in VBA

VBA provides a wide array of debugging tools to help you find and correct errors in your code. You can use debugging tools like breakpoints, procedure stepping, watching variables, and the call stack to see the order of procedure execution.

Displaying the Debug Toolbar

The debugging commands can be found on the **Debug** menu on the Visual Basic Editor menu bar. There is also a separate Debug toolbar. To display the Debug toolbar, right-click any blank area on the Visual Basic Editor menu bar and select the **Debug** checkbox on the shortcut menu.

The image below shows the buttons on the Debug toolbar in the Visual Basic Editor.

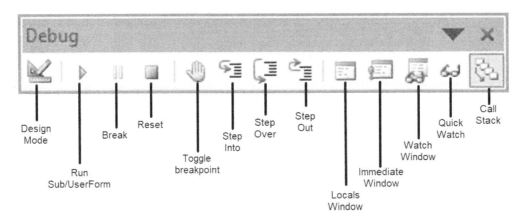

Figure 8-1: The Debug toolbar.

> **Tip**: The Debug menu initially displays as a floating menu, but you can dock it to the Visual Basic Editor menu bar by dragging it over the space to the right of the default menu commands.

Break Mode

Break mode pauses code execution at the line where you have inserted a breakpoint. At this point, the program is still running, but it has been paused. While in break mode, you can examine the current values in the variables, properties, and expressions that are in scope. You can also step through your code one line at a time to examine the program flow and how any variables and properties are being changed. This method is one of the most effective ways of identifying logic errors in your code.

In break mode, the following actions occur:

- **Execution is paused**: When VBA encounters a condition that causes it to enter break mode, it will stop code execution and switch control to the Visual Basic Editor.

- **Variables and properties are preserved**: As the code is still effectively running but paused, the variables and properties are preserved. Hence, you can check the current values of variables, properties, and expressions. You can change the values of variables and properties to observe the effect on other objects. You can also call other procedures.

You can enter break mode by doing the following:

- **Set a breakpoint:** You use this to pause the execution of an application in a specific line in your code.

- **Run the code with one of the Step commands on the Debug menu:** When you use one of the **Step** commands, execution starts, but VBA enters break mode at the beginning of the procedure. Break mode allows you to step through the code using one of the **Step** commands.

Setting a Breakpoint

You can set a breakpoint by either using the **Breakpoint** feature or using the **Stop** statement in your code. When code execution reaches that point, it will enter break mode.

To set a breakpoint in the Code window, use any of the following methods:

- Click a spot on the Margin Indicator Bar next to the line where you want execution to pause.

- Click anywhere in the line where you want execution to pause and do one of the following:
    - Press F9.
    - On the Visual Basic Editor menu bar, select **Debug > Toggle Breakpoint**
    - On the **Debug** toolbar, click the **Toggle Breakpoint** button.

Chapter 8: Debugging

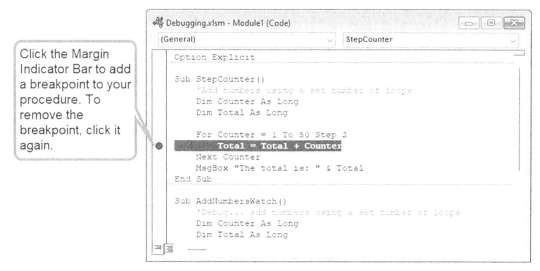

Figure 8-2: Setting a breakpoint in the Code window.

Note You cannot place a breakpoint on a line that is a comment, variable, constant, array, or any other declaration statement.

To clear a breakpoint, do the following:

- Place the cursor anywhere in the line containing the breakpoint and toggle it off by repeating any of the commands described above for setting a breakpoint.

    –or–

- To clear all breakpoints in your project, select **Debug > Clear All Breakpoints** (or press **Ctrl+Shift+F9**).

Displaying the Margin Indicator

If the Margin Indicator Bar is not visible in your Code window, follow these steps to display it:

1. On the Visual Basic Editor menu bar, select **Tools > Options** to display the **Options** dialog box.
2. On the **Editor Format** tab, select the **Margin Indicator Bar** checkbox.
3. Click **OK** to dismiss the Options dialog box.

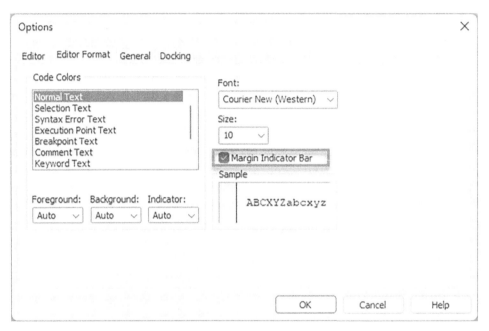

Figure 8-3: Displaying the Margin Indicator.

Note The breakpoints described above are not preserved when you save and close the project. If you want breakpoints that remain available when you close and reopen a project, use the **Stop** statement anywhere in the code where you want to enter break mode. Just remember to remove all **Stop** statements when debugging is complete.

Stepping Through Code Execution

After entering break mode using one of the methods described above, you can step through the code using the **Debug** toolbar in the Visual Basic Editor. This method allows you to execute one line of code at a time and observe the results. Stepping through code is particularly useful if you are new to programming. You can observe the program flow and better understand how programming constructs like conditional statements and loops work.

The following section describes the three **Step** buttons on the Debug toolbar and how each one works.

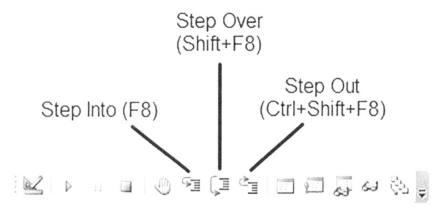

Figure 8-4: The Debug toolbar has three Step buttons for stepping through code.

- **Step Into:** This button executes the code, one line at a time. When you click the Step Into button, it will highlight the next line to be executed. When you click the button again, it will execute that line and highlight the next line. You can just click on this button to start the process of stepping through the code without needing to set a breakpoint.

- **Step Over:** This command is similar to **Step Into**. However, code execution does not branch into any called procedure. A called procedure is executed as a unit, and the debugger steps to the next statement in the current procedure. Use this command if you don't think the problem is in a called procedure.

- **Step Out:** The **Step Out** command executes the remaining lines in the current procedure. If the procedure was called from another procedure, execution passes back to the calling procedure.

To step through your code one line at a time using **Step Into**, do the following:

1. Enter break mode using one of the methods described under **Setting a Breakpoint**.
2. On the **Debug** menu, click **Step Into**. Continue clicking the **Step Into** button to run the code one line at a time.

   –or–

   Press F8 to run the next line of code. Continue pressing F8 to run the code one line at a time.

Using the Immediate Window

You can use the Immediate window to display information from your program while it's in break mode. For example, you can use it to display the output from debugging statements in your code, like **Debug.Print**. You can use the Immediate window to check the current value of variables, properties, and statements by typing them directly into the Immediate window. You can also use the Immediate window to experiment by assigning new values to variables and properties to see how they affect other variables, properties, or objects in your code.

When you first open the Visual Basic Editor, the Immediate window may not be visible as it is not one of the windows opened by default.

To display the Immediate window at any time, do the following:

- On the Visual Basic Editor menu bar, click on **View** and select **Immediate Window** from the menu.

   –or–

- Click the **Immediate Window** button on the **Debug** toolbar.

   –or–

- Press Ctrl+G.

The following image shows how to view the value of a variable, *Total*, and the value of an expression, *Total + Counter*. The procedure in which they're located is in break mode. Type

Chapter 8: Debugging

a question mark followed by the statement you want to evaluate and press Enter. The result will be displayed in the line below it.

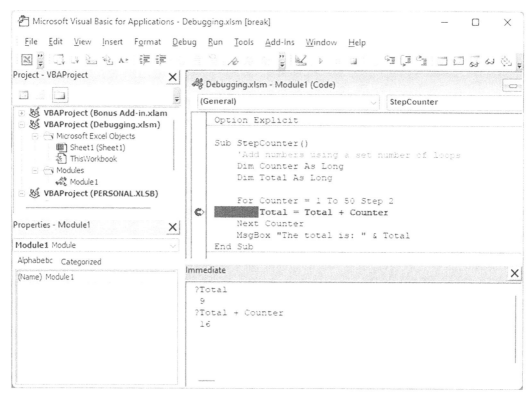

Figure 8-5: Checking the contents of variables in the Immediate window.

The question mark (?) is a shorter form of the VBA **Print** statement that you can use in the Immediate window. You can use the following lines to display the value in the *Total* variable in the Immediate window.

```
Print Total
```

—or—

```
?Total
```

The Immediate window's scope is limited to the current procedure or variables available to it, which include:

- Local variables declared in the procedure that is currently in break mode.

171

- Variables declared at the module level and available to all procedures in the current module.
- Public variables that are available to all procedures in the project.

Variables or properties that are out of scope can't be accessed in the Immediate window.

Using the Debug.Print Statement

One way to monitor what is happening to variables in your code at runtime is to insert the **Print** method of the **Debug** object in your code to send an output to the Immediate window.

For instance, you may want to view the history of a variable or property as the program runs. You can use **Debug.Print** to track the value of the variable or property at each stage in your code by sending outputs to the Immediate window. When code execution pauses or completes, you can review the printed values in the Immediate window.

In the following example, the **Debug.Print** statement prints the value of *Total* to the Immediate window with each iteration of the loop.

```vba
Sub DebugPrint()
    Dim i As Long
    Dim Categories(5) As String
    
    'Populate the array with values
    Categories(0) = "Chairs"
    Categories(1) = "Tables"
    Categories(2) = "Sofas"
    Categories(3) = "Footstools"
    
    'Print values to Immediate window
    For i = 0 To 3
        Debug.Print Categories(i) & " is in element " & i
    Next i
End Sub
```

Chapter 8: Debugging

The following image shows the output in the Immediate window:

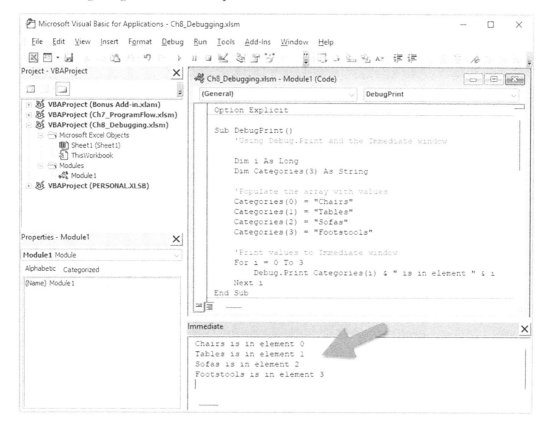

Figure 8-6: Sending information to the Immediate window with Debug.Print.

Using the Locals Window

You can use the **Locals** window to monitor the values of variables while your application is running. The Locals window shows the variables declared in the currently running procedure and their values. For example, you could use the **Locals** window to observe how the variables change when stepping through code. This process could help you determine when an error was introduced due to a variable change and what action caused it.

The Locals window displays the information in three columns:

- **Expression:** The expression column lists the names of the variables. You can't change the data in this column.
- **Value:** This column lists the values of variables. You can edit the values here to test how your code responds to the new values.
- **Type:** Contains the data type of the variables. You can't change the data in this column.

To display the Locals window, do the following:

- On the Visual Basic Editor menu bar, select **View** > **Locals Window**.

    –or–

- Click the **Locals Window** button on the **Debug** toolbar.

In the following example (image below), the *AddNumbersWatch* procedure is in break mode. The **Locals** window shows the value and data type for all expressions in the procedure.

For example, the *Counter* variable is of type Long, and its current value is 4, as shown in the following illustration:

Chapter 8: Debugging

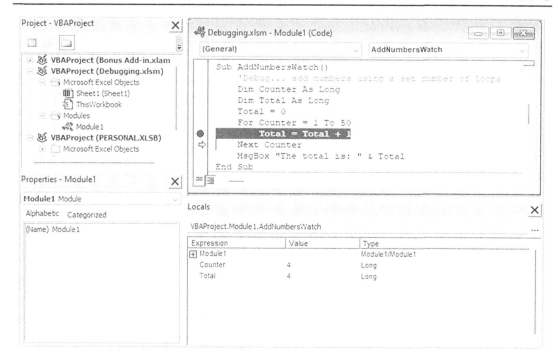

Figure 8-7: Using the Locals window.

Using the Watch Window

Use the **Watch** window to monitor expressions as your code runs. The **Locals** window lets you observe the value of variables in your code at runtime. On the other hand, the **Watch** window lets you observe expressions that you enter in the window. The expression can be a variable, a call to a function, or any other valid expression.

A watch expression can be particularly useful when running a loop with many iterations, and you want to enter break mode near the end of the counter. Using a command like **Step Into** to step through the code can be time-consuming if the loop has many iterations. With the **Watch** window, you can set an expression that watches the loop counter and then breaks when it reaches a certain value.

175

To display the **Watch** window, do the following:

- On the Visual Basic Editor menu bar, select **View > Watch Window**.

  –or–

- Click the **Watch Window** button on the **Debug** toolbar.

Watch Expressions

There are three watch types in VBA:

- **Watch Expression**: This displays the expression being watched and its value in the Watch window when the program enters break mode.
- **Break When Value Is True**: Causes a procedure to enter break mode when the expression being watched becomes true during code execution. This option helps you to determine the point at which an expression passes a test and what happens next.
- **Break When Value Changes**: Causes a procedure to enter break mode when the value of a variable or property changes from its initial value. This option helps you to observe exactly when a variable or property changes at runtime and the cause of the change.

Adding a Watch Expression

Suppose we have a loop with 100 iterations. We want to enter break mode when the loop counter reaches 98 so that we can observe changes to other variables. We can add a watch expression that puts the procedure in break mode when the counter variable is 98.

To add a Watch expression to your application, do the following:

1. On the Visual Basic Editor menu bar, select **Debug > Add Watch** to display the **Add Watch** dialog box.
2. In the **Expression** box, enter the expression that you want to monitor. In the case of our example, it would be *Counter = 98* (assuming the variable name is *Counter*).

3. Under **Context**, select the Procedure and Module to add the watch expression.

4. Under **Watch Type**, select one of the three options. For our example, we want to break when the value is True.

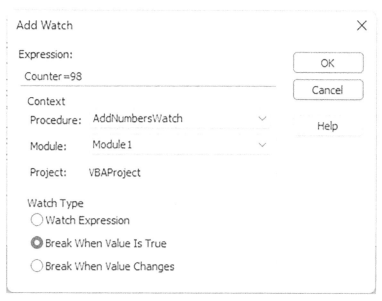

Figure 8-8: Adding a watch expression.

5. Select **OK** to start the Watch.

When the code is executed, VBA enters break mode when the Counter variable reaches 98.

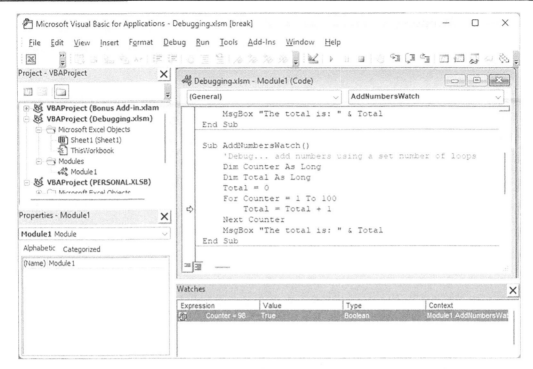

Figure 8-9: Going into break mode when a watch expression is True.

Tip: Another way to add a watch expression in a procedure is to select the expression in the Code window, right-click the expression, and select **Add Watch**.

Editing or Deleting a Watch Expression

To edit a watch expression, do the following:

- Right-click the watch expression in the Watch window and select **Edit Watch**. Then, edit the watch expression in the **Edit Watch** dialog box.

  -or-

- Select the watch expression in the Watch window, and on the Visual Basic Editor, select **Debug** > **Edit Watch**.

To delete a watch expression, right-click the watch expression in the Watch window and select **Delete Watch**.

> **Note** Just closing the Watch window does not remove watch expressions. To remove them from your project, delete them manually.

The Call Stack

Suppose your project has nested procedures. For example, one procedure calls another procedure, and within the second procedure, a third procedure is called. Like a complex hierarchy of nested Excel formulas, keeping track of many levels of nested procedure calls could become difficult.

The **Call Stack** is a debugging tool that traces program execution through multiple procedures and shows the flow of execution. This tool is useful for projects with several nested procedure calls. To debug your code, you may want to keep track of the order in which the procedures are being called. With the **Call Stack**, you can check whether your code follows the correct sequence of procedures.

The following image shows three nested procedures in the Call Stack window. The *Customer* procedure calls *Order*, and the *Order* procedure calls *OrderLines*.

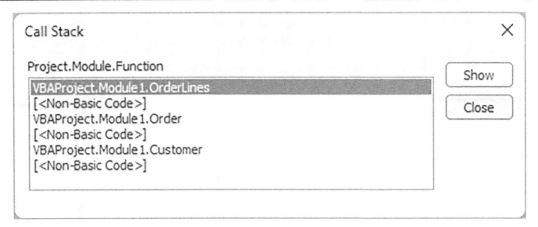

Figure 8-10: The Call Stack.

The last executed procedure is at the top of the Call Stack, and the first is at the bottom. If there are many called procedures in your code, you can examine the **Call Stack** at any point in break mode. You can only display the Call Stack when your code is in break mode.

To display the **Call Stack** while in break mode, do the following:

- On the Visual Basic Editor menu, select **View** > **Call Stack** to display the Call Stack.

    —or—

- Click the **Call Stack** button on the Debug toolbar.

Chapter 9

Handling Runtime Errors

In this chapter:

- Understanding runtime errors in VBA.
- Using the On Error and Resume statements to trap and handle runtime errors.
- Using the Err object to identify which error occurred and how to handle it.
- Writing code to handle inline errors.
- Using the Raise method to raise runtime errors with custom information.

A runtime error in VBA is an error that occurs when your application is running. A runtime error will cause VBA to stop execution and display an error message. Another way to put it is that the application crashed! You don't want your application to crash upon encountering an unexpected error. Hence, a need to incorporate error-handling routines, especially in production applications.

Understanding Runtime Errors

Runtime errors differ from syntax errors and can happen to perfectly designed applications. For example, a user could forget to insert a memory stick in the USB slot when your application needs to read the memory stick drive; the system can run low in memory; files may not be where the application expects to find them when reading files from disk.

In the code below, if the user enters a string instead of a number, a runtime error occurs in the line where we try to convert the value to the currency format:

```
Sub GetUserInput01()
    Dim UserInput As Variant

    ' Prompt for a value
    UserInput = InputBox("Please enter a number")

    ' Insert the value in cell A1 in the active worksheet
    Range("A1").Value = CCur(UserInput)

End Sub
```

If the user enters a string, the code above generates a "Type mismatch" runtime error, as shown in the image below:

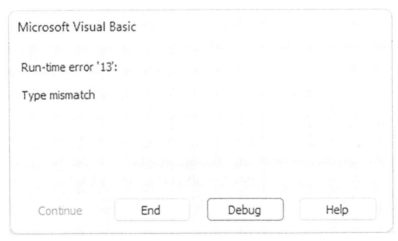

Figure 9-1: A type mismatch runtime error.

Chapter 9: Handling Runtime Errors

Sometimes, you can avoid easily anticipated errors by using logical tests. For example, you can check the value entered by a user. If your code expects a number, but the user enters a string, you can check the value and prompt the user to enter the correct value.

The modified example below ensures the entry is a numerical value before use. If the value isn't numerical, a message box informs the user of the error before exiting the program. VBA doesn't run the statement, which would have generated an error.

```
Sub GetUserInput02()
    Dim UserInput As Variant

    ' Prompt for a value
    UserInput = InputBox("Please enter a number")

    ' Check that the user input is numerical
    If Not IsNumeric(UserInput) Then
        MsgBox "You must enter a number."
        Exit Sub
    End If
    Range("A1").Value = CCur(UserInput)

End Sub
```

The code above is still not error-proof. For example, if you run this code while the active sheet is a Chart sheet, you'll get the following error:

Figure 9-2: Runtime error due to an object mismatch.

The code is quite basic, but even if we add further checks to avoid the error above, we still can't anticipate all possible errors in different scenarios. There could be many ways

183

that an error could occur in a procedure. The good news is that VBA provides a method to trap and deal with all possible errors. You can trap the error, deal with it in various ways, and exit the routine gracefully without letting the application stop and display an unintelligible error message to the user.

You can add error handling code to your procedures to ensure any unforeseen issue triggering an error is trapped and handled gracefully. Note that error handling differs from debugging, which is a process used to identify and fix errors in code before an application is released.

The error handling process in VBA involves the following steps:

1. At the beginning of your procedure, set an error trap that specifies the label of the error handling code.
2. In the error handling section, handle the error by either resolving the issue that caused the error, displaying a message informing the user of the issue and how to resolve it, or exiting the application gracefully.
3. Exit the error handling code.

On Error Statement

The **On Error** statement basically says, "*If an error occurs, do this…*". So, the statement sets an error trap and specifies the location of the error handler, which execution will jump to when an error occurs.

Chapter 9: Handling Runtime Errors

There are three forms of the **On Error** statement:

Statement	Description
On Error GoTo *line*	Sets the error handling trap and specifies the location in the procedure where the error is handled.
	The *line* argument can be any line label or line number and must be in the same procedure as the **On Error** statement. Otherwise, a compile error occurs.
On Error Resume Next	Tells VBA to skip the statement that caused the error and continue execution from the statement immediately after. Use this statement if you anticipate an error that can be ignored so it doesn't require an error handler.
On Error GoTo 0	This statement disables any error handler that was previously set. In some scenarios, you may need to temporarily disable the error handler to perform certain operations before enabling it again.

If a run-time error occurs, execution jumps to the label indicated in the On Error GoTo statement.

The example below shows the structure of an error handler in a VBA procedure:

```
Sub CodeHandlingExample()

    On Error GoTo ErrorHandler 'Set the error trap

    'The main code of the procedure goes here.

    Exit Sub

ErrorHandler: 'Line label to start error handler.

    'Your error handling code goes here.

    Resume 'Exit the error handling code.

End Sub
```

In the example above, the label is named *ErrorHandler*. Any trapped errors are handled in the section under the ErrorHandler label. The **Resume** statement specifies where processing continues. In this example, processing continues with the line that caused the error, assuming we ran code to fix the issue. The **Exit Sub** statement prevents normal code execution from reaching the error handler. Thus, in an error-free run, the procedure ends without running the error-handling code at the end of the routine.

Note If the On Error statement does not work as described, it may be due to a setting in VBA Options. Excel ignores all On Error statements when **Break on All Errors** is selected in VBA Options.

To fix the issue, follow the steps below:

1. In the Visual Basic Editor, select **Tools** > **Options**.
2. In the **Options** dialog box, select the **General** tab.
3. Under **Error Trapping**, select **Break on Unhandled Errors**.

Resume Options

Use the **Resume** statement to specify where your application will continue execution after handling an error. There are different types of resume statements you can use in VBA:

Statement	Description
Resume	Used to continue execution from the statement that caused the error. For example, if the user forgets to insert a memory stick in the USB slot when the application requires it, you can tell the user to resolve the issue and then run that statement again.
Resume Next	Resumes execution with the statement immediately following the statement that caused the error. If the error occurred in a called procedure, execution continues with the statement after the called procedure.
Resume *line*	Execution resumes at the *line label* or *line number* specified in the Resume statement. The line number or line label argument must be inside the same procedure as the error handler.

If there is no Resume statement in the error handler, code execution in the procedure ends.

The following procedure displays an input box prompting the user for a number. The number is then inserted in cell A1 in the active worksheet. The code has an error handler used to catch errors occurring in the procedure's main part.

For example, if the user enters a string, the program will generate an error when converting it to currency. Execution then jumps to the error handler, *ErrorHandler*. The user is informed of the error and can re-enter the value or cancel. If the user selects Yes, the **Resume** statement sends execution to the *TryEntry* label at the beginning of the routine to restart the entry process.

```
Sub ErrorHandlerDemo01()
    'Generates an error if user input is not a number

    Dim UserInput As Variant
    Dim Msg As String
    Dim Response As Long

    On Error GoTo ErrorHandler

TryEntry:
    ' Prompt for a value
    UserInput = InputBox("Please enter a number")
    If UserInput = "" Then Exit Sub

    'Generates an error if the input is not numerical
    Range("A1").Value = CCur(UserInput)
    Exit Sub

ErrorHandler: ' Error handling label
    Msg = "Error " & Err.Number & ": " & _
          Err.Description & vbNewLine
    Msg = Msg & "Enter a number" & vbNewLine
    Msg = Msg & "Try again?"
    Response = MsgBox(Msg, vbYesNo + vbCritical)
    If Response = vbYes Then Resume TryEntry
End Sub
```

The preceding code example still has some issues, as it provides one message for all errors. The message box is a modal dialog box that temporarily locks the user from the rest of Excel until it is closed. The user cannot correct any issues in Excel while the message box is displayed. Hence, the prompt needs to be dismissed before the issue can be corrected in Excel.

You can improve the error handler by creating a customized message for each anticipated runtime error by accessing the error number in the **Err** object.

The Err Object

The **Err** object holds the number and other properties of the last generated error. You can use the properties and methods of the Err object in your error handling code to check which error has occurred, clear an error value, or raise an error. The **Number** property of the Err object is an integer that indicates the last error that occurred. To check the last error that occurred, use the following statement:

```
Err.Number
```

Sometimes, you can fix the issue and continue the process without interrupting the user. In other cases, you'll use the error code to determine the error that occurred, inform the user of the error with a custom message, and perform any necessary actions based on their response.

The **Description** property of the **Err** object is a string that holds a description of the last error generated. To access the description of the error, use the following statement:

```
Err.Description
```

Normally, you pass the description to a string variable for later use.

The **Source** property holds the name of the object that generated the error. For example, if you opened a file in your code that resulted in an error, you would use **Err.Source** to identify the application that caused the error.

VBA resets the properties of the Err object to zero (0) or zero-length strings when a procedure ends or when a **Resume Next** statement is executed within an error-handling routine. Using a Resume statement outside an error-handling routine will not reset the properties of the Err object. You can use **Err.Clear** to explicitly reset Err.

The following example code is a revised version of the user entry code discussed previously in this chapter. The procedure displays an input box prompting the user for a number. The user's input is then inserted in cell A1 in the active worksheet. This example uses **Err.Number** to catch anticipated errors and provide a customized response for each one:

```
Sub ErrorHandlerDemo02()
    Dim UserInput As Variant
    Dim Msg As String
    Dim Response As Long

    On Error GoTo ErrorHandler

TryEntry:
    ' Prompt for a value
    UserInput = InputBox("Please enter a number")
    If UserInput = "" Then Exit Sub
    Range("A1").Value = CCur(UserInput)
    Exit Sub

ErrorHandler: ' Error-handling routine.
    Select Case Err.Number
        Case 13 ' Type mismatch
            Msg = Msg & "Invalid entry." & vbNewLine
            Msg = Msg & "Do you want to try again?"
            Response = MsgBox(Msg, vbYesNo + vbCritical)
            If Response = vbYes Then Resume TryEntry
        Case 1004 ' Protected sheet or a chart
            Msg = "Error " & Err.Number & ": " & _
                Err.Description & vbNewLine
            Msg = Msg & "Ensure the active sheet is "
            Msg = Msg & "not protected or a chart sheet."
            MsgBox Msg, vbCritical
            Exit Sub
        Case Else ' catches all other errors
            Msg = "Error " & Err.Number & ": " & _
                Err.Description & vbNewLine
            Msg = Msg & "Please contact support."
            MsgBox Msg, vbCritical
            Exit Sub
    End Select
End Sub
```

In the procedure above, if **Err.Number** is 13, it indicates that the user entered a string instead of a number. The message box informs them of the error while allowing them to try again.

If the error number is 1004, the range in the Excel sheet couldn't be accessed. A protected sheet or a chart sheet can cause this error. Thus, error 1004 is handled by displaying a message box telling the user to ensure the sheet is not protected or a chart sheet. The message box also only has one button, which dismisses it when clicked, as it needs to be closed before the user can correct the issue.

Finally, the error handler uses a **Case Else** statement to catch other errors not specifically handled and displays a generic message to the user to contact support.

Inline Error Handling

In some scenarios, you may want to address an error as it happens rather than branch off to a separate error handler. This method is called inline error handling. For example, you can use the **On Error Resume Next** statement to ignore an error and continue execution at the line immediately following the line that caused the error.

In the following example code, we are attempting to access a workbook named *Book1.xlsx* and to assign it as a workbook object to a variable named *wkb*. If the workbook doesn't exist, the statement will attempt to assign a non-existent object to the variable and cause a runtime error. The **On Error Resume Next** statement enables us to ignore the error, allowing execution to go to the line where we can check the value in the variable before attempting to use it.

```
Sub OpenFile()
    Dim wkb As Workbook

    On Error Resume Next
    Set wkb = Workbooks("Book1.xlsx")

    On Error GoTo 0
    If wkb Is Nothing Then
        MsgBox "The file does not exist."
    End If
End Sub
```

After using an inline error handler for an anticipated error, you don't want to continue ignoring errors for the rest of your procedure. Therefore, after using On Error Resume Next to handle a potential error, use On Error GoTo *label* to resume your procedure's error handling process. The procedure above uses On Error GoTo 0 to disable the error handler and resume the normal error reporting behavior in VBA.

Passing Back Errors

If you have invoked several procedures in your code, error handling becomes a little more complicated, as an error could occur in any of the called procedures. If an error occurs in a called procedure that doesn't have an error handler, VBA passes the error back to the calling procedure.

For example, suppose you have an *Orders* procedure that calls a *GetProduct* function. If an error occurs in *GetProduct* and the procedure doesn't contain any error handling code, VBA passes the error up to *Orders*. If *Orders* also has no error handler, VBA displays an error message and stops code execution.

The problem with this process is that you may not know precisely where the error originated if you have several levels of called procedures in your code. In a scenario like this, you can use the **Raise** method of the **Err** object to specify the origin of an error.

The Raise Method

If you want the calling procedure to handle all errors, avoid putting error handlers in called procedures so VBA automatically passes any errors back to the calling procedure.

Alternatively, you can use the **Raise** method of the **Err** object to raise custom errors in called procedures. When an error occurs in a called procedure, one way of handling it is to raise the error again with custom properties and pass it back to the calling procedure. This technique lets you identify where an error originated and how to handle it.

Syntax:

Err.Raise *number, source, description, helpfile, helpcontext*

The *number* argument is required, while the other arguments are optional.

In the example below, *GetData* is invoked inside *CalculateInterest* to get the user input. If an error occurs in *GetData*, a custom error is raised and passed to *CalculateInterest*, where the error is handled with a customized block of code.

Calling procedure:

```
Sub CalculateInterest()
    Dim UserInput As Currency
    Dim Response As Long

    On Error GoTo ErrorHandler

    'Call function
    UserInput = GetData

    'Insert value in Excel cell
    Range("A1").Value = CCur(UserInput)
    Exit Sub

ErrorHandler:
    If Err.Source = "GetData" Then
        'Handle error from called function here
        MsgBox "Error: " & Err.Number & vbNewLine & _
        "Description: " & Err.Description & vbNewLine & _
        "Source: " & Err.Source
    Else
        'Handle all other errors here
    End If
End Sub
```

Called procedure:

```
Function GetData()
    Dim UserInput As Variant
    Dim InterestRate As Double

    On Error GoTo ErrorHandler

    InterestRate = 0.0575

    'Prompt for a value
    UserInput = InputBox("Please enter the value.")

    'Return the value
    GetData = UserInput * InterestRate
    Exit Function

ErrorHandler:
    Err.Raise Err.Number, "GetData"
End Function
```

In the code above, when an error occurs in GetData, execution goes to the ErrorHandler label. The error handling code then uses **Err.Raise** to raise the error again with custom information specifying the name of the procedure in the **Source** argument. You can use other arguments of the **Raise** method, for example, *description*, to provide additional custom information about the error.

After raising the error in *GetData*, execution passes back to *CalculateInterest*, where the error is handled under the *ErrorHandler* label. **Err.Source** allows us to identify the procedure in which the error occurred so we can process it accordingly.

When you have several levels of procedure calls, raising an error in this manner helps you handle errors better based on their source.

Chapter 10

Introducing Excel Objects

In this chapter:

- Introducing the concept of objects.
- Understanding the Excel object model.
- Referencing objects in the object hierarchy.
- Accessing and setting object properties.
- Performing actions with object methods.
- Working with the Application object.
- Using worksheet functions in code.

This chapter introduces the concept of objects and how they are applied in VBA. As VBA was designed to enable you to create and manipulate Excel objects programmatically, understanding Excel objects is an important part of becoming proficient with VBA. Excel objects are where you begin to get into the meat of VBA programming. You will learn to reference Excel objects in the object hierarchy and expose the properties and methods you want to use. You'll also use the Application object to access and use its members to perform tasks in Excel.

Overview of Objects

Objects are packaged functionality of an application that you can use to create solutions programmatically. You can imagine programming objects like real-life physical objects.

For example, a car is an object with **properties** like its *make, color, engine capacity, fuel level,* etc. The properties describe the car. Some properties, like the engine capacity, are read-only, while others, like the fuel level, can be changed. The same concept applies to Excel objects. Some properties are read-only, while others are updatable.

To access a property of an object, use the following syntax:

```
Object.Property
```

For the car example, we can access its properties like this:

```
Car.Color
Car.Make
Car.Capacity
```

A car also has **actions** it can perform like *drive, reverse, signal,* and *brake*. The actions you can perform with a car are equivalent to *methods* of objects that you can use to perform tasks.

To call a method of an object, use the following syntax:

```
Object.Method
```

Similarly, we can call actions for our car example with the following:

```
Car.Drive
Car.Signal
Car.Brake
```

An Excel **object** can be an element in an application like a worksheet, a range, or a UserForm. An object can also be a piece of code in the object library, without a graphical interface, that you use to perform tasks, like the **Err** object.

A **collection** is also an object with zero or more objects of the same type. For example, Excel has a **Workbooks** collection, representing a collection of all the open Workbook objects. If no workbook is open, then the Workbooks collection has zero objects. A collection has its own properties and methods, enabling a group of similar objects to be referred to as a unit. For example, the Workbooks collection in Excel has an **Add** method that allows you to programmatically create a new Workbook object.

Object Properties, Methods, and Events

Each object can have properties, methods, and events that allow you to manipulate them programmatically and use the functionality they provide:

- **Properties**: Properties define the characteristics of an object. For example, the Excel Worksheet object contains properties such as *Name*, *Rows*, and *Visible*.
- **Methods**: Methods are the actions you can perform with an object. For example, the Worksheet object contains methods such as *Copy*, *Move*, and *Delete*.
- **Events**: An event is an action that can be triggered when something happens to an object, such as opening a workbook, activating a worksheet, closing a UserForm, or clicking a button on a UserForm. You can write code that runs when an event is triggered. These are called *event handlers*. In VBA, events are mostly associated with Excel objects with a graphical interface, like Worksheets, UserForms, and UserForm controls.

Advantages of Objects

Using an already packaged object in your code enables you to create complex programming solutions without writing too much code. For instance, you can write code using the **Chart** object to visually represent data without creating the chart from scratch. VBA already has a **Chart** class, which you can use to create a new instance of a **Chart** object and then use its built-in properties and methods to display your data.

Chapter 10: Introducing Excel Objects

Object Library References

An object library defines the types of objects an application provides and their associated methods and properties. After setting a reference to an object library, you can use the **Object Browser** to view its properties and methods. A standard installation of Excel automatically references the libraries required to manipulate Excel objects in VBA. However, it is important to know where these references are set so that you can fix any potential issues related to missing object library references.

To view the object library references, on the Visual Basic Editor menu, select **Tools > References** to display the **References** dialog box.

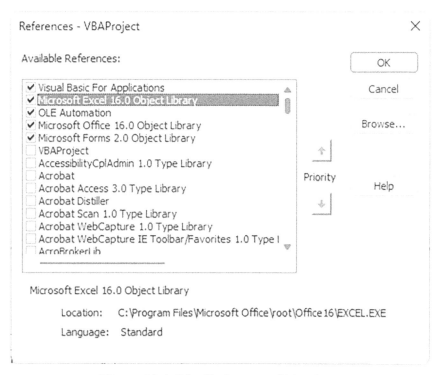

Figure 10-1: The References dialog box.

The default object libraries required to manipulate Excel objects in code are:

- Visual Basic For Applications.
- Microsoft Excel 16.0 Object Library.
- OLE Automation.

- Microsoft Office 16.0 Object Library.

Sometimes, you'll need to set references to the libraries of other applications here. For example, if you want to access external data, you need to set a reference to the ADO Object Library. If you want to write code to automate a Microsoft Word document from Excel, you'll need to set a reference to the Microsoft Word 16.0 Object Library.

To close the References dialog box, select **Cancel**.

The Excel Object Model

The Excel object model is a conceptual map of the objects and collections in Excel. The object model defines which objects the application exposes (i.e., makes available to be manipulated programmatically) and how the objects relate.

A VBA object represents each Excel element. For example, the Workbook, Worksheet, and Range objects represent a workbook, worksheet, and a range of cells, respectively. You can automate tasks in Excel with code that manipulates these objects. You can create powerful custom solutions by using the methods and properties of these objects.

The Hierarchy of Objects

Excel provides a multitude of objects, most of which have methods and properties. VBA uses these objects to automate Excel. You can manipulate Excel objects with VBA code from within Excel or from other Microsoft 365 applications, like Microsoft Word or Microsoft Access. Becoming familiar with Excel's object hierarchy and how the objects relate to each other is especially useful when referencing objects in VBA.

The **Application** object, which represents the application itself, is at the top of the hierarchy. In this case, it is the Excel application. The illustration below shows a portion of Excel's VBA object hierarchy. A rectangle represents a collection, and an oval represents a single object:

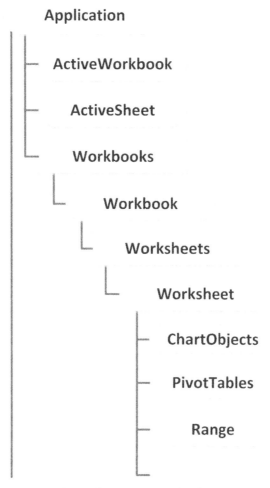

Figure 10-2: The Excel VBA object model.

The image above represents a small section of the Excel object model. For more information on objects in the hierarchy, search for "Excel object model VBA" in VBA Help.

The following table describes some of the most commonly used objects in Excel:

Object	Description
Application	This object represents the Excel application itself. The Application object provides a lot of information, including the current open objects.
Workbook	The Workbook object represents a single Excel workbook within the application.
Worksheet	The Worksheet object is part of the Worksheets collection within a Workbook object.
Range	A Range object represents a single cell or a selection of cells within a worksheet. You must define a Range object before you can manipulate data in specific cells in a worksheet using its properties and methods.
Chart	The Chart object represents a chart in Excel. A chart can be a member of the ChartObjects collection in a worksheet or a separate chart sheet in the workbook.
PivotTable	Represents a PivotTable in a worksheet, an interactive table summarizing large data sets.

Navigating the Object Hierarchy

You use VBA code to navigate the Excel object model and reference the object you want to work with. To refer to an object in code, visualize moving down the object hierarchy. For example, to access a particular range in a workbook, you can visualize the hierarchy like this:

Excel Application > Workbook > Worksheet > Range.

A visual understanding of the hierarchy helps determine what object should logically come next when referencing an object in code. As illustrated in the Excel object model above, all Excel objects are under the **Application** object. Thus, you start with the Application

Chapter 10: Introducing Excel Objects

object to navigate to an object down the hierarchy, separating each object with the dot operator (.).

The example code below navigates to a particular workbook named *Book1.xlsx* in the Workbooks collection of the Application object:

```
Application.Workbooks("Book1.xlsx")
```

Note that the workbook's name in the collection is in quotation marks. You can also use an index number to refer to a workbook in the Workbooks collection. The code below references the first workbook in the Workbooks collection:

```
Application.Workbooks(1)
```

Using an index number is useful when you want to loop through several workbooks in a collection and apply the same actions to them.

The following example navigates to a worksheet within Book1.xlsx:

```
Application.Workbooks("Book1.xlsx").Worksheets("Sheet1")
```

We can navigate further down the object hierarchy to a range within Sheet1:

```
Application.Workbooks("Book1.xlsx").Worksheets("Sheet1").Range("A1")
.Value
```

The example above accesses the **Value** property of the specified **Range** object, Range("A1"). This reference points to cell A1 in a worksheet named *Sheet1*, which is in a workbook named *Book1*. This reference is also called "fully qualified" because it specifies the full path to the object.

Using Simpler References

The fully qualified reference used above is quite long. If you have to use fully qualified references each time you refer to an object, it can get tedious quickly! VBA allows you to shorten the references by making assumptions based on the default or active objects.

For example, you can omit referencing the Application object when writing code in Excel to manipulate Excel objects. Excel is the default application in this case.

201

So, we can simplify the reference by omitting the Application object to make the code look like this:

```
Workbooks("Book1.xlsx").Worksheets("Sheet1").Range("A1").Value
```

The reference above is still quite long. We can shorten it further by assuming we are referencing the active workbook. For instance, if we only have one workbook open, that would be the active workbook. The shortened reference will look like this:

```
Worksheets("Sheet1").Range("A1").Value
```

This reference is looking more like it. However, we can shorten it even further by assuming we are referencing the active worksheet. The example below rewrites the code without explicitly referring to the worksheet:

```
Range("A1").Value
```

This short piece of code refers to cell A1 in the active worksheet in the active workbook.

Referring to a worksheet range using the above shortcuts is great for small pieces of informal code. However, it could cause errors in certain circumstances. For example, the workbook or worksheet we assume in our code may not be the active object when the code is executed. This discrepancy could generate an error or produce inaccurate results. Hence, it is best to explicitly specify the names of workbooks and worksheets in scenarios where there is room for ambiguity.

You can use a **With** statement to avoid repeating long object references when referring to the same object. The **With** statement is discussed later in this chapter.

Setting Properties and Calling Methods

The preceding sections showed how to access an object by navigating the object hierarchy. However, objects on their own aren't of much use without their properties, methods, and events. Objects become useful when you can read/set properties or call methods to perform actions in Excel. Changing the properties of an object enables you to change its characteristics. Generally, you use properties to set or retrieve attributes, while methods are used to perform actions.

Setting Object Properties

To assign a value to an object, use the general format:

`Object.Property = Value`

The example code below sets the **Value** property of the Range object, *range("A1")* to 300. The value in the range is retrieved using the Value property again and displayed with a message box.

```
Sub ObjectProperties()
    'Assigns a value to cell A1 of Sheet1 in the active workbook.
    Worksheets("Sheet1").Range("A1").Value = 300
    MsgBox Range("A1").Value
End Sub
```

Calling Object Methods

A method is used to perform an action. You can think of methods as verbs. For example, you can *drive* a car. So, if we were to translate that to VBA code, it would be:

`Car.Drive`

Some methods return a value, and others don't. Some methods have arguments, and others don't.

> **Note** A *parameter* is a variable that is part of a method's definition or syntax. When you call the method in your code, the values passed into its parameters are called *arguments*. These terms are often used interchangeably.

How you invoke a method depends on whether the method returns a value and if you want to use the value in your code. Use the following syntax to call a method that either doesn't return a value or the return value is not used in your code. The arguments are optional as some methods do not have parameters:

```
Object.Method [arg1, arg2, …]
```

The arguments in the syntax above are not enclosed in parentheses because the method does not return a value.

An example of a method that does not have a parameter or a return value is the **Select** method of the **Range** object:

```
Range("A1:A10").Select
```

Likewise, the following statement runs the **AutoFit** method of the **Columns** collection to fit text in the selected columns but does not return a value:

```
Selection.Columns.AutoFit
```

If a method returns a value, and you want to assign it to a variable, you must place its arguments in parentheses. Generally, use parentheses when the method is on the right side of an equal sign. Use the following syntax to call a method and pass its return value to a variable:

```
Variable = Object.Method ([arg1, arg2, ..])
```

The code statements below show different ways to call a method:

```
Sub CallingMethods()
    'Calling a method and using the return value.
    Range("A1").Value = WorksheetFunction.Average(45, 73, 67, 43, 60)

    'Calling a method with an argument and no return value.
    Range("A1").AddComment "Score Average"

    'Calling a method with no argument and no return value.
    Range("A2:A10").Clear
End Sub
```

The example above has three method calls:

- The first statement calls the **Average** method of the WorksheetFunction object. The statement passes the result to a range object, cell A1, in the active worksheet.
- In the second method call, **AddComment** is used to insert a comment in cell A1 of the active worksheet. This method has no return value.
- The third method call uses the **Clear** method of the Range object to clear cells A2:A10 in the active worksheet.

In the first statement, the method's arguments are in parentheses because it returns a value. The second method call doesn't return a value, so the argument is not in parentheses. The third method call has no arguments or return value.

You can also use a named argument to specify an argument for a method. It is not necessary to specify the name of an argument, as shown below, but in certain scenarios, it can make your code easier to read.

The code below calls the **AddComment** method of the Range object by explicitly naming the **Text** argument for which we provided a value:

```
Range("A2").AddComment Text:= "Score Average"
```

To identify the name of arguments, as you enter the syntax for a method, pay attention to VBA's *Auto Quick Info* feature. This feature provides help regarding method arguments and their names, as shown in the image below:

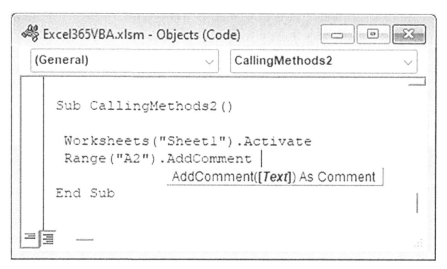

Figure 10-3: VBA's Auto Quick Info feature.

Using the With Statement with Objects

The **With** statement allows you to access a member of an object, like a property or method, multiple times without using the fully qualified name every time. You specify the fully qualified object name once in the **With** block and use the dot notation to access its members subsequent times within the block.

Syntax:

With *objectExpression*
　[statements]
End With

objectExpression is an expression that evaluates to an object.

Often, when working with members of an object, you need to refer to the same object or structure multiple times to perform actions. The With...End With structure simplifies the code used to access members of the object. Also, using With...End With can make code run more efficiently as the object is fully referenced just once in the With block.

The following code example selects a range in the active worksheet and sets various formatting options using With...End With.

```vba
Sub UsingWith()
    'Formats the selected range in the active worksheet
    Range("A1:A10").Select
    With Selection.Font
        .Name = "Calibri"
        .Size = 20
        .Bold = True
        .Italic = True
        .Underline = True
    End With
    Selection.Columns.AutoFit
End Sub
```

Using Object Variables

The **Dim** statement is used to declare an object variable. The declaration doesn't refer to an actual object until you use the **Set** statement to assign an object to it.

The code below declares a **Range** object variable called MyRange and uses the Set statement to assign a new worksheet range to it:

```
Dim MyRange As Range

Set MyRange = Range("A1:A10")
```

Triggering Object Events

An event is an action that can be triggered when something happens to an object, such as opening a workbook, a mouse click, or a key press. You can write code that runs when an event happens. User actions, code instructions, or system events can trigger object events. In VBA, events are like predefined empty procedures in which you can insert code that runs when the event is triggered.

For example, if you have several worksheets in a workbook, selecting a worksheet triggers the **Activate** event of that worksheet. You can insert code in the **Worksheet_Activate** event that runs every time the worksheet is activated. Some Excel objects have predefined events for which you can write code, but not all objects have or respond to events. The image below shows the events attached to a worksheet object for which you can write code.

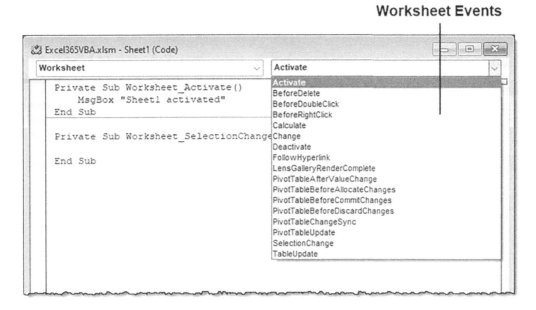

Figure 10-4: Worksheet events.

Events are covered in chapters 15, 16, and 18.

Using the Object Browser

The Visual Basic Editor has a great tool called the Object Browser that you can use to browse the objects available to you and their associated properties, methods, and events. When you select a member of an object in the **Members Of** list, you get information about the object on the **Details** pane, including the syntax of methods and their arguments.

Chapter 10: Introducing Excel Objects

Figure 10-5: The Object Browser allows you to identify the properties, methods, and events of objects.

To open the Object Browser, select **View > Object Browser** on the Visual Basic Editor menu.

Tip: In the Visual Basic Editor, you can quickly open the Object Browser by pressing **F2** on your keyboard or selecting the **Object Browser** icon on the Standard toolbar.

At the top of the dialog box, The **Project/Library** drop-down list contains a list of objects that are currently available to you. The default selection is *All Libraries*. If you have references to libraries from several Microsoft 365 applications, you can narrow down your search by selecting a library from the drop-down list.

209

The **Search Text** box enables you to search for an object. For instance, if you're looking for all Worksheet objects, enter "worksheet" in the search box and select the **Search** button (with the binoculars icon).

The Object Browser displays the search results in the **Search Results** list. All objects containing the words "worksheet" are displayed in the results list.

Select an item in the **Search Results** list box to highlight it in the **Classes** list box and display its members in the **Members Of** list box (on the right side of the dialog box).

To get help for an object in any of the lists, select the object name and press F1 on your keyboard. The Visual Basic Editor opens the help webpage for that item. You can also use the **Help** button (the question mark icon) to get help for an object.

 Note You need an internet connection to view VBA help online.

Tip: To get a full list of the methods and properties of an Excel object, you can also use the format "VBA *[object name]* properties" or "VBA *[object name]* methods" to search for it using your internet search engine. Where *[object name]* is the name of the object. One of the top search results will be the VBA help page for that object.

Using Auto List Members with Objects

In certain scenarios, when referencing objects in code, the **Auto List Members** feature helps by listing the objects' available properties, methods, and events.

The list is displayed when you type a dot after the referenced object, as shown in the following image.

Chapter 10: Introducing Excel Objects

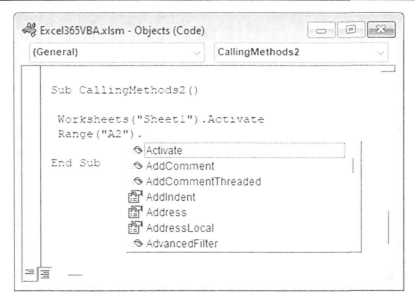

Figure 10-6: The Auto List Members feature is the IntelliSense equivalent in VBA.

You can type a letter to narrow the list to items that begin with that letter. Each letter you type narrows down the list further. Select the item you need and press the **Tab** key to enter it in your code. This feature allows you to more easily identify properties and methods of objects as you type your code. If you wish to change your selection, press Ctrl+J to redisplay the list of members.

The Application Object

The **Application** object, which represents the entire Excel application, contains properties and methods that affect the application and any active objects. For example, the Application object contains worksheet functions you can use in your code.

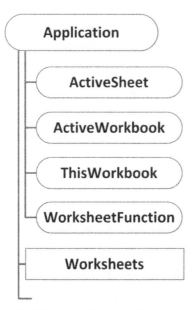

Figure 10-7: The Application object hierarchy.

Using Worksheet Functions from VBA

A commonly used property of the Application object is the **WorksheetFunction** property, which returns the **WorksheetFunction** object. Each built-in function in Excel is represented by a method in the WorksheetFunction object.

To see all available functions in the WorksheetFunction property, search for "WorksheetFunction" in the Object Browser.

Use the WorksheetFunction property when you want to use a built-in Excel function to perform a calculation or evaluation in code. Any built-in function you can use manually

Chapter 10: Introducing Excel Objects

in a worksheet is available in VBA through the **WorksheetFunction** property. For example, the code below uses the **CountBlank** function to search for blank cells in the range A1:C14 on the active worksheet. A message box informs the user if blank cells are found.

```
If Application.WorksheetFunction.CountBlank(Range("A1:E14")) > 0 Then
        MsgBox "There are blank cells in the range!", vbCritical
End If
```

> **Note** Using functions from the WorksheetFunction property in code is different from using built-in functions as part of formulas in Excel cells. For information on how to add formulas to worksheet cells, see my Mastering Excel 365 book.

Working with the Active Object

The **ActiveWorkbook** and **ActiveSheet** properties can be accessed from the **Application** object. These properties return the active objects in the application workspace. Suppose the currently open workbook is named *Book1* and contains a worksheet named *Sheet1*. The **ActiveWorkbook** property would return *Book1*, while the **ActiveSheet** property returns *Sheet1*. Thus, you can use these properties to access and manipulate the active objects without using their fully qualified references.

The Application object also has a **Selection** property, which returns any selected range of cells in the active worksheet as a Range object. You can use the selection property to reference the ranges currently selected in the active worksheet. You can use the **ThisWorkbook** property to return a reference to the workbook containing your code anytime.

The following code used properties of the Application object to display some information regarding the active workbook:

```vba
Sub CheckActiveObjects()
    ' Activate Sheet1
    Worksheets("Sheet1").Activate
    
    'Display the name of these active objects
    Debug.Print ActiveWorkbook.Name
    Debug.Print ActiveSheet.Name
    
    'Display the type of the selected object
    Debug.Print TypeName(Selection)
End Sub
```

Chapter 11

Working with Workbooks

In this chapter:

- Referencing existing workbooks.
- Creating new workbooks.
- Working with workbook properties and methods.
- Working with workbook events.

This chapter will cover how to create and manipulate workbooks programmatically in Excel. You will learn how to open or create new workbooks, create workbook event procedures, save a workbook, and close a workbook.

The Workbook Object

Each workbook in Excel contains one or more worksheets that allow you to store and organize information. The currently open workbooks in Excel can be accessed through the **Workbooks** collection. You can access each workbook using a Workbook object. The **Workbook** object allows you to access objects within the workbook, like worksheets, charts, etc.

The illustration below shows the hierarchy of the Workbooks collection:

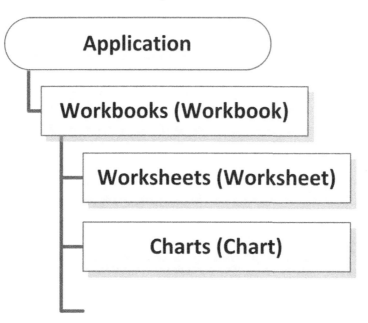

Figure 11-1: The Workbook object hierarchy.

Opening a Workbook

To open an existing workbook, call the **Open** method of the **Workbooks** collection. The following code opens the SalesReport.xlsx workbook:

```
Application.Workbooks.Open "C:\Data\SalesReport.xlsx"
```

Adding a New Workbook

To create a new workbook and add it to the Workbooks collection, call the **Add** method of the **Workbooks** collection. The code below creates and adds a new workbook to the running instance of Excel:

```
Workbooks.Add
```

Referencing a Workbook

When you create a new workbook or open an existing one in code, it becomes the active workbook by default. Hence, you can refer to the workbook with the **ActiveWorkbook** property of the Application object. You can also assign the workbook to an object variable using a **Set** statement, as shown in the example code below:

```
Dim wkbAnalysis As Workbook
Set wkbAnalysis = Workbooks.Add
```

After setting the object variable, you can refer to that workbook using the variable, regardless of the currently active workbook in Excel.

You can also use the **ThisWorkbook** property to return a Workbook object for the current workbook.

The following code example references a new workbook and an existing workbook before using the object variables:

```
Sub WorkbookObjects()
    Dim wb1 As Workbook
    Dim wb2 As Workbook
    
    'Create a new workbook
    Set wb1 = Workbooks.Add
```

```
        'Reference an existing open workbook
        'Change the path here to point to a file on your PC
        Application.Workbooks.Open "C:\Data\Excel\SalesReport.xlsx"
        Set wb2 = Workbooks("SalesReport.xlsx")

        'Use object variables
        MsgBox "First workbook: " & wb1.Name & vbNewLine & _
               "Second workbook: " & wb2.Name
End Sub
```

Saving a Workbook

You can save a workbook in VBA using the **Save**, **SaveAs**, or **SaveCopyAs** methods of the **Workbook** object. After saving the workbook, you can close it using the **Close** method.

Save a workbook with the following "Save" methods:

- **Save**: Saves the specified workbook.
- **SaveAs**: Used for saving the workbook as a different file.
- **SaveCopyAs**: Used for saving the workbook as a different file without modifying the open workbook.

The following example code saves all workbooks that are currently open:

```
Sub SaveFiles()
    Dim wkb As Workbook

    For Each wkb In Application.Workbooks
        wkb.Save
    Next wkb
End Sub
```

To save a workbook as a different file, use the **SaveAs** method of the Workbook object. The following example creates a new workbook and then automatically displays a **SaveAs** dialog box to get the file name from the user:

```
Sub FileSaveAs()
```

```
    Dim wkb As Workbook
    Dim FName As Variant

    Set wkb = Workbooks.Add

    ' Get file name from user
    Do
        FName = Application.GetSaveAsFilename
    Loop Until FName <> False
    wkb.SaveAs FileName:=FName
End Sub
```

The **Path** property of a workbook returns its location directory path. The following code uses the **Path** property of the active workbook to save it with a different name in the same folder:

```
ActiveWorkbook.SaveAs ActiveWorkbook.Path & "\" & "SalesReport2.xlsx"
```

Closing a Workbook

After working with a workbook, you can use the **Close** method of the Workbook object to remove it from the application workspace. You can save the workbook as you close it with the Close method or cancel any changes you have made.

The following code example saves the active workbook as SalesReport2 before closing it:

```
Sub SaveAndClose()
    'Save and close the active workbook
    Dim FName As String
    FName = ActiveWorkbook.Path & _
            Application.PathSeparator & "SalesReport2.xlsx"
    ActiveWorkbook.Close SaveChanges:=True, FileName:=FName
End Sub
```

You can use the **PathSeparator** property of the **Application** object as another way to insert a backslash "\" in a Windows file path (or a forward slash "/" in a MacOS file path). Some shared network drives also use a forward slash as a path separator. Using **Application.PathSeparator** ensures the correct path separator is used regardless of the platform in which your workbook is saved.

Workbook Events

Workbooks have a predefined set of events in VBA that are triggered automatically in response to an action. You can use these events to perform specific actions based on user or system actions. For example, you can write code that runs when the workbook is opened, printed, or closed.

Workbook event procedures must be stored in the workbook where the events will occur. Hence, the workbook must be a macro-enabled file (xlsm, xlsb, or xltm), as VBA code cannot be saved in a standard Excel workbook.

The following table lists some of the useful workbook events:

Event	Occurs
Open	Triggered when the workbook is opened.
Activate	This event is triggered when the workbook is activated.
Deactivate	Occurs when the workbook is deactivated.
BeforeClose	This event occurs before the workbook closes. If changes were made to the workbook, you can insert code here that executes before the user is asked to save changes.
BeforePrint	This event is triggered before the workbook is printed.
BeforeSave	Triggered before the workbook is saved.
NewSheet	Occurs when a new sheet is added to the workbook.

For a full list of workbook events, search for "Workbook object" in VBA Help.

> **Note** Excel often disables macros in a workbook that is from an external source. Remember this when creating event procedures that are executed automatically when the workbook opens. In cases where Excel initially disables macros, any macros set to run when the workbook opens will not run until the workbook is Trusted on the computer.

Adding Code to Workbook Events

Follow the general steps below to add code to a workbook event:

1. Create a new Excel Macro-Enabled Workbook (xlsm file) or open an existing one.
2. In Excel, switch to the Visual Basic Editor by pressing Alt+F11.
3. In the Project Explorer window, expand the VBAProject for the workbook to which you want to add code.
4. Under **Microsoft Excel Objects**, double-click **ThisWorkbook** to open the Code window for your workbook.
5. In the Code window, select **Workbook** in the **Object** box (if it's not already selected).
6. In the **Procedure** box, select the event you want from the dropdown list.

   The Visual Basic Editor enters the starting and ending statements for the procedure.
7. Insert your code between the starting and ending statements of the event procedure in the Code window.
8. To insert a different event procedure for the workbook while in the Code window, repeat steps 5 to 7 above.

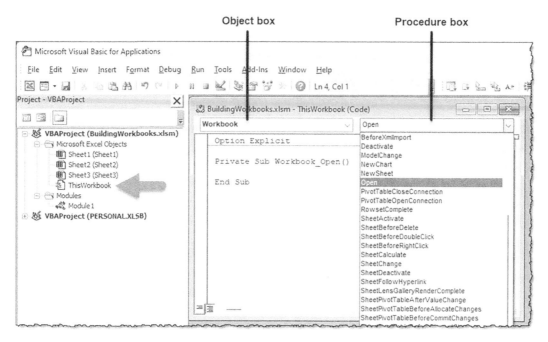

Figure 11-2: Selecting an event procedure for a workbook in the Code window.

Workbook event procedures are named in the following format: *Workbook_Event*. For example, the **Open** event procedure is named **Workbook_Open**, and the **Activate** event procedure is named **Workbook_Activate**.

Order of Workbook Events

When creating event procedures related to opening or closing a workbook, it's important to know the order in which the event procedures are triggered. Knowing the order of events enables you to determine the appropriate event procedure to place code for a particular action. Placing code in the wrong event procedure may produce unexpected results.

When a workbook is opened, events are triggered in the following order:

- Open
- Activate

- WindowActivate

When a workbook is closed, events are triggered in the following order:
- BeforeClose
- WindowDeactivate
- Deactivate

When a workbook is closed with unsaved changes, events are triggered in the following order:
- BeforeClose
- BeforeSave
- AfterSave
- WindowDeactivate
- Deactivate

Open Event

One of the most commonly used workbook events is the **Open** event, triggered whenever the workbook is opened. This event is useful for performing initializing actions to prepare a workbook.

The example code below was entered in the Code window of the **ThisWorkbook** object. When the user opens the workbook, the routine checks whether it is a Monday. If it is Monday, the procedure reminds the user to submit their timesheet.

```
Private Sub Workbook_Open()
    Dim MsgText As String
    If WorksheetFunction.Weekday(Now(), 2) = 1 Then
        MsgText = "Today is Monday! "
        MsgText = MsgText & "Don't forget to submit your "
        MsgText = MsgText & "timesheet for last week."
        MsgBox MsgText, vbInformation
    End If
End Sub
```

The code above, contained in the **ThisWorkbook** object, is executed each time the user opens the workbook, but they'll only get the message (shown below) on Mondays.

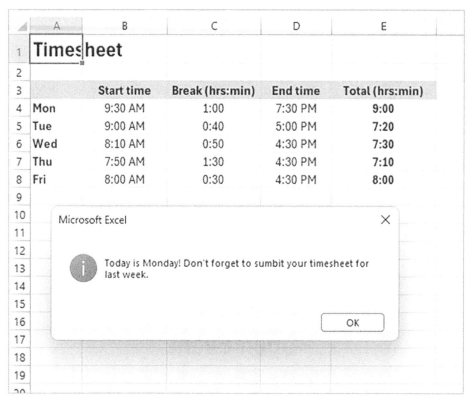

Figure 11-3: The Open event of the workbook displays a message box to the user.

The Workbook_Open event procedure can be used for many actions, including the following:

- Displaying a welcome message to the user.
- Displaying a UserForm if it is required for data entry.
- Activating a specific worksheet in the workbook.
- Opening other workbooks required for the task at hand.
- Setting window options like maximizing the window.

Activate and Deactivate Events

The **Activate** event occurs when a workbook becomes the active window. You can use this event to apply predefined settings to the selected workbook. Conversely, the **Deactivate** event occurs when the workbook is no longer selected. You can use this event to return to a previous view after a workbook loses the focus.

> **Note** The **Activate** event is not triggered when you create a new window for the same workbook or switch between windows showing the same workbook. Switching between windows showing the same workbook triggers the **WindowActivate** event rather than the Activate event.

The example code below, placed in the **Workbook_Activate** procedure, hides the Excel ribbon whenever the workbook is activated:

```
Private Sub Workbook_Activate()
    ' Hide the ribbon
    If Application.CommandBars("Ribbon").Height >= 150 Then
        Application.CommandBars.ExecuteMso "MinimizeRibbon"
    End If
End Sub
```

The "MinimizeRibbon" argument of the **ExecuteMso** method can be used to toggle the ribbon on or off. The above routine checks the height of the ribbon to determine whether it is currently visible. If the ribbon is visible, it is then hidden.

It is always important to reverse any temporary changes you made to the view when you exit the workbook. The following code in the **Workbook_Deactivate** event procedure restores the ribbon when the workbook is deactivated.

```
Private Sub Workbook_Deactivate()
    ' Show ribbon if it's currently hidden
    If Application.CommandBars("Ribbon").Height < 100 Then
        Application.CommandBars.ExecuteMso "MinimizeRibbon"
    End If
End Sub
```

BeforeClose Event

The **BeforeClose** event occurs when the workbook is closed. You can use this event to catch unintended close actions and allow the user to cancel the close process.

The following example prompts the user to confirm that they want to close the workbook. If the user selects **OK**, the workbook is saved and closed. If they select **Cancel**, the close process is canceled.

```
Private Sub Workbook_BeforeClose(Cancel As Boolean)
    Dim Response As Variant
    Response = MsgBox("Save and close this workbook?", _
                    vbOKCancel + vbQuestion, "Close?")
    If Response = 1 Then
       If Me.Saved = False Then Me.Save 'Save this workbook
    Else
        Cancel = True 'Cancel the close process
    End If
End Sub
```

BeforePrint Event

The **BeforePrint** event is triggered before a user prints the workbook or any object inside it. You can add code to this event procedure to save the workbook before printing, as shown in the example below:

```
Private Sub Workbook_BeforePrint(Cancel As Boolean)
    ActiveWorkbook.Save
End Sub
```

NewSheet Event

The **NewSheet** event is triggered when a new worksheet is created in the associated workbook. The following example moves any new worksheet added to the workbook before the first sheet. It then renames the worksheet with an incremental number based on the number of sheets in the workbook.

```
Private Sub Workbook_NewSheet(ByVal Sh As Object)
    Sh.Move Before:=Sheets(1)
    Sh.Name = "Report " & Sheets.Count + 1
End Sub
```

In the code above, the parameter **Sh** is a Worksheet object representing the newly created sheet.

Chapter 12

Working with Worksheets

In this chapter:

- Creating new worksheets in code.
- Referencing existing worksheets.
- Using worksheet properties and methods.
- Working with worksheet events.

This chapter covers creating and manipulating worksheets using the Worksheets collection, Worksheet object, and worksheet events. You will programmatically create and delete worksheets within a workbook. You will deploy worksheet event procedures triggered by user actions to perform actions in Excel.

The **Worksheets** collection is different from the **Sheets** collection. The Sheets collection contains all sheets in the workbook, which can include chart sheets and worksheets. Conversely, the Worksheets collection only contains the worksheets in the workbook.

Chapter 12: Working with Worksheets

The Worksheet Object

Worksheets are the main objects in a workbook used to create and manipulate data. A worksheet consists of cells that are organized into rows and columns. The image below illustrates some of the main objects in the Worksheet object hierarchy.

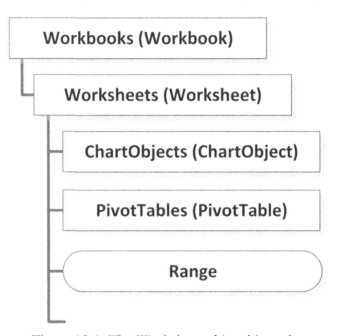

Figure 12-1: The Worksheet object hierarchy.

Adding a New Worksheet

> **Note**: When creating a new workbook in VBA, the number of sheets created in the workbook is determined by the setting in **Excel Options** specifying the default number of sheets in a new workbook. The current default for Excel is one worksheet named *Sheet1*.
>
> To change the default number of worksheets in a workbook, do the following:
> 1. On the ribbon, select **File** > **Options** > **General**.
> 2. Under the **When creating new workbooks** section, change the value in the **Include this many sheets** box to the number of default worksheets you want in a new workbook.

To programmatically add a new worksheet to a workbook, use the **Add** method of the **Worksheets** collection.

Syntax:

expression.Add (*Before, After, Count, Type*)

The **Add** method adds the new worksheet before the active worksheet unless you specify a value for the *Before* or *After* parameters.

The example below is a Sub procedure in a module. The statement adds two new sheets after *Sheet1* in the active workbook.

```
Sub AddWorksheets()
    ActiveWorkbook.Worksheets.Add After:=Worksheets("Sheet1"), Count:=2
End Sub
```

To return the number of worksheets in a workbook, use the **Count** property of the Worksheets collection. This property enables you to perform actions where you need to know the number of sheets in the workbook. For example, the code below adds a new sheet after the last sheet in the workbook:

```
ActiveWorkbook.Worksheets.Add After:=Worksheets(Worksheets.Count)
```

Chapter 12: Working with Worksheets

By default, the last worksheet you add to the workbook becomes the active worksheet. So, you can use the **ActiveSheet** property to refer to the new worksheet.

Naming a Worksheet

After adding the worksheet to the workbook, you can use the **Name** property of the **Worksheet** object to change its name. The code below renames all the sheets in the active workbook based on the current date and the sheet's index number in the **Worksheets** collection.

```
Sub RenameWks()
    Dim Ctr As Long
    
    ' Loop through sheets in the book and rename them
    For Ctr = 1 To Worksheets.Count
        Worksheets(Ctr).Name = Format(Now + Ctr, "mmm dd, yyyy")
    Next Ctr
End Sub
```

The image below shows the result of using the **Name** property to programmatically rename all worksheets in the active workbook:

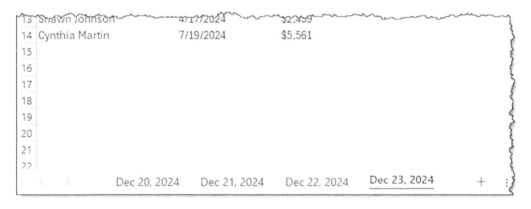

Figure 12-2: Worksheets renamed programmatically using the Name property.

231

Activating a Worksheet

To select a specific worksheet and work with its data, use the **Activate** method of the Worksheet object.

The code below loops through the worksheets in the active workbook to find and select the *Orders* worksheet. If the worksheet is not found, the procedure informs the user with a message box.

```
Sub FindWorksheet()
    Dim wks As Worksheet
    
    'Find the Orders sheet and activate it
    For Each wks In Worksheets
        If wks.Name = "Orders" Then
            wks.Activate
            
            'Exit the Sub after the sheet is activated
            Exit Sub
        End If
    Next
    'Inform user if sheet is not found
    MsgBox "The Orders sheet was not found!", vbExclamation
End Sub
```

After adding a worksheet to a workbook, you can change its position using the **Move** method of the **Worksheets** collection.

Syntax:

expression.Move(*Before*, *After*)

The example below moves the worksheet named *Orders* to a position before the first worksheet in the workbook:

```
ActiveWorkbook.Worksheets("Orders").Move Before:=Worksheets(1)
```

Deleting a Worksheet

You can delete worksheets from a workbook using the **Delete** method of the **Worksheets** collection. Each workbook must have at least one worksheet by default, so you can't delete all the worksheets in a workbook.

The code below finds and deletes all but the last worksheet in the active workbook where the name starts with the string "*Temp*."

```
Sub DeleteWs()
    Dim wks As Worksheet
    
    'Find and delete all worksheets starting with "Temp"
    For Each wks In ActiveWorkbook.Worksheets
        If ActiveWorkbook.Worksheets.Count > 1 Then
            If wks.Name Like "Temp*" Then
                wks.Delete
            End If
        End If
    Next wks
End Sub
```

When you delete a worksheet, Excel displays a message prompting you to confirm the delete action. You may want to turn off these notifications when you delete worksheets programmatically. To turn off these notifications, set the **DisplayAlerts** property of the **Application** object to **False**.

Worksheet Events

Like workbooks, worksheets have a predefined set of events executed automatically in response to an action. You can insert code in these events to run when the event happens. For example, you can write code that runs when a worksheet is activated.

Each worksheet in a workbook has an object listed in the **Microsoft Excel Objects** folder in the Project Explorer window (as shown in the image below).

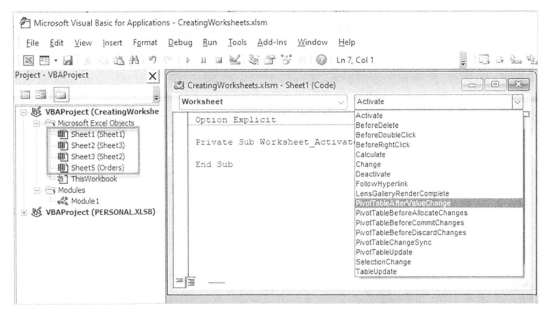

Figure 12-3: Each worksheet is represented by an object in the Project Explorer window. You can write code for worksheet events.

Tip: You can quickly open the Code window for a worksheet by right-clicking the sheet's name tab in Excel and selecting **View Code**.

Some of the examples below use the **Range** object, which is discussed in Chapter 13.

Activate and Deactivate Events

Excel runs the **Activate** event when a sheet gets the focus and the **Deactivate** event when it loses the focus. The example code below activates cell A1 in the sheet that has been activated:

```
Private Sub Worksheet_Activate()
    Range("A1").Activate
End Sub
```

You can use the **Deactivate** event to perform actions when the worksheet loses the focus. The code below prompts the user to decide whether to run the spelling checker:

```
Private Sub Worksheet_Deactivate()
    Dim Response As Long

    Response = MsgBox("Run spelling checker?", vbYesNo)
    If Response = vbYes Then
        ActiveSheet.CheckSpelling
    End If
End Sub
```

Calculate Event

The **Calculate** event is triggered whenever the worksheet is recalculated. Excel automatically recalculates a worksheet when a formula is added or when cells with dependent formulas are changed. A user can also calculate a worksheet manually by selecting **Formulas** > **Calculation** > **Calculate Sheet** on Excel's ribbon.

The following code adjusts the widths of columns A to H to fit the value whenever the sheet is recalculated:

```
Private Sub Worksheet_Calculate()
   Columns("A:H").AutoFit
End Sub
```

Change Event

The **Change** event is triggered when any cell in the worksheet is changed. In the example below, the **Worksheet_Change** event procedure changes the background color of a cell in column B based on the number the user enters in an adjacent cell in column A:

```
Private Sub Worksheet_Change(ByVal Target As Range)
    Dim ThisRow As Variant
```

```
    'Apply a different color for each number range
    If Not IsArray(Target) And Target.Column = 1 Then
        If IsNumeric(Target) Then
            ThisRow = Target.Row
            Select Case Target.Value
            Case 1 To 9
                Range("B" & ThisRow).Interior.Color = vbRed
            Case 10 To 20
                Range("B" & ThisRow).Interior.Color = vbBlue
            Case Is > 20
                 Range("B" & ThisRow).Interior.Color = vbGreen
            Case Else
                Range("B" & ThisRow).Interior.ColorIndex = xlColorIndexNone
            End Select
        End If
    End If
End Sub
```

In the code above, the **Target** argument in the **Worksheet_Change** procedure represents the changed cell. When a cell is changed in the first column (A), the routine checks whether the user entered a number. If the value is a number, the routine applies a background color (based on the range of the number) to the adjacent cell in column B.

You can perform the same task manually using the **Conditional Formatting** command on the **Home** tab. However, if you have a more complex set of actions to apply to multiple sheets, using code in a Sub procedure in a module would be more efficient. You can then call the Sub procedure from the **Worksheet_Change** event procedure of the sheets where it is required.

Practice: Working With Worksheets

In this practice, you'll programmatically create a new workbook containing a worksheet for each month of the year. The number of worksheets automatically created in a new workbook can vary depending on the setting in **Excel Options**. The procedure should count how many worksheets were automatically added to the new workbook. Then, the procedure should add or delete worksheets to ensure there are 12 worksheets in the workbook. After adding the worksheets, you'll rename them for each month of the year.

> **Note** The solution for this practice can be found in Module2 of the workbook, **Ch12_WorkingWithWorksheets.xlsm**.

▶ **Defining the CreateMonthsWorkbook procedure.**

1. Start Excel.

2. Create a new Macro-Enabled Workbook (xlsm file) or use an existing workbook you used for a previous example.

3. Open the Visual Basic Editor and insert a new standard module.

4. In the module, enter a new Sub procedure called **CreateMonthsWorkbook**.

▶ **Creating the new workbook in code.**

1. Declare three local variables:

    ```
    Dim NumSheets As Long
    Dim Ctr As Long
    Dim FName As String
    ```

    The NumSheets variable will contain the number of worksheets in the new workbook. The Ctr variable is the counter used to loop through the worksheets in the workbook. The FName variable will contain the file save path.

2. Use the **Add** method of the Workbooks collection to create a new workbook:

    ```
    Workbooks.Add
    ```

3. Use the **Count** property of the Worksheets collection to get the number of worksheets in the workbook. Then, assign the number to the NumSheets variable:

```
NumSheets = Worksheets.Count
```

4. Use an If statement to determine if the value in NumSheets is less than 12. If it is less than 12, add enough new worksheets to the workbook to increase the count to 12. If NumSheets is greater than 12, delete the extra worksheets:

```
If NumSheets < 12 Then
      Worksheets.Add Count:=12 - NumSheets
    Else
      For Ctr = 1 To NumSheets - 12
          Worksheets(Ctr).Delete
      Next Ctr
End If
```

5. The **MonthName** function returns the month's name based on a number (between 1 and 12) passed as its argument. Use this function with a For…Next loop to name each worksheet in the workbook with the name of the month based on the loop's counter:

```
For Ctr = 1 To 12
      Worksheets(Ctr).Name = MonthName(Ctr)
Next Ctr
```

> **Note** You can set **Application.DisplayAlerts** to False if you want to disable the notifications displayed by Excel before worksheets are deleted.

6. Save the new workbook with the name *Months Report* to the same folder as the workbook containing the procedure:

```
FName = ThisWorkbook.Path & _
      Application.PathSeparator & "Months Report"
ActiveWorkbook.SaveAs FName
```

▶ **Testing the procedure.**

- In the Visual Basic Editor, use the **Run Sub** button to run the procedure (or press F5). Excel should create a new workbook containing 12 worksheets, each sheet representing a month in the year.

Chapter 13

Working with Range Objects

In this chapter:
- Referencing Range objects.
- Accessing and changing Range object properties.
- Performing actions with Range object methods.
- Understanding selection versus direct referencing.
- Understanding A1 versus R1C1 references.
- Using the A1 referencing style.
- Using the R1C1 referencing style.
- Working with named ranges.

Chapter 13: Working with Range Objects

The **Range** object is one of the most frequently used objects when accessing and manipulating data in worksheets. A Range object can be a cell, a row, a column, a group of cells, or multiple selections in a worksheet. The Range object has properties and methods that enable you to change properties and values in worksheet cells.

This chapter shows you different ways of referencing ranges, such as specifying a row or several rows. You'll learn how to access and change values in ranges, resize a range, and select a range based on others. You'll understand the difference between the A1 and R1C1 reference styles and which scenarios best suit each style.

Returning a Range Object

You can use the properties of the **Range** object to manipulate cell ranges in the worksheet. In this section, we will cover how to return a **Range** object for known cell ranges or cell ranges relative to other cells in the worksheet. After returning a Range object, you can use it to programmatically manipulate values, formulas, or formatting in a worksheet.

Referencing a Range at Design Time

Referencing a range through the Excel object hierarchy is straightforward if you know the cell(s) at design time. See Chapter 11 for how to navigate the object hierarchy. For example, the statement below references cell A1 in the active worksheet and passes the value to a variable named *Num*:

```
Num = Range("A1").Value
```

You can return a Range object using several properties of the Worksheet object, like **Cells**, **Rows**, **Columns**, and **Range**. Each of these properties returns a Range object representing the specified cell(s). Other properties such as **Selection**, **Offset**, **Resize**, and **CurrentRegion** also return a Range object.

Cells Property

The **Cells** property returns a Range object representing all the cells on a worksheet. You can return a reference to a specific cell by using the **rowIndex** and **columnIndex** parameters.

Syntax:

expression.Cells(*rowIndex, columnIndex*)

expression is a variable representing a **Worksheet** object. If you omit the object, Cells returns a Range object representing cells on the active worksheet.

The example below returns a Range object that points to cell E12 on the active worksheet:

```
Cells(12, 5)
```

The **Cells** property is especially useful for looping through several cells using counter variables. The following example creates a multiplication table in the active worksheet by using counters and the Cells property:

```
Sub MultiplicationTable()
    Dim MyRow As Long
    Dim MyCol As Long
    
    For MyRow = 1 To 10
        For MyCol = 1 To 10
            Cells(MyRow, MyCol).Value = (MyRow * MyCol)
        Next MyCol
    Next MyRow
End Sub
```

Rows and Columns Properties

You can also use the **Rows** and **Columns** properties of the Worksheet object to return a range. The Rows property returns a collection of all rows in the worksheet or range. Likewise, the Columns property returns all the columns on the specified worksheet. You can return a reference to specific rows or columns with the index parameter.

In the code below, *FirstRow* is set to the first row in the active worksheet. *SubTotal* is set to the fifth column in the active worksheet.

```
Dim FirstRow As Range
Dim SubTotal As Range

Set FirstRow = Rows(1)
Set SubTotal = Columns(5)
```

Range Property

The **Range** property returns a **Range** object for the specified cell or range of cells. You can use this property to return a Range object for a contiguous or non-contiguous cell range.

Syntax:

expression.Range (Cell1, Cell2)

The object qualifier *expression* is a variable representing a **Worksheet** object.

Cell1 is required, while *Cell2* is optional. The Range property accepts a reference entered as a string or a Range object. When used without an object qualifier, this property returns a Range object from the active sheet (the property fails if the active sheet isn't a worksheet, for example, a chart).

The following examples are all valid ways to use the Range property:

```
Set MyRange = Range("1:4")          'Returns rows 1 to 4.
Range("A:D").Select                 'Selects columns A to D
Range("Sales").Select               'Selects a named range
Range("SalesTable").Select          'Selects a table
Range("A1:A12").Select              'Selects the range A1:A12
Range("A1, A12").Select             'Selects cells A1 and A12.
Range("A1:C10, E1:G10").Select      'Selects non-adjacent ranges
Range(Range("A1"), Range("A12")).Select 'Selects the range A1:A12.
```

Resizing and Repositioning a Range

Previously, we covered returning a Range object for a range of cells known at design time. However, in some situations, you may need to return a range where the cells are unknown at design time. For example, the data you retrieve from a data source could have a different number of rows or columns each time. Also, if your application is interactive and requires user input, the range of cells to reference at runtime could vary. Hence, you may need to dynamically adjust cell references if your code changes certain ranges at runtime, like inserting formulas or applying formatting. Cell references like these are relative to a range offset from another range reference. You can use properties like **CurrentRegion**, **Offset**, **Resize**, and **Selection** to resize and offset ranges.

Selection Property

The **Selection** property of the **Application** object returns the currently selected object in the active worksheet. You can use the **Select** method to select an object and then use the **TypeName** function to return the object type. The Selection property returns **Nothing** if no object is selected.

The following code entered into the **Immediate** window selects range A1:E5 in the active worksheet and then counts the number of columns in the selection to return 5:

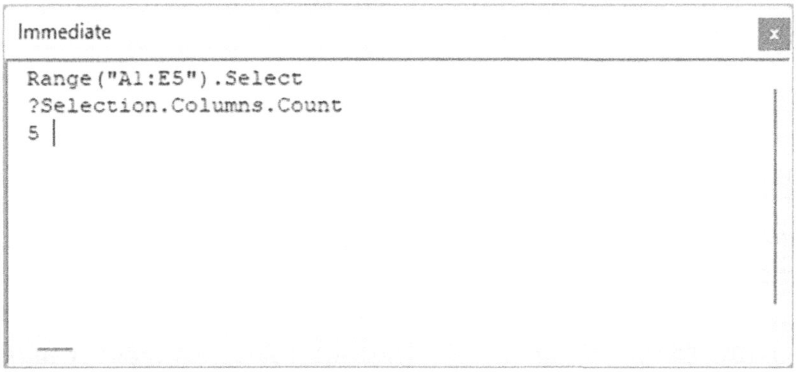

```
Range("A1:E5").Select
?Selection.Columns.Count
5
```

Figure 13-1: Using the Selection property in the Immediate window.

CurrentRegion Property

The **CurrentRegion** property of the **Range** object returns a range representing a region of data on the worksheet bordered by blank rows and columns. The CurrentRegion property is useful for working with ranges that will change over time.

For example, if you're working with data imported from an external source, the number of rows (or records) returned may differ each time the data is updated. The CurrentRegion property allows you to define a range representing the data list regardless of the number of rows or columns in the data.

If you have data on a worksheet starting from cell B3 at the top left, you can reference the whole region containing data with the following code:

```
Dim Orders As Range

Set Orders = Range("B3").CurrentRegion
```

The CurrentRegion property allows you to return the whole region of data as a Range object by applying the property to any cell in the region. The code below produces the same results as the previous example even though CurrentRegion is applied to cell D8 instead of B3:

```
Set Orders = Range("D8").CurrentRegion
```

The following illustration shows the region referenced when either of the preceding statements is executed against this worksheet. The range returned is B3:E19.

	A	B	C	D	E
1				CurrentRegion	
2					
3		**Orders**			
4		Name	Unit Price	Quantity	Total
5		Collection Belvoir Console Table	$519.00	2	$1,038
6		Harley Fabric Cuddle Chair	$700.00	3	$2,100
7		House Kent Oak Console Table	$609.00	1	$609
8		Collection New Bradley Manual Recliner Chair	$1,179.00	4	$4,716
9		Collection Bradley Riser Recline Fabric Chair	$1,059.00	6	$6,354
10		Lumina Console Table	$898.00	7	$6,286
11		Collection Belvoir Console Table	$1,091.00	3	$3,273
12		Fabric Chair In A Box	$1,149.00	4	$4,596
13		Fabric Chair In A Box - Denim Blue	$300.00	2	$600
14		Fabric Tub Chair	$247.00	3	$741
15		Fabric Wingback Chair	$289.00	6	$1,734
16		Floral Fabric Tub Chair	$686.00	4	$2,744
17		Habitat Oken Console Table	$586.00	1	$586
18		Collection Belvoir Console Table	$1,149.00	2	$2,298
19		Total			$37,675
20					

Figure 13-2: Using the CurrentRegion property to select a group of cells and return a Range object.

The example code below names the range returned by the CurrentRegion property:

```
Range("B3").CurrentRegion.Name = "OrdersReport"
```

Offset Property

The **Offset** property returns a **Range** object offset from the specified range by a specified number of rows or columns. When you call this property, you can specify the offsetting rows and columns in its arguments. The Offset property returns a Range object that has the same size as a specified range but is offset by one or more rows and/or columns. The following is the syntax for the Offset property:

Syntax:

expression.Offset (*RowOffset*, *ColumnOffset*)

The object qualifier *expression* represents a **Range** object.

The following example uses the Offset property to return a range that is offset by three rows and five columns from the original range A1:C10:

```
Range("A1:C10").Offset(3, 5).Select
```

The code above returns a range F4:H13, as shown in the following illustration.

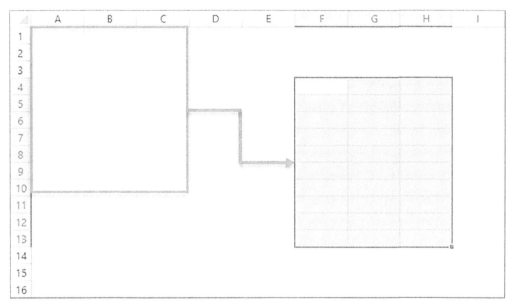

Figure 13-2: Using the Offset property to select a range relative to another range.

Resize Property

The **Resize** property resizes the specified range based on the dimensions provided in the RowSize and ColumnSize arguments. This property returns a **Range** object.

Syntax:

expression.Resize(*RowSize, ColumnSize*)

The object qualifier *expression* represents a **Range** object variable.

The following example resizes the range A1:D10 to the range A1:B5:

```
Range("A1:D10").Resize(5, 2).Select
```

The image below illustrates the resize operation performed in the example above:

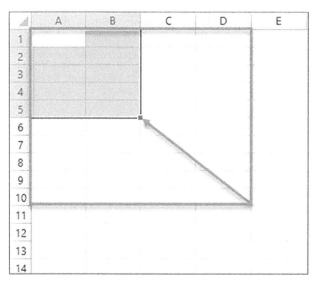

Figure 13-3: Using the Resize property to resize a range.

You can combine the **Offset** and **Resize** properties to change the position and size of a range. The example below sets a Range object variable to the first blank column to the right of a region in the *Orders* worksheet:

```
Sub RefFirstBlankColumn()
    'Reference the 1st blank column to the right of the current region
    Dim DataRange As Range
    Dim RowsCount As Long, ColumnsCount As Long
    
    Worksheets("Orders").Activate
    Set DataRange = Worksheets("Orders").Range("A1").CurrentRegion
    RowsCount = DataRange.Rows.Count
    ColumnsCount = DataRange.Columns.Count
    
    'Identify first blank column after the CurrentRegion
    Set DataRange = _
```

```
        DataRange.Offset(0, ColumnsCount).Resize(RowsCount, 1)
    DataRange.Select
End Sub
```

The illustration below shows the selected range after the offset and resize operations.

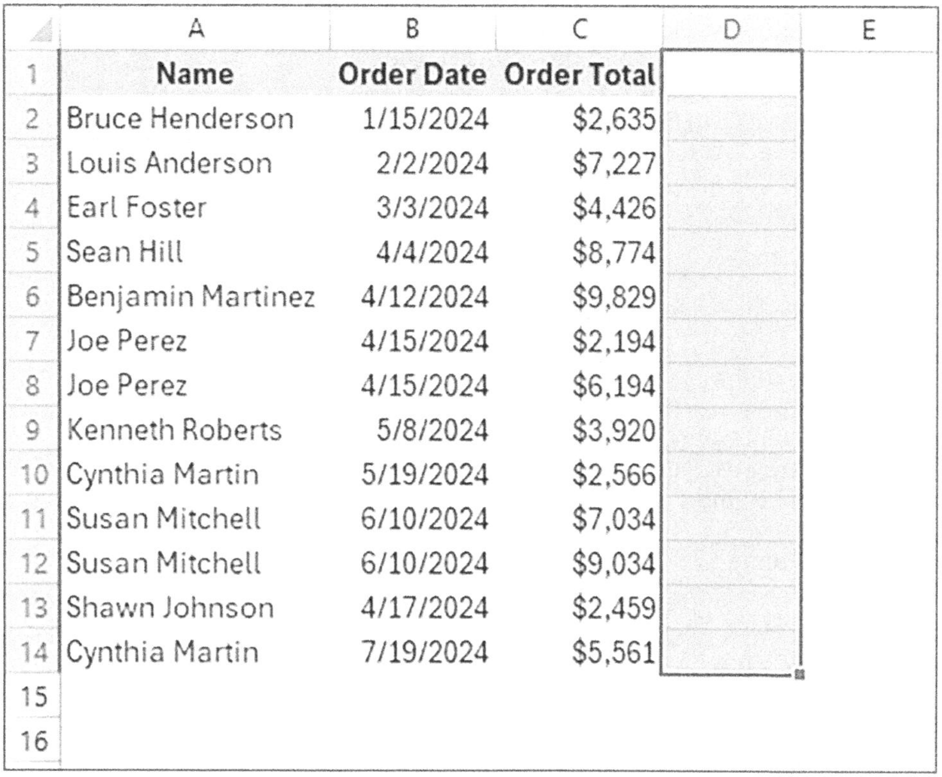

	A	B	C	D	E
1	Name	Order Date	Order Total		
2	Bruce Henderson	1/15/2024	$2,635		
3	Louis Anderson	2/2/2024	$7,227		
4	Earl Foster	3/3/2024	$4,426		
5	Sean Hill	4/4/2024	$8,774		
6	Benjamin Martinez	4/12/2024	$9,829		
7	Joe Perez	4/15/2024	$2,194		
8	Joe Perez	4/15/2024	$6,194		
9	Kenneth Roberts	5/8/2024	$3,920		
10	Cynthia Martin	5/19/2024	$2,566		
11	Susan Mitchell	6/10/2024	$7,034		
12	Susan Mitchell	6/10/2024	$9,034		
13	Shawn Johnson	4/17/2024	$2,459		
14	Cynthia Martin	7/19/2024	$5,561		
15					
16					

Figure 13-4: Using the Offset and Resize to return a range based on another range.

Range Selection versus Direct Referencing

When working with cell ranges in Excel, there are times when you need to work with a selected range. For example, when the user selects the range before a routine is executed. However, it is often unnecessary to programmatically select the range before working with it.

The two examples below demonstrate the difference between selecting a range before using it or directly referencing the range.

The following procedure selects each cell before bolding its contents:

```
Sub UsingASelection()
    Dim CellRange As Range
    For Each CellRange In Range("A1:P100")
        CellRange.Select
        If IsNumeric(Selection.Value) Then
            Selection.Font.Bold = True
        End If
    Next CellRange
End Sub
```

The following procedure uses direct references to apply the **Bold** format:

```
Sub UsingAReference()
    Dim CellRange As Range
    For Each CellRange In Range("A1:P100")
        If IsNumeric(CellRange.Value) Then
            CellRange.Font.Bold = True
        End If
    Next CellRange
End Sub
```

The code example above performs the same action but runs six times faster than the previous code using a selection. It is more efficient to use direct referencing when working with ranges as the code executes faster.

Tip: When recording a macro in Excel, you normally select a range of cells before performing actions on the range. Thus, the code recorded by the macro recorder often uses the **Selection** property to reference cells. Changing cell selections to direct cell referencing can make macro-recorded code more efficient.

Practice: Returning a Range Object

In this example, you'll use properties of the Range object to return a reference to a range relative to another range. If the price of a product on the list is greater than or equal to $1,000, you will apply bold formatting to the row. You will then format the *Price* column to the **Currency** format using a custom format.

> **Note** The sample data used and source code for this practice are in the **ProductList_Solution.xlsm** workbook, which is in the practice files folder for Chapter 13.

▶ **Create a new workbook.**

1. Create a new macro-enabled workbook. You can name it **ProductList.xlsm**.
2. Copy the **Products** sheet from **ProductList_Solution.xlsm** to your new workbook.
3. Review the data in the **Products** worksheet (shown in the following image).

	A	B	C	D
1	ProductID	Product Name	In Stock	Price
2	1	Collection Belvoir Console Table	9	413.00
3	2	Collection Bradley Riser Recline Fabric Chair	6	519.00
4	3	Collection Martha Fabric Wingback Chair	5	1,200.00
5	4	Collection New Bradley Manual Recliner Chair	7	609.00
6	5	Collection New Malvern Console Table	10	499.00
7	6	Cora Fabric Chair	10	1,054.00
8	7	Fabric Chair	5	348.00
9	8	Fabric Chair In A Box	4	1,423.00
10	9	Fabric Chair In A Box - Denim Blue	4	264.00
11	10	Fabric Tub Chair	5	300.00
12	11	Fabric Wingback Chair	9	247.00
13	12	Floral Fabric Tub Chair	9	289.00
14	13	Habitat Oken Console Table	10	686.00
15	14	Harley Fabric Cuddle Chair	10	586.00
16	15	House Kent Oak Console Table	10	1,179.00
17	16	Hygena Fabric Chair	5	898.00
18	17	Hygena Fabric Chair In A Box	4	1,091.00
19	18	Hygena Lumina Console Table	10	1,149.00
20				

Figure 13-5: Product list requiring formatting.

▶ Create the FormatData Procedure

1. Open the Visual Basic Editor.

2. Insert a new module in the VBA project for your workbook, **ProductList.xlsm**.

3. In the module, enter a Sub procedure called **FormatData**.

4. In the FormatData procedure, declare two local variables named ListData and ListRow as Range objects, as shown below:

```
Dim ListData As Range
Dim ListRow As Range
```

Suppose that the list of products is periodically downloaded from a data source, and it can have a different number of records. You want the ListData variable to

Chapter 13: Working with Range Objects

always reference all the records in the Products worksheet regardless of the number of rows. The ListRow variable will be used in a **For...Each** loop that iterates through the records in the referenced range in ListData to apply the formatting.

5. Set the value of ListData as equal to the current region of cell A2:

```
Set ListData = ThisWorkbook.Worksheets("Products") _
               .Range("A2").CurrentRegion
```

6. Write a **For...Each** loop that runs once for each row in the ListData range, using its **Rows** property.

```
For Each ListRow In ListData.Rows

Next ListRow
```

7. Inside the loop, write an **If** statement that checks the price of the product. If the price is 1000 or more, apply the bold format to the whole row. Use the **Cells** property of the ListRow Range object to return the value in the fourth column of the row.

The following example shows how the **For...Each** loop should look:

```
For Each ListRow In ListData.Rows
    If ListRow.Cells(1, 4).Value >= 1000 Then
        ListRow.Font.Bold = True
    End If
Next ListRow
```

8. Use the **Offset** and **Resize** properties to move and resize the range. Then, use the **NumberFormat** property to format the fourth column to the Currency number format, as shown in the example below:

```
ListData.Offset(0, 3).Resize(ListData.Rows.Count, 3). _
NumberFormat = "[$$-en-US]#,##0.00_ ;-[$$-en-US]#,##0.00"
```

The code above offsets the range by three columns to the right and then resizes the range to one column. The last column, *Price*, becomes the first in the new range. The **NumberFormat** property of the resultant range is then set to a **Currency** number format.

The full procedure should look like this:

```
Sub FormatData()
    'Solution for Practice: Returning a Range Object

    Dim ListData As Range
    Dim ListRow As Range

    Set ListData = ThisWorkbook.Worksheets("Products") _
                .Range("A2").CurrentRegion
    For Each ListRow In ListData.Rows
        If ListRow.Cells(1, 4).Value >= 1000 Then
            ListRow.Font.Bold = True
        End If
    Next ListRow
    ListData.Offset(0, 3).Resize(ListData.Rows.Count, 3). _
    NumberFormat = "[$$-en-US]#,##0.00_ ;-[$$-en-US]#,##0.00"
End Sub
```

▶ **Test and Save Your Work**

- Run the FormatData procedure in the Visual Basic Editor.

    The rows with products priced $1,000 or more should appear bold, and the last column should be formatted as **Currency**.

Figure 13-6: The formatted product list.

Using a Range Object

After referencing a range of cells with a **Range** object, you can perform several actions on the specified worksheet using the Range object. In this section, you'll learn how to use a Range object to format cells, enter values and formulas in cells, and programmatically create local and global named ranges.

Formatting a Range

You can write code to perform any formatting action that can be performed manually. However, an easier way to write code to format a worksheet is to apply the desired formatting manually while recording your actions with the macro recorder. After the code is recorded, you can copy and paste it into your procedure and apply it to a Range object you have defined.

Most of Excel's formatting commands are in the **Format Cells** dialog box. To display the **Format Cells** dialog box, click the dialog box launcher in the **Font** group on the **Home** tab (a diagonal arrow on the bottom-right of the group).

The **Format Cells** dialog box allows you to perform various formatting actions, including specifying number formats, aligning cell content, changing fonts, and applying fill colors.

The example below uses the **NumberFormat** property of the **Range** object to apply a custom currency format to the specified range:

```
Range("D2:D20").NumberFormat = _
    "[$$-en-US]#,##0.00_ ;-[$$-en-US]#,##0.00"
```

The format codes required for the **NumberFormat** property are the same as those found on the **Format Cells** dialog box under **Number > Category > Custom > Type**. You can determine the format code you want by testing it on the worksheet before copying and pasting it into your VBA procedure.

Chapter 13: Working with Range Objects

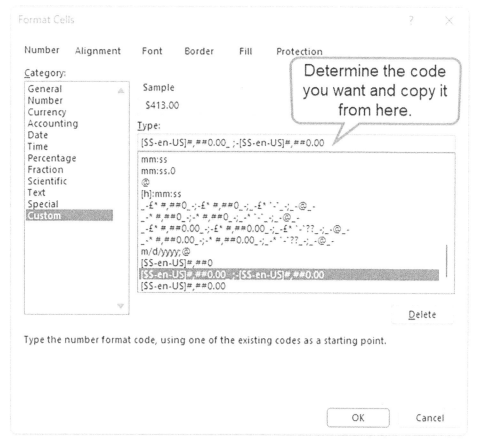

Figure 13-7: Identifying and copying a custom number format from Excel's interface to use in code.

You can also change other formatting properties of a range, like font, alignment, and fill color, as shown in the example below:

```
With Range("A1:D1")
     With .Font
           .Name = "Aptos Display"
           .FontStyle = "Bold"
           .Size = 12
           .ColorIndex = 2 'White color
     End With
     .HorizontalAlignment = xlCenter
     .Interior.ColorIndex = 47 ' Gray color
End With
```

You can use the **AutoFit** method of the Range object to adjust the width of columns or the height of rows in a range to achieve the best fit. The Range object must return one or more rows or columns. Otherwise, **AutoFit** generates an error.

The following example Autofits the columns in range A1:D20 to ensure they fit the values:

```
Range("A1:D20").Columns.AutoFit
```

An alternative way to format a range of cells is using the **Style** property of the **Range** object. The following example formats the referenced range in the accounting **Currency** style based on the regional settings of the host computer:

```
Range("A1:A10").Style = "Currency"
```

To view the various styles that you can programmatically apply to a range of cells, select **Home > Styles > Cell Styles** on the Excel ribbon.

Using a Preformatted Template File

Using a preformatted workbook template is one way to reuse formatting in a worksheet without writing code. For example, if you periodically produce a report that requires the same formatting, you can apply it to a blank worksheet and save it as an Excel workbook template. Whenever you need to create the report, create a new workbook based on the template and insert your data. A workbook template is not ideal for all situations, but it allows users to make small changes to the appearance of the workbook without requiring coding.

Overview of Formula Referencing

Before delving into programmatically entering formulas in cells, it is important to review how cells are referenced in Excel. This section compares and contrasts the A1 and R1C1 referencing styles.

A1 Reference versus R1C1 Reference

An Excel worksheet can use either the **A1** or **R1C1** reference style:

- **The A1 Reference Style**

    Excel uses the A1 reference style by default. In this reference style, the columns have letters (A-IV, for 256 columns), while the rows have numbers (1-65,536). To reference a cell, pair the column letter with the row number. For example, A10 refers to the cell at the intersection of column A and row 10.

- **The R1C1 Reference Style**

    In the R1C1 reference style, both the columns and rows use numbers. To reference a cell, an R followed by a number (1-65,536) indicates the row, while a C followed by a number (1-256) indicates the column. For example, the cell reference at the intersection of column A and row 10 is R10C1.

Note To change your workbook from the default A1 reference style to the R1C1 reference style, go to **Excel Options** > **Formulas**. Under the section **Working with formulas**, select **R1C1 reference style**. You don't necessarily need to change Excel's referencing style to R1C1. The R1C1 reference style is useful when creating formulas in code.

Absolute versus Relative Referencing

Worksheet cell referencing can be relative or absolute:

- **Relative reference**

    By default, Excel uses a relative cell reference, meaning that the location the reference points to depends on the location of the cell containing the reference. For instance, if you copy the formula **=A1+B1** from cell C1 to D2, the formula changes to **=B2+C2**. Therefore, the formula now references different cells on the worksheet.

- **Absolute reference**

    An absolute reference points to a particular location on the worksheet, regardless of the location of the cell containing the reference. If you copy an absolute reference from one cell to another, it continues pointing to the same location on the worksheet.

If you intend to use a formula in only one place, it makes no difference whether you use a relative or an absolute reference. However, the reference type becomes very important if you intend to fill or copy that formula into other cells.

You can use a combination of absolute and relative referencing in the same formula, which is known as mixed referencing.

 Note See my *Mastering Excel 365* book to learn more about cell referencing in Excel.

Using A1 Referencing Style

Suppose you have the following formula in cell E1:

=C1+D1

Referring to cell C1 from cell E1 is pointing to a cell two columns to the left (E minus C) and on the same row. Likewise, referring to cell D1 from cell E1 is pointing to a cell one column to the left (E minus D) and on the same row.

When you copy or fill the formula down to cells E2:E3, each cell reference changes to reflect its relative position:

Cell	Formula
E1	=C1+D1
E2	=C2+D2
E3	=C3+D3

To convert the previous formula to an absolute reference, insert a dollar sign ($) before the column letter and row number. For example, $C$2 is an absolute reference that points to cell C2 regardless of where it is copied & pasted in the worksheet. The dollar sign before the column and row tells Excel that the cell reference does not change when the formula is copied to other cells.

Imagine that you have the following formula in cell E1:

=$C$1+$D$1

When you copy this formula down to the range E2:E3, the formula remains the same as shown below:

Cell	Formula
E1	=$C$1+$D$1
E2	=$C$1+$D$1
E3	=$C$1+$D$1

Using the R1C1 Referencing Style

A relative cell reference in the R1C1 referencing style has the row and/or the column number in square brackets ([n]). For example, R[-2]C[-2] indicates two rows above and two columns to the left of the cell containing the reference. Likewise, R[2]C[3] indicates two rows below and three columns to the right of the cell containing the reference.

The following example shows a formula in row one and column three. The formula is =A1+B1 (in the A1 referencing style):

=RC[-2]+RC[-1]

In the formula above, the first cell reference RC[-2] points to a cell on the same row and two columns to the left of the formula's location. The second cell reference in the formula RC[-1] points to a cell on the same row and one column to the left of the formula's location.

An absolute reference using the R1C1 referencing style uses an R followed by the row number and a C followed by the column number. For example, cell C1 is specified as R1C3 as an R1C1 style absolute reference. To convert the previous formula to an absolute reference in the R1C1 reference style, remove the square brackets so that the formula looks like this:

=R1C1+R1C2

The formula above points to specific cells. The first cell reference in the formula points to the cell in row 1 and column 1. The second cell reference in the formula points to a cell in row 1 and column 2. This formula will reference the same cells no matter where the formula is placed on the worksheet.

Entering Values and Formulas

The **Range** object has several properties for entering values and formulas. This section covers several properties, including the **Value**, **Formula2**, **Formula2R1C1**, and **FormulaArray** properties.

Value Property

The **Value** property is used to set or retrieve the value in a cell, and it is the default property of the Range object. The following example calculates 10% of the value in cell A1 and inserts the result in cell B1:

```
Range("B1").Value = Range("A1").Value * 0.1
```

Formula2 Property

The **Formula2** property supersedes the **Formula** property in Excel versions that support Dynamic Arrays. Use the **Formula2** property to return or enter a formula in a cell or range of cells in the A1 referencing style. The **Formula** property is still supported in VBA for backward compatibility. However, if you're using Excel 2019 and later, you should use **Formula2** instead of the **Formula** property in your code.

Formulas entered with the **Formula2** property are always evaluated as an array, and if more than one result is returned, the results spill to adjacent cells.

The example below inserts the specified formula in cell A11:

```
Range("A11").Formula2 = "=SUM(A1:A10)"
```

Formula2R1C1 Property

With the **Formula2** property described above, you must refer to a particular range at design time. Conversely, the **Formula2R1C1** property allows you to enter a formula at design time relative to the active cell or range. This property requires the formula to be entered in the R1C1 referencing style.

The example below enters a formula in the active cell that sums the five cells directly above the active cell:

```
ActiveCell.Formula2R1C1 = "=SUM(R[-5]C:R[-1]C)"
```

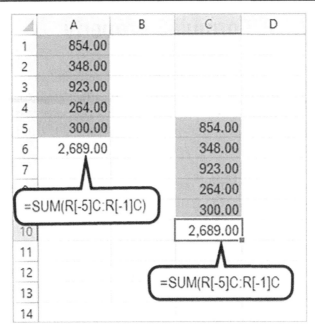

Figure 13-8: With relative references, you don't need to know specific ranges at design time.

As shown in the illustration above, if the active cell at runtime is A6, the formula entered would be: =SUM(A1:A5). If the active cell at runtime is C10, the formula entered would be: =SUM(C5:C9).

As the formula uses a relative reference, you don't need to know the specific cells referenced at design time. This method is useful if the referenced range can change at runtime.

Address Property

The **Address** property returns the address of a range. The **Address** property is useful for building a formula where the referenced cells can change at runtime. Suppose you want to programmatically insert a formula directly below a list of values the user selected at runtime, as shown in the illustration below. You can use the **Address** property to determine the selected range and then work with that reference.

The following example inserts a formula that sums the contents of the currently selected range of cells in the cell directly below the selected range.

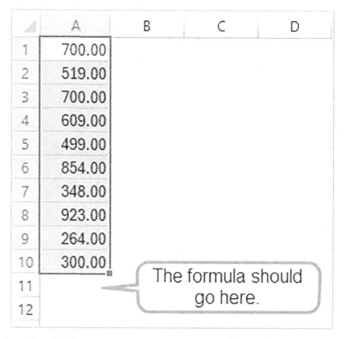

Figure 13-9: Using the Address property to create a formula to calculate a range that is not known at design time.

```
Sub RangeAddress()
    Dim DataRange As Range
    Dim TotalCell As Range
    Dim RowsCount As Long

    'Set the data range to the selection on the worksheet
    Set DataRange = Range(Selection.Address)
    RowsCount = DataRange.Rows.Count

    'Reference the first empty cell below the data range
    Set TotalCell = DataRange.Offset _
        (RowsCount, 0).Resize(1, 1)

    'Sum selection and insert in cell directly below
    TotalCell.Formula2R1C1 = "=SUM(" _
        & Selection.Address(ReferenceStyle:=xlR1C1) & ")"
End Sub
```

The formula above does not explicitly reference any range, so it would work for any selected range at runtime.

AutoFill Method

The **AutoFill** feature in Excel lets you fill cells with sequential dates and numbers. It enables you to automate repetitive tasks as it is smart enough to figure out what data goes in a cell (based on another cell) when you drag the fill handle across cells. For example, you can enter January in one cell and use the AutoFill feature to automatically enter the rest of the months.

Figure 13-10: Using the AutoFill feature in Excel.

For more on how to use AutoFill in Excel, see my Excel Basics book.

The **Range** object has an **AutoFill** method that you can use to programmatically fill a range of cells with less code to produce the same results that would be required without the method.

Syntax:

expression.AutoFill (*Destination*, *Type*)

The object qualifier *expression* represents a Range object containing the data. The *Destination* parameter is the range of cells you want to fill with values, and the *Type* parameter specifies how the target range is filled.

The *Type* parameter takes a constant, which is an **XlAutoFillType** enumerated type. The default Type is **xlFillDefault** (or 0), which causes Excel to use the most appropriate fill type. If you omit the Type, Excel uses the **xlFillDefault**.

The example below fills a range of dates (in a weekly interval) in cells A1:A2 on the active worksheet to cells A1:A10:

```
Sub AutoFillDates()
    Dim FillRange As Range
    Set FillRange = Range("A1:A10") 'range on the active worksheet
    Range("A1:A2").AutoFill Destination:=FillRange
End Sub
```

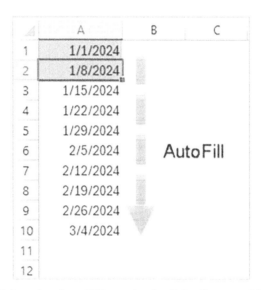

Figure 13-11: Using the AutoFill method of the Range object to fill dates.

Practice: Working with a Range Object

In this practice, you'll use several properties of the **Range** object to insert a formula that adds a total to the Sales column in the list.

> **Note** The sample data and code for this practice are contained in the **SalesByProduct_Solution.xlsm** workbook. This workbook is in the practice files folder for Chapter 13.

▶ **Create a New Workbook and Copy the Sample Data**

1. Create a new workbook named **SalesByProduct.xlsm**.

2. Copy the data from *Sheet1* in **SalesByProduct_Solution.xlsm** to your new workbook.

3. Review the sales data in your workbook, **SalesByProduct.xlsm** (shown in the image below).

Figure 13-12: Sales report to be calculated.

Chapter 13: Working with Range Objects

▶ **Create the AddFormula Procedure.**

1. Open the Visual Basic Editor.

2. Insert a new module in the VBA project for the **SalesByProduct.xlsm** workbook.

3. Inside the new module, insert a new Sub procedure called **AddFormula**.

4. In the AddFormula procedure, declare two local variables named **DataList** and **SalesTotal** as Range objects, as shown below:

   ```
   Dim DataList As Range
   Dim SalesTotal As Range
   ```

   Suppose the sales report is generated periodically and can have a different number of rows. You want the DataList range to always reference all the records in the report regardless of the number of rows. The SalesTotal range will reference the first blank cell at the bottom of the Sales column (see the image of the sales report at the start of this practice).

5. Set the value of DataList to the current region of cell A3:

   ```
   Set ListData = Worksheets("Products").Range("A3").CurrentRegion
   ```

   This statement creates a range made up of the area with values bordered by blank cells.

6. Set the value of the SalesTotal variable to the first blank cell directly below the values of the Sales column (column E).

   ```
   Set SalesTotal = _
       DataList.Offset(DataList.Rows.Count, 4).Resize(1, 1)
   ```

   The code above offsets the range down by the number of rows in the list and by four columns to the right. Then, the range is reduced to one cell, **E16**, for the sample data used in this example.

7. Use the **Formula2R1C1** property of the SalesTotal range to insert a formula that sums up the Sales column (column E), as shown below:

```
SalesTotal.Formula2R1C1 = "=SUM(R3C:R[-1]C)"
```

R3C:R[-1]C means the referenced range is from row 3 of the worksheet to one row above the SalesTotal range, on the same column as SalesTotal. This reference is equivalent to E3:E15. SUM ignores text values, so the column title is ignored.

▶ **Test and Save Your Work.**

- Run the AddFormula procedure in the Visual Basic Editor.

    The procedure should insert the formula that sums up the *Sales* column at the bottom of column E.

	A	B	C	D	E
1	**Sales Report**				
2					
3	ProductID	Product Name	Price	Qty	Sales
4	1	Collection Belvoir Console Table	$413.00	2	$826.00
5	6	Cora Fabric Chair	$1,054.00	6	$6,324.00
6	7	Fabric Chair	$348.00	1	$348.00
7	8	Fabric Chair In A Box	$1,423.00	5	$7,115.00
8	9	Fabric Chair In A Box - Denim Blue	$264.00	4	$1,056.00
9	10	Fabric Tub Chair	$300.00	3	$900.00
10	11	Fabric Wingback Chair	$247.00	5	$1,235.00
11	12	Floral Fabric Tub Chair	$289.00	1	$289.00
12	13	Habitat Oken Console Table	$686.00	2	$1,372.00
13	14	Harley Fabric Cuddle Chair	$586.00	3	$1,758.00
14	15	House Kent Oak Console Table	$1,179.00	1	$1,179.00
15	16	Hygena Fabric Chair	$898.00	5	$4,490.00
16					$26,892.00
17					

Figure 13-13: A formula sums up the Sales column using the Formula2R1C1 property.

Defining Named Ranges

In Excel, it is sometimes useful to identify a single cell or a group of cells with one name to make it easier to reference and read in formulas. A named range is one or more cells in Excel selected and given a name that can be used anywhere in the worksheet (or workbook if it is a global name). After you specify a name, the range can now be referenced using that name in Excel formulas and functions.

For example, on a worksheet, you can name a cell containing a sales total as **SalesTotal** and another cell containing the tax rate as **TaxRate**. You can then reference the cells using their names in place of the cell references in a formula, as shown in the example below:

= SalesTotal * TaxRate

Named ranges provide similar benefits when referencing ranges programmatically. A named range is an absolute reference by default. When you create a formula with a named range, you can use the formula anywhere in the worksheet, and it will always refer to the same cell or group of cells.

The Scope of Named Ranges

Named ranges can be either standard or local:

- **Standard**

    A standard name is global to the sheet and can be used inside any sheet in the workbook. For example, if the name Orders refers to the range A2:D20 in one worksheet, you can use that name in other worksheets in the workbook to refer to the range. You can only have one instance of a standard name in a workbook.

- **Local names**

    A local name is only available in the sheet where it was created. When you define the name, you can define the scope. You can define the name in a specific sheet or make it global to the whole workbook. If you intend to create copies of sheets within a workbook or give ranges similar names in different sheets, make the names local to avoid name conflicts. An example of a local named range is **Print_Area**, which Excel creates when you select the **Set Print Area** command in a worksheet. A local name is used because each worksheet will likely have a different print area.

Defining a Name Manually

You can define a named range with the **Define Name** command on the **Formulas** tab in Excel. Follow the steps below to define a name:

1. In the worksheet, select the cells you want to include in the named range.

2. On the Excel ribbon, select **Formulas > Defined Names > Define Name**.

   Excel displays the **New Name** dialog box.

3. In the **New Name** dialog box, specify the following settings:

   - In the **Name** box, enter the name of your range.

   - In the **Scope** dropdown list, select the name of a sheet for a local name or select **Workbook** for a standard name.

   - The **Refers to** box shows the range selected on the worksheet in step 1. If you haven't selected a range or wish to change it, click the Expand Dialog button on the box and select the range.

Chapter 13: Working with Range Objects

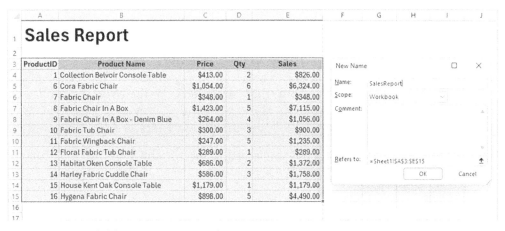

Figure 13-14: Adding a new named range.

4. Click **OK** when done.

> **Note** If you set the scope of a named range to **Workbook**, the name will be available in all worksheets in the workbook. You can't create another named range using the same name in that workbook. If the scope is set to a particular sheet, the name can be used only within the sheet. Also, you can use that name for named ranges within the scope of other sheets.

Defining a Name Programmatically

To programmatically define a named range, use the **Add** method of the **Names** collection. The **Names** collection holds all the Name objects in the workbook or application. A **Name** object is a defined name for a range of one or more cells.

Syntax for the **Add** method:

expression.Add (*Name, RefersTo, Visible, MacroType, ShortcutKey, Category, NameLocal, RefersToLocal, CategoryLocal, RefersToR1C1, RefersToR1C1Local*)

The object qualifier *expression* represents a **Names** object.

> **Note** For more details about the parameters in the **Add** method, search for "Names.Add method VBA" in VBA Help.

The example below defines a new standard name for the range A1:C15 on the *Orders* worksheet in the active workbook:

```
Sub StandardNamedRange()
    'Create standard/global named range
    ActiveWorkbook.Names.Add _
        Name:="OrdersGlobal", _
        RefersTo:="=Orders!$A$1:$C$15"
End Sub
```

The following example defines a new local name that refers to cells A1:C15 on the *Orders* worksheet:

```
Sub LocalNamedRange()
    'Create a local named range
    ActiveWorkbook.Names.Add _
        NameLocal:="Orders!OrdersLocal", _
        RefersToLocal:="=Orders!$A$1:$C$15"
End Sub
```

If the name already exists, Excel overwrites it with the new definition. If the specified sheet doesn't exist, the **Add** method returns **Nothing**.

You can return a **Name** object using its index number or name in the **Names** collection. For example, Names(1) returns the first **Name** object in the workbook, and Names("Orders!OrdersLocal") returns the **Name** object called OrdersLocal in the *Orders* worksheet.

The example below deletes the local name OrdersLocal stored in the *Orders* worksheet of the active workbook:

```
ActiveWorkbook.Names("Orders!OrdersLocal").Delete
```

The following code loops through the **Name** objects in the **Names** collection of the active workbook and displays them in column A of *Sheet1*:

```
Sub DisplayNames()
    'Display all saved names in Sheet1
    Dim NamedRange As Name
    Dim BlankRow As Long
    
    Worksheets("Sheet1").Activate
    For Each NamedRange In ActiveWorkbook.Names
        'Determine the next blank row
        BlankRow = WorksheetFunction.CountA(Range("A:A")) + 1
        Cells(BlankRow, 1).Value = NamedRange.Name
        Range("A:A").Columns.AutoFit
    Next NamedRange
End Sub
```

Chapter 14

UserForms

In this chapter:

- Introducing UserForms.
- Getting familiar with the Properties window.
- Working with UserForm controls.
- Working with the Toolbox.
- Creating a dialog box example.
- Working with UserForm events.
- Working with control events.
- Creating a room booking form example.

UserForms allow you to create custom dialog boxes that users can use to interact with your application. UserForms allow you to gather user input and display information. In this chapter, you will learn how to add a UserForm to your project, add controls to it, set control properties, and add event procedures (code) that respond to user actions.

Introduction to UserForms

A UserForm is useful when you need to interact with users, either by getting information from them or displaying information. In previous examples covered in this book, we used the InputBox to get information from the user. The input box is quite simple and limited in that it only allows the user to enter one value at a time. Thus, if you need to collect multiple values from the user, you must call the input box multiple times to get all the input values required.

On the other hand, a UserForm provides more flexibility and an efficient way of collecting user input. For example, you can use option buttons, text boxes, dropdown lists, Yes/No options, and several other data input modes. UserForms provide a richer way of communicating information to users than the basic message box. Thus, use a UserForm instead of a message box if you need to provide a message requiring more complex user interaction.

Note This chapter uses the terms "UserForm" and "dialog box" interchangeably, as UserForms are used to create custom dialog boxes. However, "dialog box" is mostly used to refer to a UserForm at runtime.

Examining an Input Box Example

To demonstrate the difference between using a UserForm and an input box, we can explore an example that requires collecting information from the user to run the program. We'll first examine a solution using an input box before solving the same problem with a UserForm.

The following code example enables users to format the numbers in the selected worksheet range to currency.

The program offers three currency options from which users can select:

- USD (US dollar) = 1
- GBP (Pound sterling) = 2
- EUR (Euro) = 3

An input box is displayed at the start of the process, allowing users to enter a number (between 1 and 3) representing the currency format they want. The value entered by the user is then assigned to the variable *CurrOption*. The **Select Case** statement determines which option was selected and which statement to execute.

```
Sub CurrencyFormat()
    Dim CurrOption As Variant
    Dim MsgTxt As String
    
    'Check that a range is selected before proceeding
    If TypeName(Selection) <> "Range" Then
        MsgBox "Please select the range you want to format."
        Exit Sub
    End If
    
    MsgTxt = "Enter 1 for USD; 2 for GBP; and 3 for EUR."
    
    ' Get input from the user
    CurrOption = InputBox(MsgTxt)
    
    ' Apply the currency format selected
    Select Case CurrOption
        Case Is = 1
            Selection.NumberFormat = "[$$-en-US]#,##0.00"
        Case Is = 2
            Selection.NumberFormat = "[$£-en-GB]#,##0.00"
        Case Is = 3
            Selection.NumberFormat = "[$€-x-euro2] #,##0.00"
        Case Else
            Selection.NumberFormat = "General"
    End Select
End Sub
```

When we select the target range (A2:A16 in this case) and run the procedure from the Code window, Excel displays the following input box.

Chapter 14: UserForms

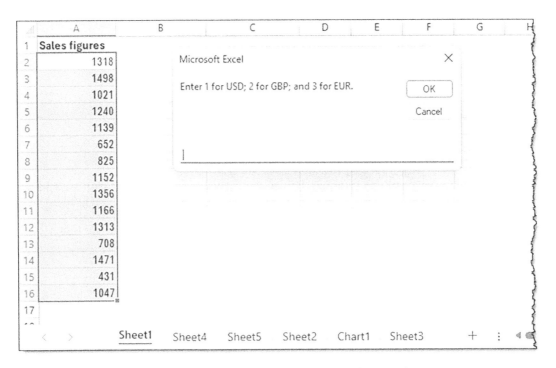

Figure 14-1: Using an input box to select options.

Entering number 1 formats the selected range as US dollar currency, 2 formats the range as pound sterling, and 3 formats the range as Euro.

The example above requires the input box to be redisplayed each time we want to format a range. It is also not user-friendly, as the options are not clear. A UserForm will provide a cleaner and more user-friendly approach.

Inserting a new UserForm

This section will walk you through adding a UserForm to your VBA project.

Follow the steps below to insert a new UserForm in your project:

1. On the ribbon, select **Developer** > **Code** > **Visual Basic** to open the Visual Basic Editor. Alternatively, select Alt | F11.
2. In the Project Explorer window, select the project to which you want to add the new UserForm.
3. On the Visual Basic Editor menu, select **Insert** > **UserForm**.

   A new UserForm is added to the **Forms** folder in the project.

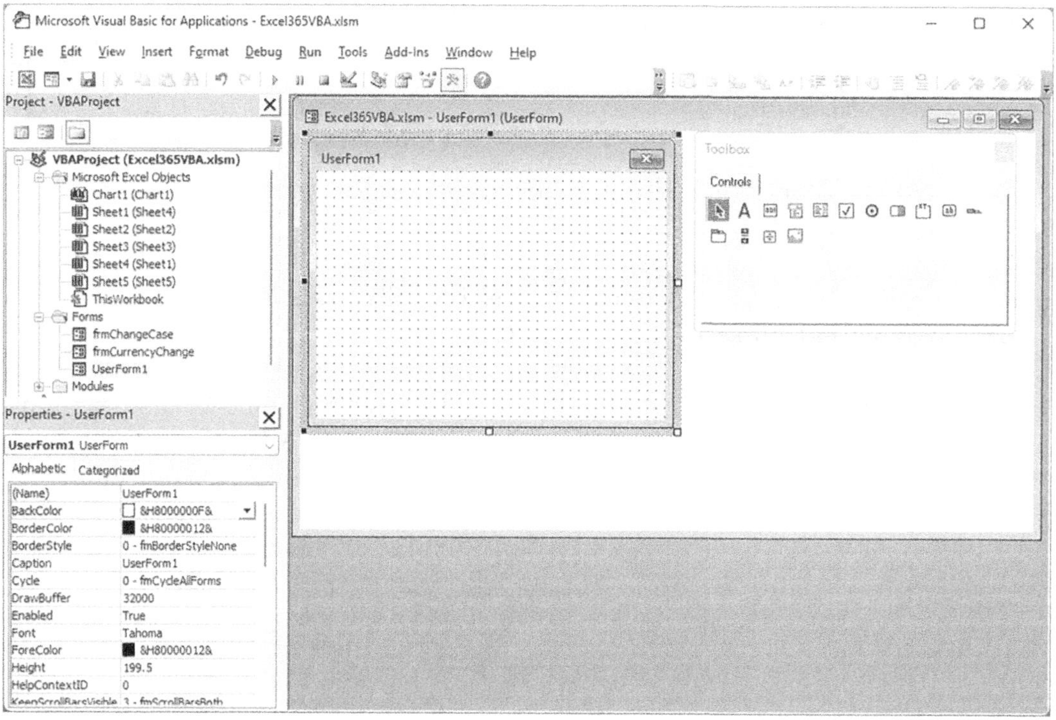

Figure 14-2: Adding a new UserForm to a VBA project.

Chapter 14: UserForms

> **Note** To remove a UserForm from a project, right-click the UserForm in the Project Explorer window and select **Remove *[UserForm name]***.

Running a UserForm

You can run a UserForm from within the Visual Basic Editor. During the development process of your application, you'll need to run your UserForm from inside the Visual Basic Editor several times to test and refine the dialog box.

Running a UserForm From the Visual Basic Editor

To quickly run a UserForm inside the Visual Basic Editor, activate the UserForm by clicking its title bar. Then, do one of the following:

- Click the **Run Sub/UserForm** button on the Standard toolbar.

  -or-

- Press F5.

  -or-

- On the menu, select **Run** > **Run Sub/UserForm**.

Displaying a UserForm Programmatically

To display a UserForm from code, invoke its **Show** method from a procedure in a module or another UserForm, as shown in the example code below:

```
frmAddUser.Show
```

> **Tip**: An easier way to enter UserForm control names in code is to type the first 2-3 characters of the name and press Ctrl+Space. VBA displays an IntelliSense menu of the available object names starting with the entered characters. Select the name you want from the list and press Tab to enter it in your code. Ctrl+J can also be used for this purpose.

Closing a UserForm

UserForms are displayed as modal by default, which means the user must close the UserForm before returning to the workbook. UserForms can also be set to modeless, meaning the user can return to the workbook while the UserForm is open. The **ShowModal** property determines the mode of a UserForm. When **ShowModal** is True, the UserForm is modal; when set to False, the UserForm is modeless.

To close a UserForm opened from the Visual Basic Editor, do one of the following:

- Click the **Close** button (x) on the right side of the UserForm's title bar.

    -or-

- Click the **Reset** button on the Standard toolbar.

To close a UserForm in code, use the **Unload** statement. Typically, you would place a Close or Cancel button on the UserForm and enter an Unload statement in its **Click** event, as shown in the example code below:

```
Private Sub CloseButton_Click()
    Unload frmAddUser
End Sub
```

The Properties Window

The Properties window lets you change UserForm and control properties at design time. If the Properties window is not visible, display it using one of the following methods:

- Press the F4 key.
- Click the **Properties window** button on the Standard toolbar (between the Project Explorer and the Object Browser buttons).
- On the Visual Basic Editor menu, select **View** > **Properties window**.

To hide the Properties window, click the **Close** button in its title bar. You can always display it whenever needed by pressing F4.

By default, the Properties window is displayed on the left side of the Visual Basic Editor. However, it is best to dock it to the right side of the Visual Basic Editor when working with UserForms.

To dock the Properties window to the right side of the window, click its title bar and drag it over the right edge until a transparent rectangle appears. Release the mouse to dock the window to that location.

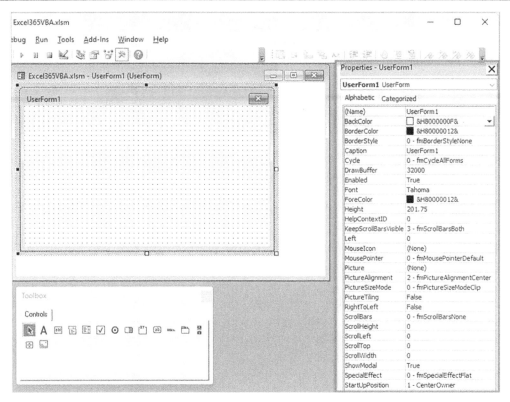

Figure 14-3: Repositioning the Properties window.

Setting UserForm Properties

You can set several properties for your UserForm at design time (using the Properties window) or runtime in code. The following section covers some common properties to set at design time.

Name

The default name given to a new UserForm is *UserFormN*, where N is a unique number. For example, the first new UserForm is *UserForm1*, the second is *UserForm2*, and so on. It is important to set the **Name** property as soon as you create a UserForm, as you'll likely use the name to reference it in code.

To change the name of a UserForm, click the **Name** property and change the default name to something that reflects the functionality of the UserForm.

 Note UserForms share the same naming rules as variables, covered in Chapter 4.

Caption

Use the **Caption** property to set the text in the UserForm's title bar. The default caption is *UserFormN* (with N representing a unique number). Change the caption from the default name to make the UserForm more user-friendly and identifiable.

The **Name** and **Caption** are different properties. The Caption property does not have the same naming rules as the Name property. For example, the Caption property can have spaces and other characters that can't be used in the Name property of a UserForm.

Font

Another UserForm property you can change early in the development process is the **Font** property. This property is for instances where you want to use a different font from the default font. Controls placed on a UserForm will use the font set on the UserForm. However, controls placed before you change the **Font** property of the UserForm are unaffected. So, if you intend to use a different font from the default, set the **Font** property of the UserForm before placing controls on it.

Width and Height

You can resize a UserForm with your mouse by grabbing the resize handle on the lower-right corner and dragging it. However, the **Width** and **Height** properties enable you to set more precise values. For instance, if you need several UserForms in your application to be uniform, you can use the **Width** and **Height** properties to ensure they are the same size.

BackColor and ForeColor

The **BackColor** property sets or returns the background color of a UserForm, while the **ForeColor** property sets or returns the color used to display text on the UserForm. If applicable, you may need to set the **BackColor** and **ForeColor** properties of your application to your organization's color scheme.

> **Tip**: To become familiar with UserForm properties, you can try changing some properties in the Properties window and then run the UserForm to see the effect. To run a UserForm in the Visual Basic Editor, press F5 or click the **Run** button on the Standard toolbar.

> **Tip**: You can get contextual help for each property by selecting the property and pressing F1. The Visual Basic Editor takes you to the online help for that property.

UserForm Controls

After creating a UserForm, you will notice a floating window called the Toolbox displayed next to the UserForm.

The Control Toolbox

If the toolbox is not visible (after creating a UserForm), you can display it by:

- Selecting **View** > **Toolbox** on the Visual Basic Editor menu.

    -or-

- Selecting the **Toolbox** button on the Standard toolbar.

Figure 14-4: The controls toolbox.

To identify the name of an icon in the toolbox, hover your mouse over the icon. A help tip displays the name.

Note Unlike other windows in the Visual Basic Editor, the toolbox is not dockable. Occasionally, the toolbox may disappear behind other windows on your desktop. If you can't see the toolbox, click the **Toolbox** button on the Standard toolbar to bring it into focus.

The table provides an overview of the default controls in the toolbox:

Control	Description
Label	Use this control to display titles, captions, and instructions.
TextBox	Used to capture and display information entered by a user. You can set the MultiLine property to true to create a multi-line box.
ComboBox	Provides a dropdown list of values. Allows you to enter a new value or select a value from the dropdown list.
ListBox	Displays a list of values, enabling you to select one or more values (multi-select).
CheckBox	Displays the selection status of an item. Allows the user to select one of two values, like True/False, Yes/No, or On/Off.
OptionButton	Use this control to show which item is selected in a group of options.
ToggleButton	Use this control to toggle a selection On or Off. The control's value is True when selected and False when not selected.
Frame	Use the Frame control to create an option group or visually group controls that are closely related.
CommandButton	Used to trigger, stop, or interrupt an action or process.
TabStrip	Enables you to display different sets of information for the same controls. This control is rarely used because it is easier to create a tabbed dialog box with the MultiPage control.
MultiPage	Use this control to group related items on a tab. You can use it to create a dialog box with multiple tabs.
ScrollBar	Provides a stand-alone scroll bar that you can place on a UserForm. It sets or returns the value of another control based on the position of the scroll box.
SpinButton	You can use this control to increase or decrease the displayed value of another control. For example, you can write code to update the number displayed on a label using the SpinButton.
Image	Allows you to display an image on a UserForm. This control supports various file formats, including *.jpg, *.bmp, *.gif, and *.wmf.

Adding Controls to a UserForm

There are three ways you can add controls to a UserForm:

Method 1

Select the control in the toolbox and drag it to the position on the UserForm where you want it.

> **Tip:** To quickly duplicate a control on a UserForm, like an OptionButton, select the control, hold down the Ctrl key, and drag it down with your mouse. The drag action creates a new instance of the control instead of moving it.
>
> To duplicate multiple controls simultaneously, for example, a Label and a TextBox, select both controls, hold down Ctrl, and drag the selection down with your mouse. The selected controls are duplicated.

Method 2

Use the following method to place multiple instances of the same type of control on a UserForm.

1. Double-click the control's icon in the toolbox to select it.

   Your mouse pointer changes to a plus sign (+) and a small icon when moved over the UserForm.

2. Position the pointer where you want to place the control and click once.

   The Visual Basic Editor adds the control to the UserForm.

3. Subsequent clicks add new instances of the control to the UserForm.

4. When you've added the instances of the control you want, click the control's icon in the toolbox once to clear the selection.

You can reposition and arrange the controls individually after adding them to the UserForm.

Method 3

The third method, described below, lets you position and size the control as you draw it on the UserForm. This method is useful for adding larger controls like a ListBox, Frame, or an Image to a UserForm.

Follow the steps below to draw a control on your UserForm:

1. In the toolbox, select the icon for the control you want to add to the UserForm.
2. Move your mouse pointer to the position on the UserForm where you want the upper-left corner of the control to start.
3. Click and hold the mouse button. Then, drag to the lower right corner.

    A rectangle is displayed, showing the size and location of the control.
4. Once the control is sized to your liking, release the mouse button.

After adding the control, you can position, resize, and format the control using commands on the format menu.

Setting Control Properties

Each type of control has properties related to its appearance and behavior that you can set at design time or runtime.

Setting Control Properties at Design Time

The **Properties window** (shown in the following image) allows you to set control properties at design time.

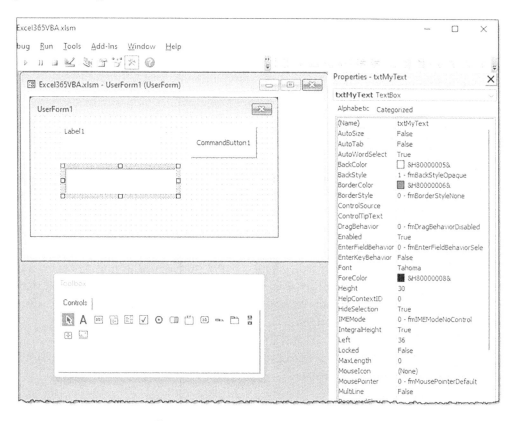

Figure 14-5: The Properties window.

The Properties window displays the properties of the control currently selected. If you select a different control, the Properties window changes to show the properties of that control.

Most controls have unique properties but share some common properties like **Name**, **Enabled**, **Visible**, **Width**, **Height**, etc.

To change a control's property, follow the general steps below:
1. Select the control on the UserForm.

If you want to change properties for the UserForm itself, click a blank area on the UserForm.

2. Press F4 to display the Properties window (if it is not visible).

3. In the Properties window, identify the property you want to change on the left column, and in the right column, enter the value (or select a value from the dropdown list if applicable).

Control Naming Rules and Conventions

UserForm controls follow the same naming rules as variables and procedures, covered in Chapter 4 under **Variable Naming Guidelines**.

There is no obligatory naming convention in VBA besides the naming rules. However, adopting a naming convention that you use consistently throughout your VBA project is good practice. A naming convention makes it easier to write and read code.

Ideally, you want to know the control type when using its name in the Code window. For example, when using a TextBox control, give it a name that identifies it as a text box. Give a ListBox control a name that identifies it as a list box, and so on. Thus, instead of naming a text box *Company*, use *TextCompany* or *txtCompany*. Instead of naming an OptionButton control *Other*, use *OptionOther* or *optOther*.

The naming convention you use is a matter of preference and what you find more suitable, but be consistent with it in your project.

Naming Controls

The **Name** property is one of the first properties you should change after adding a control to your UserForm. Naming a control is important because you use its name to identify it in the Code window. When you create a control, VBA gives it a default name (which includes a suffix number), indicating the type of control and its instance on your UserForm. For example, if you insert a TextBox control, VBA will name it *TextBox1*. If you insert another TextBox while the name *TextBox1* is currently in use, VBA names the new instance *TextBox2*, and so on. The next sequential number is given for that control type based on the names used on the UserForm.

Any code you add to an event procedure of a control is added under the current name of the control. If you rename a control after adding code, the code is not automatically moved under the new name of the control. You have to move the code manually. As the event procedure is linked to the name, it's important to rename controls on your UserForm before adding any code that references the control.

Setting Control Properties at Runtime

You can set control properties in code at runtime, just as with other Excel objects. The following code sets the **Value** property of the TextBox control to a text string:

```
TextCompany.Value = "Highland Furniture"
```

Using a With statement to Set Control Properties

When setting properties for a control, you often set several properties simultaneously. In such cases, you can write code that is more efficient and easier to read by using the **With** statement.

A **With** block is a more efficient way to access multiple properties and methods of the same object. The code runs faster as the object is only evaluated once.

For instance, instead of using the following example to set several properties of a Label control:

```
LabelConfirmation.Visible = True
LabelConfirmation.Caption = "Task successfully completed!"
LabelConfirmation.ForeColor = vbBlue
LabelConfirmation.Font.Size = 16
LabelConfirmation.Font.Bold = True
```

Use this method:

```
With LabelConfirmation
    .Visible = True
    .Caption = "Task successfully completed!"
    .ForeColor = vbBlue
    .Font.Size = 16
    .Font.Bold = True
End With
```

Returning Control Properties At Runtime

Like other Excel objects, you can retrieve the properties of controls at runtime. The following code example returns the **Text** property from a **TextBox** control and assigns it to a string variable:

```
Dim LastName As String
LastName = TextLastName.Text
```

Arranging Controls on a UserForm

After placing controls on a UserForm, you can use a command on the **Format** menu of the Visual Basic Editor to position, resize, and space them.

Selecting Multiple Controls

To select multiple controls, do one of the following:

- Hold down the **Ctrl** key while clicking the controls you want to select. The dominant control is the last one selected.

Chapter 14: UserForms

- Hold down the **Shift** key, then click the first and last control in a group of controls to select all of them. The dominant control is the first one.

- Make sure the **Select Objects** button is selected in the Toolbox. Then, click the top-left area above the topmost control and draw a rectangle over the controls you want to select. All controls within the rectangle (or touching it) are selected. The dominant control is the first one.

- Press Ctrl+A to select **all** controls on a UserForm.

Aligning, Sizing, and Positioning Controls

To reposition a control, select and drag it to the correct position with your mouse. To resize a control, drag one of the eight *sizing handles* until the control is adequately sized, then release the mouse button.

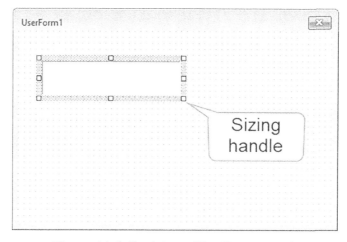

Figure 14-6: Resizing a TextBox control.

You can also use commands on the **Format** menu to align, space, and position the controls on a UserForm. To align multiple controls, select the controls using one of the selection methods described in the section above. Then, using commands on the Format menu, you can align and space the controls as needed.

295

For example, to align a group of controls to the left, do the following:

1. Drag your mouse around the controls to select them.

   You can also select multiple controls by holding down **Ctrl** and clicking each control.

2. Right-click and select **Align** > **Lefts** on the shortcut menu.

   Alternatively, select the command on the Visual Basic Editor menu by selecting **Format** > **Align** > **Lefts**.

In a multi-selection, the dominant control has white sizing handles instead of the usual black handles. This control is used as the basis for any alignment or resizing action performed on the selection. Thus, ensure the dominant control is first positioned or sized as you'd like to see the other controls in the selection.

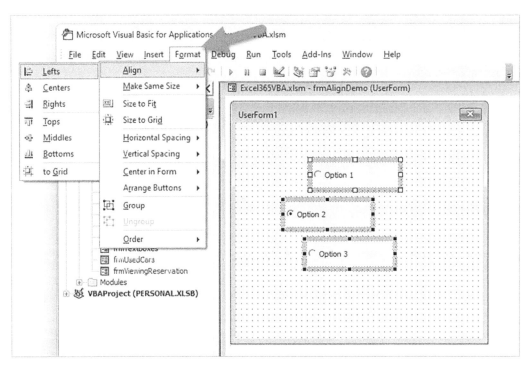

Figure 14-7: Aligning controls on a UserForm.

When you select multiple controls, the Properties window only shows the properties common to the selected controls. This feature enables you to change common properties for several controls simultaneously. For example, you can select several TextBox controls

Chapter 14: UserForms

and set the same **Height**, **Width**, and **Left** properties to make them the same size and align them to the left.

There are other self-explanatory commands on the **Format** menu for aligning, sizing, positioning, and grouping controls. You can experiment with the different menu options to see how they affect the selected controls. To undo a change, use the **Undo** button on the Standard toolbar.

Changing the Tab Order

You can organize the **Tab Order** of the controls on a UserForm to accommodate keyboard users who want to use the Tab key to move from control to control. Users can press the Tab key to circle through controls on a UserForm as they enter information.

To set the tab order of controls, do the following:

1. Select the UserForm for which you want to change the tab order.

2. On the Visual Basic Editor menu, select **View** > **Tab Order** (or right-click the UserForm and select **Tab Order** from the shortcut menu).

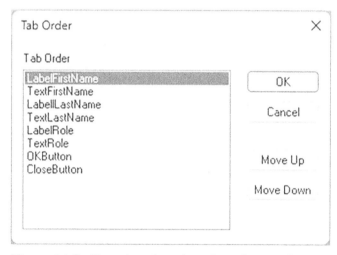

Figure 14-8: Changing the tab order of controls on a UserForm.

297

3. Set your preferred tab order by using the **Move Up** and **Move Down** buttons to position the controls on the list.
4. Select **OK** when you're done to close the Tab Order dialog box.

The tab order of a control can be found in its **TabIndex** property. The Visual Basic Editor sets the TabIndex property whenever you change the tab order of a control. Hence, you can set the TabIndex property manually in the Properties window. The first TabIndex is 0, the second is 1, and so on. To prevent a user from tabbing to a control on a UserForm, set its **TabStop** property to False.

When you place controls inside a container control (like a **Frame** or **MultiPage** control), they have their own tab order. Thus, the TabIndex property starts from 0 again for a group of controls placed inside a container control.

To change the tab order of controls inside a frame, select the Frame control, and on the Visual Basic Editor menu, select **View** > **Tab Order**. You can also right-click anywhere in the frame and select **Tab Order**. The Visual Basic Editor will display the **Tab Order** dialog box with only the controls inside the frame.

Assigning Accelerator Keys

An accelerator key (or a keyboard shortcut) allows users to go directly to a control on the UserForm by pressing the Alt key plus a letter on their keyboard. For example, Alt+F.

To specify an accelerator key for a control on a UserForm, enter a single character (usually a letter) in the **Accelerator** property in the Property window. For example, to set an accelerator for an option button, enter a letter in its **Accelerator** property.

To set accelerator keys for controls that don't have an **Accelerator** property, like a TextBox control, you can use a workaround. Place the accelerator key in a Label control that precedes the text box in the tab order. As a Label cannot receive the focus, the focus moves to the next control in the tab order. In this case, it would be your text box.

Chapter 14: UserForms

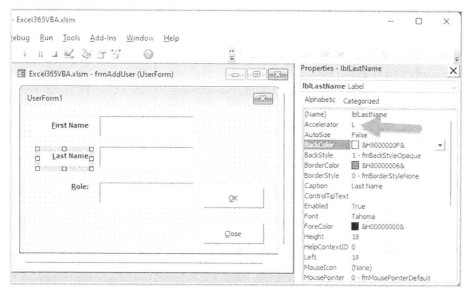

Figure 14-9: Adding keyboard shortcuts with the Accelerator property.

Note that if the accelerator key applies to a CommandButton control, the user will not see the button pressed on the interface when the accelerator keys are pressed. However, the button receives the focus, triggering its **Click** event.

Basic Controls in the Toolbox

In this section, you'll learn how to use the most commonly used controls on UserForms and their main properties. The three controls you'll most often use when building a dialog box with a UserForm are Label, TextBox, and CommandButton.

299

Label

The Label control is used to display text on a UserForm. Labels are mostly used to label text boxes, show messages to the user, or display a header on the UserForm. Users cannot edit the text in labels at runtime.

Some commonly used properties for the Label control include:

Property	Description
Name	The name of the control.
Caption	The text that is displayed on the label.
Font	This property determines the font, font style, and size of the caption.
TextAlign	Determines the alignment of the text in the Label. You can align text left, center, or right. The default is left.
AutoSize	When set to True, the label automatically resizes to display its text.
WordWrap	Determines whether the label wraps text to the next line. The default is True.
BackStyle	Determines whether a control is opaque or transparent. If you intend to change the back color of the host UserForm, you can set this Label property to **fmBackStyleTransparent** so that it always matches the color of the UserForm.

Setting the Caption

To set the text shown on a Label control, enter it in the **Caption** property. You can use the Property window to set the caption property at design time. You can also set the Caption property of a Label in code at runtime to provide updates or contextual information to the user.

The following code example sets the Caption property of a control to update the user on the progress of an action performed:

```
LabelProgressMsg.Caption = "The process was completed successfully!"
```

Chapter 14: UserForms

Aligning Label Text

The text in a Label control is left-aligned by default. The **TextAlign** property determines the alignment of the text in a Label control. You can set the TextAlign property to 1 – fmTextAlignLeft, 2 – fmTextAlignCenter, or 3 – fmTextAlignRight.

Using WordWrap and AutoSize

If the amount of text in a label exceeds its width, it is wrapped to the next line by default. This behavior is determined by the **WordWrap** property of the control, which is True by default. However, if the text exceeds a label's height, it is clipped by default. This behavior is set by the **AutoSize** property, which is **False** by default. If you anticipate that the text in your label may exceed the control's height, set the **AutoSize** property to **True**. This setting ensures the height of the control increases with its text.

The image below shows several Label controls with different **Font**, **TextAlign**, and **AutoSize** settings:

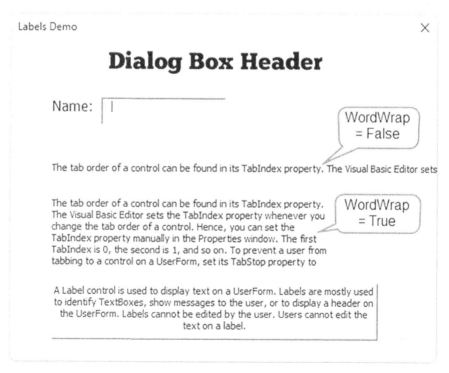

Figure 14-10: Label controls with different property settings.

301

💡 **Tip**: To ensure your labels match the color of your dialog box whenever you change its BackColor property, change the **BackStyle** property of the label to **fmBackStyleTransparent**. If the color of the dialog box changes, the label automatically matches the new color as it is transparent.

TextBox

A TextBox control is primarily used to get data input from the user. You can also display information to the user with a text box. Unlike a label, users can change the text displayed in a text box.

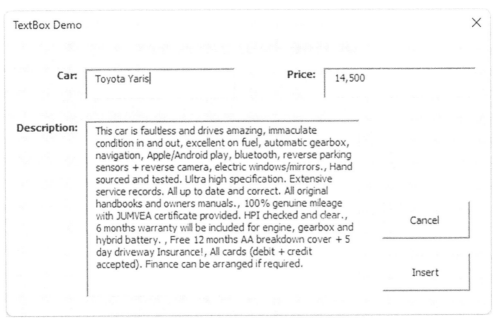

Figure 14-11: Using TextBox controls.

The following properties are some of the most useful for the TextBox control:

Property	Description
MultiLine	Set this property to True if you want the TextBox to display multiple lines of text. The default is False.
ScrollBars	This property is most useful when the MultiLine property is set to True. You can set horizontal, vertical, or both scroll bars. The default is none (0 – fmScrollBarsNone).
TextAlign	This property determines the alignment of the text in the TextBox. You can align text left, center, or right. The default is left.
WordWrap	Determines whether the TextBox wraps text to the next line. Used when MultiLine is set to True.
MaxLength	Determines the maximum number of characters the TextBox can hold. The default is 0, which is the setting for an unlimited number of characters.
AutoSize	When this property is set to True, the TextBox will resize automatically based on the amount of text entered. Note that the TextBox will grow over other controls on the UserForm when the user enters a lot of text. Only enable AutoSize if there is no chance of the TextBox growing over other controls on the UserForm. Use a scroll bar instead.

CommandButton

A command button is used to perform a task when it is clicked. You use a CommandButton control to start, pause, or end a process. The CommandButton control has several events, but the one you'll use most often is the **Click** event.

The following image shows several command buttons on a dialog box. Use the **Caption** property of a command button to set the name displayed to the user. You can enter different characters for the Caption property. The **Font** property allows you to change the font, font style, and size of the caption. You can also display an image with its **Picture** property on a command button.

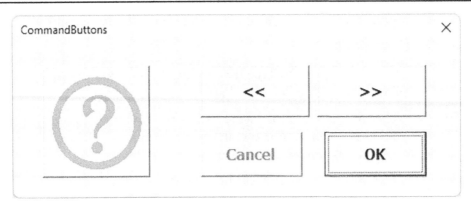

Figure 14-12: Using command buttons.

To allow a user to press the Enter key as a substitute for clicking a button, set its **Default** property to True. Only one button on the UserForm can have its **Default** property set to True. This property is usually set for the 'OK' button.

To allow a user to press Esc instead of clicking the 'Cancel' button, set its **Cancel** property to True. Similar to the **Default** property, only one button on the UserForm can have its **Cancel** property set to True.

Note For a more user-friendly dialog box, place buttons horizontally along the bottom of the UserForm or vertically along the right side of the UserForm.

ComboBox

A ComboBox control provides a dropdown list of suggested values from which users can select. A combo box combines the functionality of a text box and a list box in one control. This feature allows users to type in a value in a combo box that is not in the dropdown list, but they can't do that with a list box.

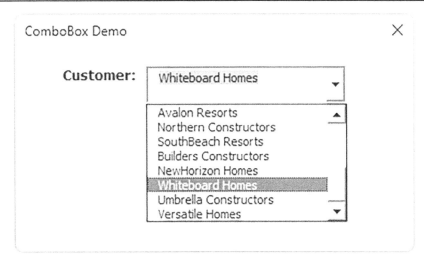

Figure 14-13: A ComboBox control.

To populate a combo box at design time, set the **RowSource** property to a worksheet range, for example, *Companies!A2:A19*, where *Companies* is the worksheet name.

The table below describes some of the common ComboBox control properties:

Property	Description
RowSource	A range containing the values to be displayed in the ComboBox. Usually, a range from a worksheet, e.g., Companies!A2:A19.
ControlSource	Stores the cell reference that holds the value selected in the ComboBox, usually a worksheet range.
Value	The value selected by the user and displayed in the ComboBox.
ListRows	Specifies the number of items to display in the list.
ListStyle	Determines whether the list is standard or displayed with option buttons.
Style	Specifies whether the control behaves like a ComboBox or a dropdown list. A dropdown list restricts the values the user can enter to the items in the list.

ListBox

A ListBox control displays a list of items from which the user can select one or more. Generally, a list box is suitable for limiting user input to the items on the list. Conversely, a combo box is best for scenarios where the user is presented with a list of options but can enter a value that is not on the list.

Figure 14-14: A ListBox control.

Like a combo box, you can populate the values in a list box at design time by setting its **RowSource** property to a worksheet, like *Companies!A2:A19*. The range can have multiple columns, for example, A2:B20, if necessary. You can also populate the list box at runtime using VBA code. If the items in a list box are more than the control's height, a scroll bar appears, allowing the user to scroll down to see the other items.

The table below describes some of the common ListBox control properties:

Property	Description
RowSource	A range containing the values to be displayed in the ListBox. Usually, a range from a worksheet, e.g., A2:A10.
ControlSource	Stores the cell reference or field that holds the value selected in the ListBox.
Value	The value selected by the user in the ListBox.
ListStyle	Determines whether the list is plain or items are displayed with option buttons.
MultiSelect	Indicates whether the ListBox allows multiple selections. There are three MultiSelect options: <ul><li>**fmMultiSelectSingle**: The user can only select one item (default).</li><li>**fmMultiSelectMulti**: Allows the selection of multiple items by clicking. Clicking a selected item clears it.</li><li>**fmMultiSelectExtended**: Allows the selection of multiple items by clicking the first item, holding down Shift, and then clicking the last item. Press Ctrl and click an item to remove it from the selection.</li></ul>

OptionButton

The OptionButton control enables users to select an option from several available options. When a user selects an option button, the other option buttons in the group are cleared.

When you place option buttons directly on a UserForm, they function as mutually exclusive controls. You can use a Frame control (a container) to organize option buttons into different groups. All option buttons within the container act as a group. The container aesthetically lets users know that the option buttons in a group are functionally distinct from other option buttons on the dialog box.

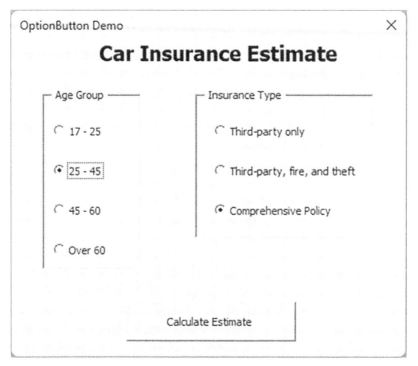

Figure 14-15: Grouping option buttons on a UserForm.

The table below describes some of the common OptionButton control properties:

Property	Description
GroupName	Allows you to create a group of mutually exclusive option buttons without a frame. You can also use a Frame control to group option buttons.
ControlSource	This property can reference a worksheet cell linked to the option button. When the option button is selected, the cell displays TRUE. When the control is not selected, the worksheet cell displays FALSE.
Value	Setting this property to **True** makes the option button the default selection in a group of option buttons.

Frame

The Frame control is used to group other controls. It can be used for visual purposes or to organize different sets of controls as a unit. A frame is useful for grouping option buttons or check boxes in a group.

The following list describes some useful Frame control properties:

Property	Description
Caption	The caption is the text displayed at the top of the frame to identify it. To display the frame without a caption, delete the default text in its **Caption** property. With no caption, the frame is displayed as an enclosed rectangle without an identifying text.
SpecialEffect	Specifies the visual appearance of the frame. You can select options to create flat, raised, sunken, etched, and bump effects.

Practice: Creating a Dialog Box

In the previous sections of this chapter, we covered UserForm basics and some of the commonly used controls. In this practice, we'll bring it all together by creating a dialog box example using several UserForm controls.

In this practice, we'll revisit the *CurrencyFormat* procedure created earlier in this chapter with an input box. This time, we'll enhance the solution using a UserForm to get the user input. The original procedure formats a worksheet range to a number format based on a number entered by the user.

The required dialog box needs to get one piece of information from the user, the currency format to apply to the text. As we have three currency options from which the user can select, we can use option buttons on the dialog box. The dialog box also needs an OK button and a Cancel button. Selecting OK runs the code that applies the format while selecting Cancel closes the dialog box and ends the process.

The program offers three currency options from which users can select:

- USD (US dollar)
- GBP (Pound sterling)
- EUR (Euro)

The solution for this practice can be found in the **CurrencyFormat_Solution.xlsm** workbook, which is in the folder for the practice files for Chapter 14.

➤ **Follow the steps below to create a new UserForm:**

1. Create a new macro-enabled workbook.
2. Switch to the Visual Basic Editor by selecting **Developer > Code > Visual Basic**.
3. In the Project Explorer window, select the VBA project for your new workbook.
4. On the Visual Basic Editor menu, select **Insert > UserForm**.

    The Visual Basic Editor adds a new UserForm to the **Forms** folder in the project.

5. In the Properties window, set the **Name** property of the UserForm to **frmCurrencyFormat**.
6. Set the **Caption** property of the UserForm to **Currency Format**.

➤ **Add OptionButton controls and a Frame to the UserForm:**

> **Note** For detailed steps on adding, sizing, and positioning controls on a UserForm, see the sections **Adding Controls to a UserForm, Setting Control Properties**, and **Arranging Controls on a UserForm** discussed earlier in this chapter.

1. Select the Frame control in the toolbox and draw it on the UserForm.
2. Add three OptionButton controls to the UserForm. Place them inside the frame.
3. Add two CommandButton controls to the UserForm.
4. Using the Properties window, change the properties for the controls you've added to the UserForm to the values listed in the table below:

Control type	Property	Value
Frame	Name	**FrameOptions**
	Caption	**Currency Options**
OptionButton	Name	**OptionUSD**
	Caption	**US Dollar ($)**
	Value	**True**
OptionButton	Name	**OptionGBP**
	Caption	**British Pounds (£)**
OptionButton	Name	**OptionEuro**
	Caption	**Euro (€)**
CommandButton	Name	**OKButton**
	Caption	**OK**
	Default	**True**

311

CommandButton	Name	**CancelButton**
	Caption	**Cancel**
	Cancel	**True**

The following image shows how the UserForm should look when the controls have been added.

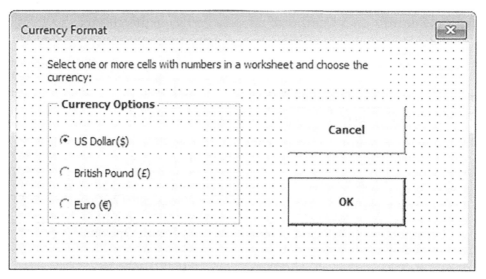

Figure 14-16: Controls on the Currency Format UserForm.

5. To see how the UserForm looks at runtime, click the title bar of the UserForm to ensure it is selected, and then click the **Run Sub/UserForm** button on the Standard toolbar (or press F5).

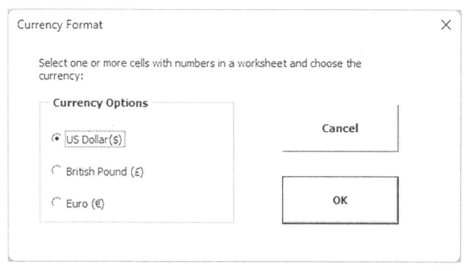

Figure 14-17: The Currency Format dialog box.

6. Note that none of the controls will work at this point, as we're yet to add events. Click the **Close** button (x icon) on the dialog box's title bar to return to design mode.

Setting the **Value** property of the option button named OptionUSD to True makes it the default selection when the UserForm is run. As the **Default** property of the OK button is set to True, pressing Enter runs the **Click** event for the OK button. Likewise, as the **Cancel** property of the Cancel button is set to True, pressing Esc activates the Cancel button.

Save the workbook containing this UserForm project. You will complete it in the next example by adding UserForm events.

Understanding UserForm Events

UserForms have a predefined set of events that can be triggered automatically when an action happens to the UserForm. Some of these events happen when the UserForm is opened or closed. You can add code to one or more of these events to perform various actions.

Common UserForm Events

The following list describes commonly used UserForm events and when each one occurs.

Initialize

The Initialize event occurs when the UserForm is loaded into memory before it is shown. This event is commonly used to initialize any variables or objects assigned initial values before displaying the UserForm. Also, you could resize or reposition controls here if necessary.

Activate

This event occurs when the UserForm receives the focus.

Deactivate

This event occurs when the UserForm loses the focus.

QueryClose

This event is typically used to ensure no unfinished tasks are in the dialog box before it closes. You can add code here to prompt the user to save the data or to cancel the closing process.

Terminate

This event occurs when the UserForm is unloaded from memory. If necessary, you can use this event to set all object references to **Nothing**.

Sometimes, you may want to disable some controls on the UserForm until all prerequisite actions have been performed. The following example uses the **Initialize** event to set the **Enabled** property of the OK button to **False** when the UserForm is loaded:

```
Private Sub UserForm_Initialize()
    cmdOK.Enabled = False
End Sub
```

Another process in the code will enable the button after other actions have been performed.

In another example, we can use the **QueryClose** event procedure to prompt users to confirm that they want to close a dialog box. The routine initially checks whether the **CloseMode** argument is 0, which is the value returned when the user clicks the **Close** button on the dialog box's title bar.

If the user clicks the **Close** button on the dialog box's title bar, they're prompted with the confirmation message. If the user selects **No** at the prompt, the routine sets **Cancel** to 1, which cancels the close process. If the user selects **Yes**, the close process continues.

```
Private Sub UserForm_QueryClose(Cancel As Integer, CloseMode As Integer)
    'frmTextBoxDemo

    Dim Answer As Variant
    Dim Message As String
    'Prompt the user to confirm the close process.
    If CloseMode = 0 Then
        Message = "Do you want to close the dialog box?"
        Answer = MsgBox(Message, vbYesNo, "Confirm close")
        If Answer = vbNo Then Cancel = 1
    End If
End Sub
```

Initializing Controls at Runtime

Besides setting control properties at runtime, you can also populate controls with initial values. The initial value of a control, like a TextBox or Label, is displayed in the control when the UserForm is displayed. Some control properties are only accessible at run time, like the **ListIndex** property of the ComboBox control.

It is always more efficient to set control properties and values at design time if possible. However, there are some scenarios where you must set control values at runtime, especially in cases where the values are not yet known at design time. For example, you may want to display a dialog box with default values based on values selected in another dialog box at runtime. Likewise, you may want to display a value on a label only known at runtime, such as the name of the user.

To initialize controls in code, you can set control properties in a separate module before displaying the UserForm, or you can set the values in the UserForm's **Initialize** event. One benefit of initializing controls inside the **Initialize** event of a UserForm is that the code is contained within the UserForm. At any point, if the UserForm is moved to another project, the initialization code will remain with it.

The code example below uses the **Initialize** event of a UserForm to populate a list box named **ListCustomers** with values:

```
Private Sub UserForm_Initialize()
    With ListCustomers
        .AddItem "Arbor Homes"
        .AddItem "Chance Fitness Co"
        .AddItem "GTech Designs"
        .AddItem "Orion Builders"
    End With
    
    LabelUser.Caption = "User: " & Application.UserName
End Sub
```

You can use the following code in a separate module to display the UserForm:

```
Private Sub GetCustomers()
    frmCustomerList.Show
End Sub
```

To set a different default value for a control each time a UserForm is displayed, you can set the value in code before invoking the **Show** method of the UserForm. The following example assigns a default value to a label (the name of the current user) and then shows the UserForm:

```
Private Sub GetCustomers()
    frmCustomerList.lblUser.Caption = "User: " & Application.UserName
    frmCustomerList.Show
End Sub
```

Note that when you reference a UserForm in code, it gets loaded into memory but is not shown.

Understanding Control Events

After creating and adding controls to your UserForm, you can add code to control event procedures to perform tasks in response to user actions.

VBA controls have a predefined set of events that are run based on user actions or system triggers. One of the most common event procedures you will write code for is the **Click** event of the **CommandButton** control. Most dialog boxes have one or more buttons to commit changes or close the dialog box. Any code you add to the Click event procedure will run when the button is clicked.

Some actions on controls can trigger several events. For example, when you select an item in the list box, the following events are triggered: **MouseDown**, **Change**, **Click**, **BeforeUpdate**, **AfterUpdate**, and **MouseUp**. The predefined events allow you to insert code at a specific point to perform a task in response to the user's action on the list box.

One way to see the order of events executed by a given action on a control is to write **Debug.Print** statements for various events for that control. For example, the code below will print the string in quotes to the Immediate window when you select an item in the associated list box:

```
Private Sub ListCustomers_AfterUpdate()
    Debug.Print "ListBox AfterUpdate event"
```

End Sub

Adding Code to Control Event Procedures

Follow the general steps below to add code to a control event procedure:

1. On the UserForm, select the control in which you want to add an event procedure. For example, a command button.

2. Right-click the control, and then select **View Code**.

   Alternatively, double-click the control to open the Code window.

3. Click the **Procedure** box and select the event procedure you want from the dropdown list.

   The Visual Basic Editor enters the starting and ending statements for the procedure.

4. Insert your code between the starting and ending statements of the event procedure in the Code window.

   You can use the **Object** box to select another control in which you want to enter an event procedure.

Chapter 14: UserForms

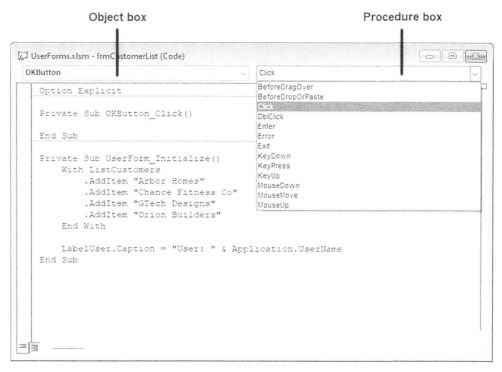

Figure 14-18: Adding code to UserForm control events.

Control event procedures include the name of the control and the name of the event. For example, the **AfterUpdate** event procedure of a ListBox named ListCustomers is ListCustomers_AfterUpdate. Likewise, the **Click** event procedure for a command button named OKButton is OKButton_Click.

Changing the Name of a Control

As the name of a control is included in its event procedures, it is important to name a control on a UserForm before adding code to its events procedures. If you change the name of the control after adding code to one or more of its event procedures, the Visual Basic Editor will not automatically move the code to the new event procedure. The code remains in the procedure with the previous name. In such instances, manually move the code to the new event procedure using cut and paste.

319

Practice: Adding Events to a UserForm

The following practice completes the **Currency Format** dialog box created earlier in this chapter. In this practice, you'll add event procedures to command buttons on the UserForm.

The solution for this practice can be found in the **CurrencyFormat_Solution.xlsm** workbook, which is in the folder for the practice files for Chapter 14.

Follow the steps below to add an event procedure to the UserForm:

1. Open the Excel macro-enabled workbook containing the UserForm named **frmCurrencyFormat** you created in the previous practice in this chapter.

2. Switch to the Visual Basic Editor by selecting **Developer** > **Code** > **Visual Basic**.

3. In the Project Explorer window, select the project containing the UserForm **frmCurrencyFormat**.

4. In the Project Explorer window, under Forms, double click **frmCurrencyFormat** to open it in design view.

    The UserForm should look like this:

Chapter 14: UserForms

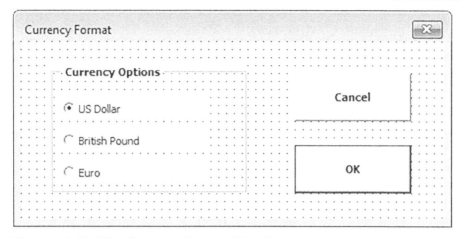

Figure 14-19: The Currency Format UserForm.

5. The UserForm has two command buttons: **OKButton** and **CancelButton**. Double-click CancelButton to open its default event procedure, which is **CancelButton_Click**.

   The CancelButton_Click event procedure is executed when the user clicks the Cancel button at runtime. As the **Cancel** property of the button is set to **True**, pressing the Esc key also triggers the CancelButton_Click procedure.

6. Add the following statement inside the CancelButton_Click procedure before the End Sub statement:

   ```
   Unload frmCurrencyFormat
   ```

   This statement closes the dialog box when the user clicks the **Cancel** button.

7. In the Object box of the Code window, select **OKButton** from the dropdown list, and select the **Click** event from the Procedure box (if it's not already selected).

   Clicking the OK button at runtime executes the OKButton_Click procedure. As the **Default** property of this button is set to **True**, pressing the Enter key also runs the OKButton_Click procedure.

8. Enter code so that the event procedure looks like this:

   ```
   Private Sub OKButton_Click()
   'Apply the currency format
   'for the option that returns True
   ```

321

```
        If OptionUSD.Value Then
            Selection.NumberFormat = "[$$-en-US]#,##0.00"
        ElseIf OptionGBP.Value Then
            Selection.NumberFormat = "[$£-en-GB]#,##0.00"
        ElseIf OptionEUR.Value Then
            Selection.NumberFormat = "[$€-x-euro2] #,##0.00"
        Else
            Selection.NumberFormat = "General"
        End If
End Sub
```

The example code above is an enhanced version of the **CurrencyFormat** procedure created at the beginning of this chapter. The code uses logical tests in the **If** block to identify the user's selected option. Then, the code block for the selected option is executed to apply the currency format to the selected range on the active worksheet.

Providing Access to the UserForm in Excel

After creating and testing a UserForm in the Visual Basic Editor, you need to create a method that allows users to open and use the UserForm in Excel. In the following examples, we'll create a macro to display the **Currency Format** UserForm. Then, we'll create access methods in Excel that enable users to open and use the UserForm as a dialog box.

You can provide user access to the UserForm with the following methods:

- A shortcut key that opens the UserForm.
- A button on the Quick Access Toolbar.
- A custom command button on the ribbon.

Creating a Macro to Open the UserForm

Follow the steps below to create a Sub procedure that can be used as a macro to display the UserForm:

1. In the Project Explorer window, select the project containing the **frmCurrencyFormat** UserForm.

2. On the Visual Basic Editor menu, select **Insert > Module**.

   The Visual Basic Editor adds a new module to the project (you can also use an existing module if you already have one in which you've stored macros).

3. Enter the following code in the module:

   ```
   Sub GetCurrencyFormat()
       'Open frmCurrencyFormat from Excel's interface
       If TypeName(Selection) = "Range" Then
           frmCurrencyFormat.Show
       Else
           MsgBox "Please select a range.", vbCritical
       End If
   End Sub
   ```

The above procedure first checks that a range is selected in the worksheet before opening the UserForm with the **Show** method. If a range is not selected, or the selection is not a worksheet range, like a chart, the user is prompted to select a range.

Assigning a Shortcut Key

Follow the steps below to assign a shortcut key that executes the GetCurrencyFormat macro:

1. Click the **View Microsoft Excel** button on the Standard toolbar or press Alt+F11 to activate the Excel window.

2. On the Excel ribbon, select **Developer > Code > Macros** (or press Alt+F8).

Excel displays the Macros dialog box.

3. In the **Macros** dialog box, under **Macro name**, select the **GetCurrencyFormat** macro.

4. Click the **Options** button.

   Excel displays the **Macro Options** dialog box.

5. Under **Shortcut key**, enter **M** (uppercase).

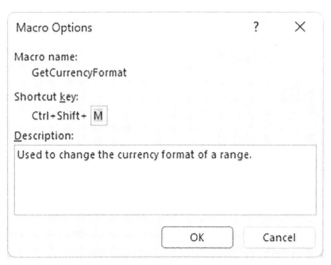

Figure 14-20: Assigning a keyboard shortcut with the Macro Options dialog box.

6. Enter a description for the macro in the **Description** box (optional).

7. Click **OK** to accept the changes and return to the Macro dialog box.

8. Click **Cancel** to dismiss the Macro dialog box.

After creating a shortcut key for the macro, as detailed above, a user can display the **Currency Format** dialog box by pressing Ctrl+Shift+M.

Creating a Button in the Quick Access Toolbar

Another way to make the UserForm accessible to users is to make the GetCurrencyFormat macro available as a button on the Quick Access Toolbar.

Follow the steps below to add the macro button to the Quick Access Toolbar:

1. Click the dropdown arrow in the Quick Access Toolbar.

2. On the dropdown menu, select **More Commands**.

   Excel displays the **Quick Access Toolbar** pane in **Excel Options**.

3. Select **Macros** from the dropdown list under **Choose commands from**.

   The list box on the left displays the macros in all open workbooks.

4. In the box on the left, select the macro you want to add to the Quick Access Toolbar and select the **Add** button to add it to the box on the right.

5. Click **OK**.

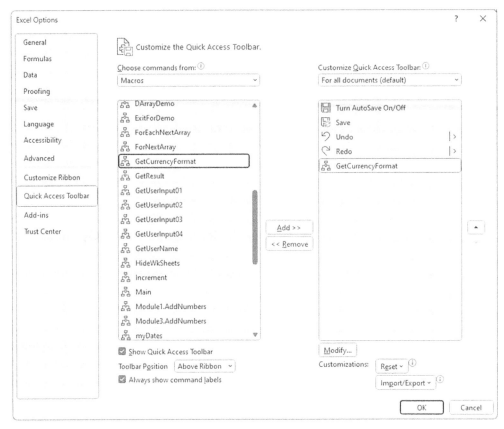

Figure 14-21: Assigning a macro to the Quick Access Toolbar.

Excel displays your macro button with a generic macro icon on the Quick Access Toolbar. To run the macro, click the button.

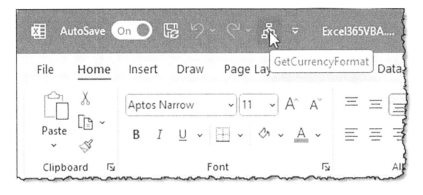

Figure 14-22: A macro button on the Quick Access Toolbar.

Note Assigning a macro to a custom button on the ribbon is covered in Chapter 2.

Testing the UserForm

Now, you can test your UserForm from Excel to ensure it works as expected.

Follow the steps below to test the UserForm:

1. Open the workbook you created containing the **frmCurrencyFormat** UserForm.
2. Enter numbers in a worksheet range, for example, in cells A2:A10.
3. Select the range.
4. Press Ctrl+Shift+M.

   Excel displays the UserForm.

5. Select a currency option, for example, **Euro**, and click **OK**.

   If the macro works as expected, Excel will format the selected cells to your chosen currency format.

6. Click **Cancel** to close the dialog box.
7. Test the dialog box again by clicking the **GetCurrencyFormat** button on the Quick Access Toolbar and following steps 5-6 above.

Mastering Excel VBA Programming

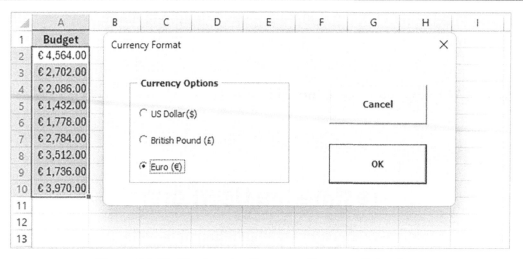

Figure 14-23: Testing the Currency Format dialog box.

As long as the workbook containing the macro is open, you can run the macro in other workbooks on the computer. If you close the workbook containing the macro, the keyboard shortcut assigned to the macro (in this case, Ctrl+Shift+M) no longer works for opening the UserForm. Conversely, if you assign the macro to a custom button on the ribbon or the Quick Access Toolbar, you can use it to run the macro even if the host workbook is closed. Excel will prompt you with a security notice, which you must **Enable** to make the workbook containing the macro available.

If the macro doesn't work, check all previous steps to find and fix the error. Debugging and troubleshooting are normal in the VBA development process. Ensure the workbook containing the macro is in a **Trusted Location** on your computer.

See Chapter 2 for how to create a trusted location for storing macro-enabled workbooks.

Practice: Room Booking Form

In this example, we'll create a UserForm that enables users to enter room booking data for meetings into a worksheet. The UserForm will be used to demonstrate the use of several UserForm controls.

The solution for this practice can be found in the **RoomBooking_Solution.xlsm** workbook that is in the practice files for Chapter 14.

When all the controls have been placed on the UserForm, it should look like this:

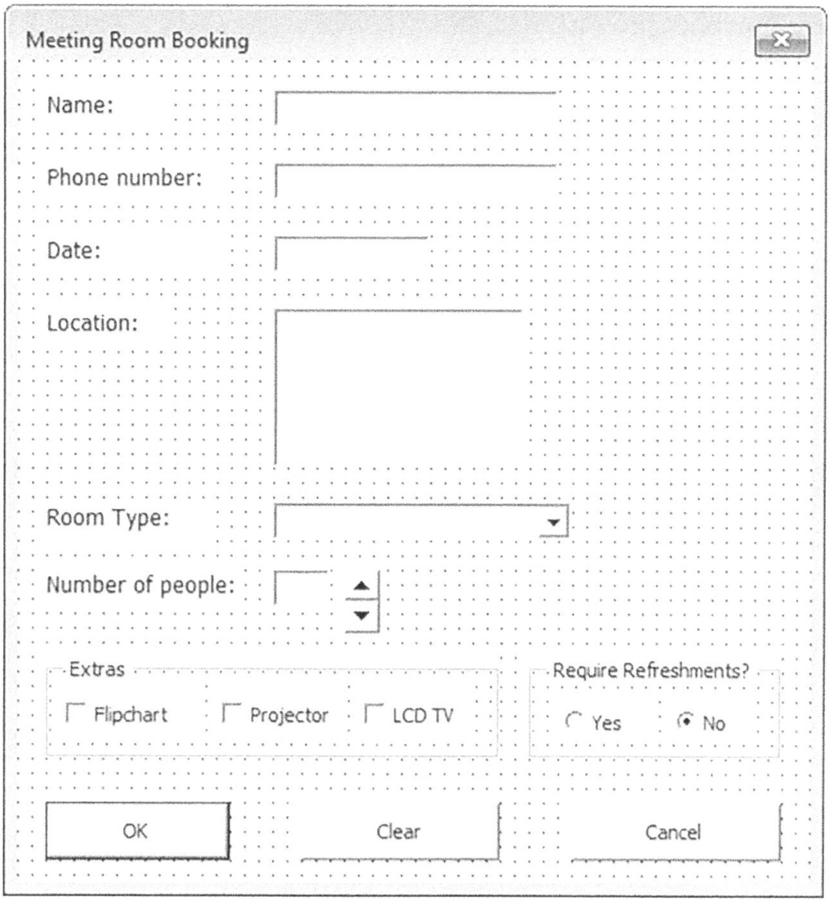

Figure 14-24: Controls placed on the 'Meeting Room Booking' UserForm.

Inserting a new UserForm

Follow the steps below to create a new UserForm:

1. Create a new macro-enabled workbook. You can name the workbook RoomBooking.xlsm.
2. In the new workbook, change the name of Sheet1 to **Bookings**.
3. On the Excel ribbon, select **Developer > Code > Visual Basic** to open the Visual Basic Editor.
4. In the Project Explorer window, select the project for RoomBooking.xlsm.
5. On the Visual Basic Editor menu, select **Insert > UserForm** to insert a new UserForm in the project.
6. In the Properties window, set the **Name** property of the UserForm to **BookingUserForm**.
7. Set the **Caption** property of the UserForm to **Meeting Room Booking**.

Adding Controls to the UserForm

1. Using the information in the table below, add controls to the UserForm:

Control	Name	Caption
TextBox	TextName	
TextBox	TextPhone	
TextBox	TextDate	
ListBox	ListLocation	
ComboBox	ComboRoomType	
TextBox	TextDelegates	
SpinButton	SpinDelegates	

Frame	FrameExtras	Extras
CheckBox	CheckFlipchart	Flipchart
CheckBox	CheckProjector	Projector
CheckBox	CheckLCDTV	LCD TV
Frame	FrameRefreshments	Require Refreshments?
OptionButton	OptionRefYes	Yes
OptionButton	OptionRefNo	No
CommandButton	OKButton	OK
CommandButton	ClearButton	Clear
CommandButton	CancelButton	Cancel

2. Set the **Default** property of the CommandButton **OKButton** to **True**.
3. Set the **Cancel** property of **CancelButton** to **True**.
4. Set the **Value** property of **OptionRefNo** to **True**.
5. Add **Label** controls to the UserForm to label the text boxes, list box, and combo box.
6. Change the **Caption** property of each label so that the labels properly identify their corresponding controls. The names of the labels do not need to be changed from the default names. See the UserForm image at the beginning of this example for how the labels are captioned.

Entering Code to Initialize the UserForm

To display the UserForm and make it ready for use, we need to write some code to initialize it. This code will be placed in the **UserForm_Initialize** event and is automatically executed whenever the form is displayed. We can use this event procedure to reset controls, populate lists, and populate controls that require default values.

Follow the steps below to enter the initialization code:

1. In the Visual Basic Explorer, double-click anywhere on **BookingUserForm** to open the Code window.
2. In the Code window, ensure **UserForm** is selected in the Object box, and **Initialize** is selected in the Procedure box.
3. Add code to the **UserForm_Initialize** event procedure so that it looks like the code shown below:

```
Private Sub UserForm_Initialize()
    'Clear text boxes
    TextName.Value = ""
    TextPhone.Value = ""
    TextDate.Value = ""
    TextDelegates.Value = ""
    
    'Clear list box
    ListLocation.Clear
    
    'Fill ListLocation
    With ListLocation
        .AddItem "Los Angeles"
        .AddItem "New York"
        .AddItem "Miami"
        .AddItem "Boston"
    End With
    
    'Clear combo box
    ComboRoomType.Clear
    ComboRoomType.Value = ""
    
    'Fill ComboRoomType
    With ComboRoomType
        .AddItem "Room 1"
        .AddItem "Room 2"
        .AddItem "Room 3"
    End With
    
    'Clear check boxes
    CheckFlipchart.Value = False
    CheckProjector.Value = False
    CheckLCDTV.Value = False
    
    'Set the default value of refreshments to No
    OptionRefNo.Value = True
```

```
        'Set focus on TextName
        TextName.SetFocus
End Sub
```

The code above performs the following actions:

- Resets all text boxes to an empty string.

- Any previously selected value in the list box is cleared. The list is then populated with items using the **AddItem** method of the ListBox control.

- Any previously selected value in the combo box is cleared. The dropdown list of the combo box is then populated with items using its **AddItem** method.

- The checkboxes for 'Extras' are cleared.

- The default value for the option buttons for 'Refreshments' is set to **No**.

- Finally, the **SetFocus** method places the cursor in the first text box on the UserForm, TextName.

Adding Event Procedures to the Controls

Currently, the UserForm looks good, but none of the controls work when clicked. We have to attach event procedures to controls on the UserForm.

Follow the steps below to add code to the Spin Button control:

1. Open the **BookingUserForm** UserForm (if it is not open).

2. Double-click the SpinButton control to open the Code window.

3. In the Code window, ensure **SpinDelegates** is selected in the Object box, and the **Change** event is selected in the Procedure box.

4. Add code so that the **SpinDelegates_Change** event procedure looks like the code below:

```
Private Sub SpinDelegates_Change()
    TextDelegates.Text = SpinDelegates.Value
End Sub
```

The code above assigns the current value of **SpinDelegates** to the text box **TextDelegates** when the spin button is clicked either up or down.

Follow the steps below to add code to the OK button:

1. Close the code window to return to the UserForm.
2. Double-click **OKButton** to open the **OKButton_Click** event procedure in the Code window.
3. Add the following code so that the **OKButton_Click** event procedure looks like this:

```
Private Sub OKButton_Click()
    Dim blankRow As Long
    Dim Extras As String
    
    'Make the Bookings sheet active
    Worksheets("Bookings").Activate
    
    'Determine the next blank row
    blankRow = WorksheetFunction.CountA(Range("A:A")) + 1
    
    'Transfer information
    Cells(blankRow, 1).Value = TextName.Value
    Cells(blankRow, 2).Value = TextPhone.Value
    Cells(blankRow, 3).Value = TextDate.Value
    Cells(blankRow, 4).Value = ListLocation.Value
    Cells(blankRow, 5).Value = ComboRoomType.Value
    Cells(blankRow, 6).Value = TextDelegates.Text
    
    'Identify selected check boxes under Extras and pass value to a variable
    If CheckFlipchart.Value = True Then
        Extras = CheckFlipchart.Caption
    End If
    
    If CheckProjector.Value = True Then
        If Extras = "" Then
            Extras = CheckProjector.Caption
        Else
            Extras = Extras & ", " & CheckProjector.Caption
        End If
    End If
    
    If CheckLCDTV.Value = True Then
        If Extras = "" Then
```

```
                Extras = CheckLCDTV.Caption
            Else
                Extras = Extras & ", " & CheckLCDTV.Caption
            End If
        End If

        ' Insert the value of the selected check boxes in the
    worksheet
        Cells(blankRow, 7).Value = Extras

        ' Identify the selected option button and enter its value
    in the worksheet
        If OptionRefYes.Value = True Then
            Cells(blankRow, 8).Value = "Yes"
        Else
            Cells(blankRow, 8).Value = "No"
        End If
    End Sub
```

The code above performs the following actions:

- First, the **Bookings** worksheet where the data will be stored is activated.

- The **CountA** method of the **WorksheetFunction** object is used to identify the next blank row in the active worksheet.

- Once the next blank row has been identified, the values in the text boxes, list box, and combo box are transferred to the active worksheet using its **Cells** property.

- The **Caption** property of each selected check box is passed into a string variable named **Extras**. The text in Extras is then transferred to the worksheet.

- The final code segment in the procedure identifies the selected option button under **FrameRefreshments** and inserts **Yes** or **No** in the worksheet accordingly.

Follow the steps below to add code to the Clear button:

1. Return to the UserForm by clicking the Minimize button of the Code window.

2. Double-click **ClearButton** to open the **ClearButton_Click** event procedure in the Code window.

3. Add code so that the event procedure looks like this:

```
Private Sub ClearButton_Click()
    UserForm_Initialize
End Sub
```

The line of code above calls the **UserForm_Initialize** event procedure when the user clicks the Clear button. As covered previously in this example, the **UserForm_Initialize** event procedure resets the UserForm by clearing any entered or selected values. The Clear button resets the UserForm to prepare it for a new entry.

Follow the steps below to add code to the Cancel button:

1. Return to the UserForm by clicking the Minimize button of the Code window.

2. Double-click the **Cancel** button to open the **CancelButton_Click** event procedure in the Code window.

3. Add code so that the event procedure looks like this:

```
Private Sub CancelButton_Click()
    Unload BookingUserForm
End Sub
```

This line of code uses the **Unload** statement to close the UserForm when the user clicks the **Cancel** button.

Designing the Worksheet to Store the Data

1. Switch to Excel by clicking the **View Microsoft Excel** button On the Visual Basic Editor.

2. Create a new worksheet named **Bookings** or rename Sheet1 to **Bookings**.

3. Copy the column headings in the first row of the Bookings worksheet from the RoomBooking_Solution.xlsm workbook to your RoomBooking.xlsm workbook. You can also manually enter the column headings.

   The column headings in the first row of the Bookings worksheet should look like the image below:

Chapter 14: UserForms

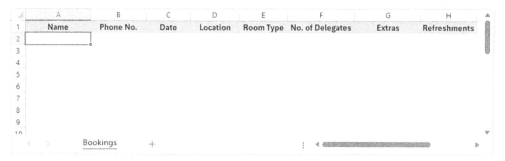

Figure 14-25: The worksheet where entries from the UserForm are inserted.

Providing Access to the UserForm

We have created the UserForm and the worksheet to store the data, but we still need to provide a method for users to open and use the UserForm. We can achieve this with a macro (Sub procedure) and a button that opens the UserForm. We can attach the macro to a button on the Quick Access Toolbar, a custom button on the ribbon, or a Form button on the worksheet.

Follow the steps below to create a macro and a Form button used to open the UserForm:

1. In the Project Explorer window, select the project for RoomBooking.xlsm.
2. On the Visual Basic Editor menu, select **Insert > Module**.

    The Visual Basic Editor adds a new module to the project.

    You can use an existing module if you already have one used to store macros.

3. Enter the following code in the module:

```
Sub ShowBookingUserForm()
    'Macro to display the room booking form.
    BookingUserForm.Show
End Sub
```

The line of code above simply displays the UserForm with the **Show** method when executed. The next steps involve creating a Form button on the worksheet to which the **ShowBookingUserForm** macro is attached.

4. Switch to Excel by clicking the **View Microsoft Excel** button on the Standard toolbar of the Visual Basic Editor.
5. On the **Developer** tab, in the **Controls** group, click **Insert**, and then select **Button (Form Control)** under **Form Controls**.
6. Draw the button on the worksheet in range J1:K2 and release the mouse.

   Excel displays the **Assign Macro** dialog box.

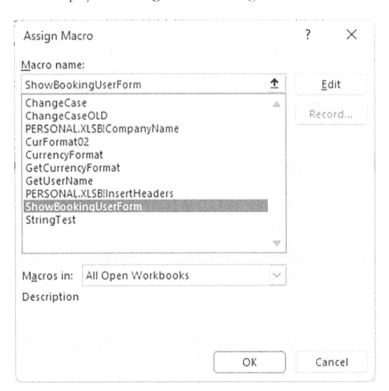

Figure 14-26: Assigning a macro to the custom button on the worksheet.

7. Select the **ShowBookingUserForm** macro and click **OK**.
8. Right-click the button, select **Edit Text**, and then change the button's text to **New Booking**.

9. Click any cell on the worksheet to exit design mode.

   The completed button and placement should look similar to the image below:

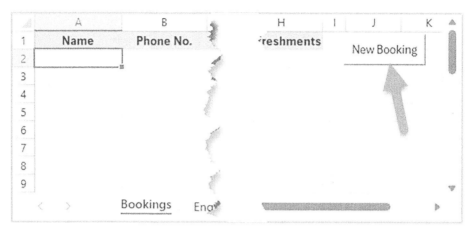

Figure 14-27: How the custom button looks on the worksheet.

Testing the UserForm

Now that we have completed the design of our UserForm, we can finally test it!

Test the UserForm by performing the following actions:

1. Open the RoomBooking.xlsm workbook.
2. On the Bookings sheet, click the **New Booking** custom button.

   Excel opens the UserForm as a dialog box.

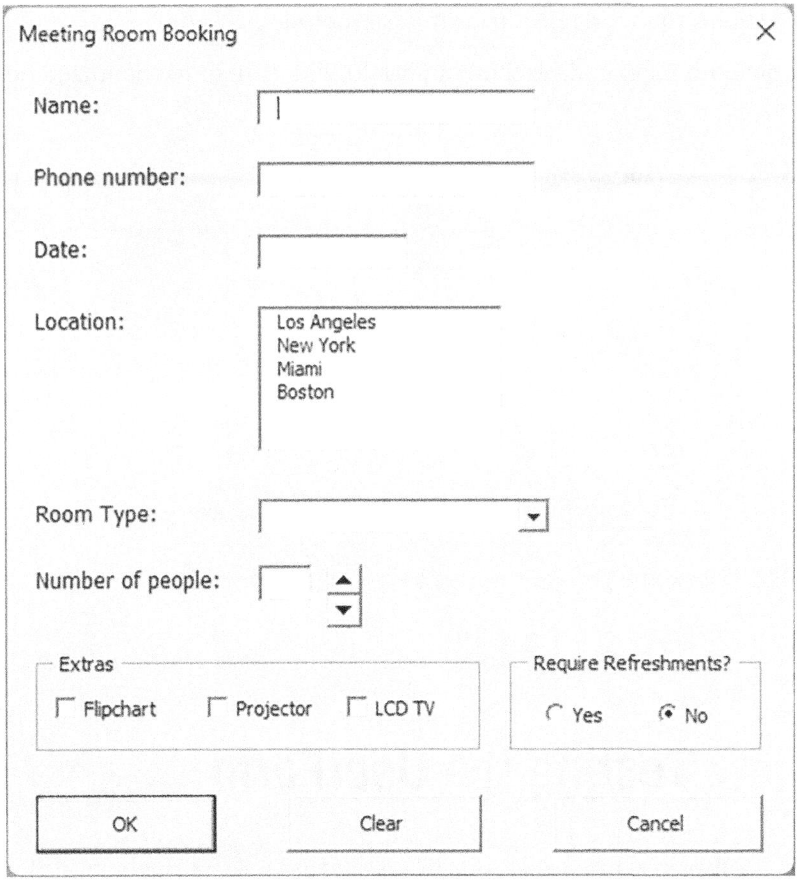

Figure 14-28: Testing the Meeting Room Booking UserForm.

3. Enter values in all boxes in the dialog box and click **OK**.

   If everything worked as expected, the information entered should be transferred to the worksheet as shown in the image below:

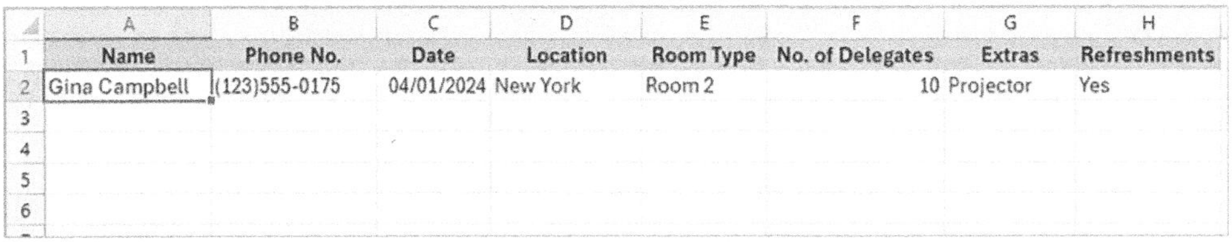

	A	B	C	D	E	F	G	H
1	Name	Phone No.	Date	Location	Room Type	No. of Delegates	Extras	Refreshments
2	Gina Campbell	(123)555-0175	04/01/2024	New York	Room 2	10	Projector	Yes
3								
4								
5								
6								

   Figure 14-29: A record inserted in the worksheet using the UserForm.

Chapter 14: UserForms

4. Use the **Clear** button to reset the dialog box and enter more records to ensure multiple records can be entered.

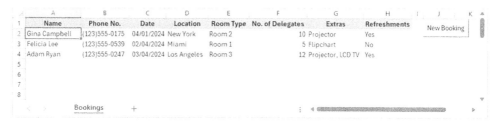

Figure 14-30: Ensuring multiple records can be inserted in the worksheet from the UserForm without overwriting previous entries.

5. Click the **Cancel** button to close the dialog box.

Adding Data Validation

So, we created the UserForm, which works as expected when transferring the entered data to a worksheet range. However, it would be customary to add data validation to a production application. One of the reasons to use a UserForm to insert data in a worksheet is that UserForms allow you to add data validation that is more complex than what you can add to worksheet cells. Data validation ensures that users properly complete the text boxes on the dialog box before the data is inserted into the worksheet. The type of data validation provided may depend on the business rules of your organization.

In this example, we'll add data validation for demonstration purposes only. So, it'll not be as comprehensive as it may need to be in a production setting.

To start, we need to create the procedure that performs the data validation.

Follow the steps below to create a Function procedure that performs the data validation:

1. In the RoomBooking.xlsm workbook, add a new worksheet named **Engine**.

    This sheet will store the names of UserForm controls that will be part of our validation routine.

2. In the Visual Basic Editor, open the UserForm **BookingUserForm**.

341

3. In the Properties Window of the UserForm, copy the **Name** property of each text box, combo box, and list box, and enter them in range A2:A7 in the **Engine** sheet in Excel.

4. On the **Engine** sheet, select the range A2:A7 and name it **ControlsToCheck**.

   We'll use the named range to reference the list of control names in our code.

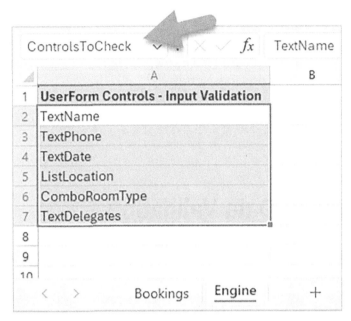

Figure 14-31: Creating a named range for the lookup list.

5. Switch to the Visual Basic Editor and double-click anywhere on **BookingUserForm** to open its Code window.

6. Enter the following code at the top of the code window just under the Option Explicit statement:

```
Function CheckControls() As Boolean
    Dim cell As Range

    For Each cell In Sheets("Engine").Range("ControlsToCheck")
        If BookingUserForm.Controls(cell.Value) = "" Then
            MsgBox "Please ensure all boxes have entries.", _
                vbCritical, "Validation Error"
            CheckControls = False
```

```
            Exit Function
        End If
    Next cell
    CheckControls = True
End Function
```

The code above uses a range variable to loop through each worksheet cell in the range named **ControlsToCheck**. The **If** block checks whether the control is empty. If the control is empty, an error message is displayed to the user. The return value of the function is then set to **False** before the **Exit Function** statement is used to exit the procedure and stop further execution. Thus, the procedure displays an error message, stops further validation checks, and returns **False** when it encounters its first missing entry.

If the **For...Each** loop is completed without finding an empty control, the procedure's return value is set to **True** before the procedure ends. Note that because we have used a Function procedure, we can return a value to the calling statement when the procedure ends.

Next, we must determine when and where to call the CheckControls procedure. For this example, the best place to call it would be at the beginning of the **OKButton_Click** procedure.

7. Insert the following line of code in the **OKButton_Click** procedure just after the variable declaration statements in the procedure.

```
If CheckControls = False Then Exit Sub
```

This statement runs the **CheckControls** Function procedure to ensure that none of the controls we're checking is empty. If the procedure returns **False**, it means that an empty control was found, and an error message was displayed to the user. The routine uses the Exit Sub statement to immediately exit the **OKButton_Click** procedure without running any further statements.

If CheckControls returns **True**, it means none of the controls was found to be empty. Hence, the rest of the code in the procedure is executed.

Testing the Data Validation Routine

To test the validation functionality added to the UserForm, do the following:

1. Open the RoomBooking.xlsm workbook (or switch to Excel if the workbook is already open).
2. On the Bookings sheet, click the **New Booking** custom button.
3. Excel opens the **Meeting Room Booking** dialog box.
4. Click **OK** without completing any of the boxes.

    The application should display the following error message to the user:

    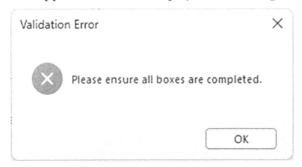

    Figure 14-32: The validation error displayed when the user does not complete the required boxes on the UserForm.

5. Click **OK** to dismiss the message.
6. In the **Meeting Room Booking** dialog box, enter values in the text boxes but not the list box or combo box, then click **OK**.

    Excel should display the same error message as those boxes are part of the validation check.

7. Dismiss the message by selecting **OK**.
8. Finally, check that Excel transfers the entered data to the worksheet when all boxes are completed. Enter values in all the boxes and click **OK**.

    If the code works as expected, the error message will not be displayed. The entered values are transferred to the worksheet.

Chapter 15

Using Built-In Dialog Boxes

In this chapter:
- Opening a file with the GetOpenFilename method.
- Saving a file with the GetSaveAsFilename method.
- Displaying different types of built-in dialog boxes with the FileDialog object.
- Using the ExecuteMso method to display dialog boxes from Excel's ribbon commands.

You can create custom dialog boxes in Excel called UserForms. However, Excel also has built-in dialog boxes for simpler and more standardized tasks. UserForms provide the opportunity for extensive customization, but they can also be time-consuming to create. Before you create a custom dialog box, see whether you can take advantage of the functionality of one of Excel's built-in dialog boxes.

GetOpenFilename

The **GetOpenFilename** method displays the standard **Open** dialog box and gets a file name from the user without opening any files. This dialog box is useful when you want the user to enter a file name or path to be used in your code. It is often difficult for users to remember the exact file path, whether to use backslashes or what extension to use. This **Open** dialog enables them to navigate to the file and select it so that the file path is passed back to the application.

Syntax:

Application.GetOpenFilename ([*fileFilter*], [*filterIndex*],[*title*],[*buttonText*], [*multiSelect*])

Description of Arguments

Name	Description
FileFilter	A string specifying the file types that appear in the dialog box. For example, *.csv. You can specify several file types to enable users to select files with different extensions.
FilterIndex	This number specifies which file filter is displayed by default for multiple file filters.
Title	A string specifying the title of the dialog box. The title is displayed as "Open" if this argument is omitted.
ButtonText	Only used for the Mac version of Excel.
MultiSelect	Users can select multiple file names if this argument is True. False allows the selection of only one file name. The default is False if this argument is omitted.

Notes:

- All arguments are optional.
- If *MultiSelect* is set to True, GetOpenFilename returns an array even if the user only selects one file name.

Chapter 15: Using Built-In Dialog Boxes

- GetOpenFilename returns False if the user cancels the dialog box.

The FileFilter Argument

Each file filter has two parts separated by a comma. The first part is descriptive, while the second is the wildcard expression. The following example is a file filter for text files:

`"Text Files (*.txt), *.txt"`

If the *FileFilter* argument has multiple file filter strings, separate them with a comma. The following example specifies two file filters: CSV and text.

`"Comma Separated Files (*.csv), *.csv,Text Files (*.txt), *.txt"`

To use several wildcard expressions for one file filter type, separate the wildcard expressions with semicolons. The following example is a filter named **Text Files** that includes file filters for text and CSV files:

`"Text Files (*.csv; *.txt), *.csv;*.txt"`.

Example 1

The following code displays a dialog box asking the user to select a file. The selected file path is then returned to the procedure:

```
Sub GetFileName()
    Dim FileName As Variant
    Dim Title As String
    Dim FilterText As String

    ' Specify file filters
    FilterText = "Text Files (*.txt; *.csv), *.csv;*.txt," & _
            "All Files (*.*),*.*"

    ' Set the dialog box title
    Title = "Get File Name"

    ' Get the filename and display it in a message box
    FileName = Application.GetOpenFilename(FilterText, 1, Title)
    If FileName <> False Then
        MsgBox "The file path is: " & FileName
    End If
```

End Sub

The procedure calls the GetOpenFilename method with a **FilterIndex** of 1, which means the first filter in the **FileFilter** argument is displayed as the default file filter. The code then checks that the return value of GetOpenFilename is not False before displaying the file name in a message box.

If the user cancels the dialog box, the GetOpenFilename method returns False (a Boolean value). Thus, the code uses a variable declared as a Variant data type to capture the return value, as it could be the file name (a String data type) or False (a Boolean data type).

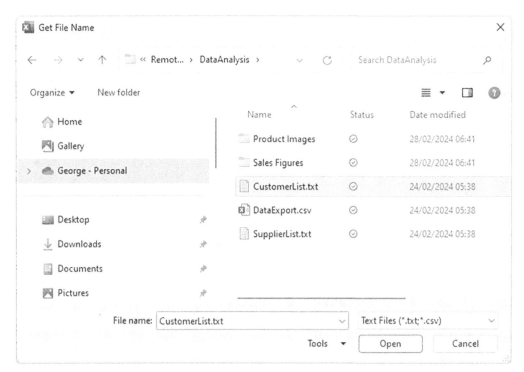

Figure 15-1: The GetOpenFilename method displays the Open dialog box.

When you select a file name and click the **Open** button on the dialog box, the routine displays the file name in a message box.

Chapter 15: Using Built-In Dialog Boxes

Figure 15-2: The File Open dialog box returns the file path.

Note This example uses a message box to display the file name for demonstration purposes only. Normally, you would use the file name to open a file.

Example 2

The following example code creates a file open dialog box using the GetOpenFilename method that allows the user to select multiple file names:

```
Sub SelectMultipleFiles()
    Dim FileNames As Variant
    Dim FilterText As String
    Dim Title As String
    Dim i As Long
    
    ' Set the file filter
    FilterText = "Text Files (*.txt; *.csv), *.csv;*.txt," & _
            "All Files (*.*),*.*"
    
    ' Set the dialog box title
    Title = "Select Files"
    
    ' Open the dialog box to select multiple files
    FileNames = Application.GetOpenFilename(FilterText, 2, Title, , True)
    
    ' Check if the user canceled the dialog
    If Not IsArray(FileNames) Then
        MsgBox "No files selected.", vbExclamation
        Exit Sub
    End If
```

349

```
    ' Loop through each selected file
    For i = LBound(FileNames) To UBound(FileNames)
        Debug.Print "Selected file: " & FileNames(i)
        ' Do something with the selected file(s)
    Next i
End Sub
```

The above code creates a dialog box where the user can select multiple files. The **MultiSelect** argument of GetOpenFilename is set to **True**, allowing multiple file selections. The selected file names are stored in the FileNames array. The code then loops through each selected file and displays its name in the Immediate Window.

GetSaveAsFilename

The **GetSaveAsFilename** method displays the standard **Save As** dialog box and gets a file name and path without saving any files. You write the code that saves the file. Use this method when you need a file path and name from the user to save a file to disk with your routine.

Syntax

Application.GetSaveAsFilename (*InitialFilename*, *FileFilter*, *FilterIndex*, *Title*, *ButtonText*)

Description of Arguments

All arguments are optional.

Name	Description
InitialFilename	Specifies the suggested file name. If omitted, Excel uses the active workbook's name.
FileFilter	A string specifying the file types that appear in the dialog box. For example, *.csv. You can specify several file types.
FilterIndex	This number specifies which file filter is displayed by default for multiple file filters. The first file filter is used if this argument is omitted.

Chapter 15: Using Built-In Dialog Boxes

Title   A string specifying the title of the dialog box. If this argument is omitted, "Open" is displayed in the title.

ButtonText   Macintosh use only.

Example

The following example creates a new workbook, prompts the user for a file name and folder using a **SaveAs** dialog box, and then saves the file to the selected folder.

```
Sub FileSaveAs()
'Create a new workbook and save it.
    Dim wkb As Workbook, Finfo As String, FilterIndex As Long
    Dim Title As String, FName As Variant

    Set wkb = Workbooks.Add

    'Set up list of file filters
    Finfo = "Excel Workbook (*.xlsx),*.xlsx," & _
            "Excel Macro-Enabled Workbook (*.xlsm),*.xlsm"

    'Make *.xlsx the default
    FilterIndex = 1

    'Set the dialog box caption
    Title = "Choose a folder and enter a name"

    'Get file name from user
    FName = Application.GetSaveAsFilename(, Finfo, FilterIndex, Title)

    If FName <> False Then
        'Save the file
        wkb.SaveAs FileName:=FName
    Else
        MsgBox "Save operation canceled."
    End If
End Sub
```

The FileDialog Object

The **FileDialog** object lets you open different Microsoft 365 file dialog boxes in code. Therefore, it is more versatile than the **GetOpenFilename** and **GetSaveAsFilename** methods discussed previously. The FileDialog property is located in the Application object of individual Microsoft 365 applications and takes a single argument, **MsoFileDialogType**, which determines the type of dialog box it returns.

There are four types of dialog boxes you can open with FileDialog:

Dialog box	Argument	Value	Description
Open	msoFileDialogOpen	1	Allows users to select one or more file names.
Save As	msoFileDialogSaveAs	2	Allows users to select a file name and path.
File Picker	msoFileDialogFilePicker	3	Enables the selection of one or more file names and paths.
Folder Picker	msoFileDialogFolderPicker	4	Allows users to select a folder name.

To display a FileDialog object, use its **Show** method. The **Show** method returns **-1** if the user selects an Action button and **0** (zero) if they select the Cancel button.

Example 1

The **FileDialog** object comes in handy if you need to get a folder location where you want to save files. The following code example creates and displays a **Folder Picker** dialog box. The selected folder path is displayed in a message box for demonstration purposes. In a functional application, you would use the folder location to perform actions.

```
Sub MyFolderPicker()
    Dim FolderPicker As FileDialog

    'Create a FileDialog object as a Folder Picker dialog box.
    Set FolderPicker = Application.FileDialog(msoFileDialogFolderPicker)
```

```
    With FolderPicker
        .InitialFileName = "C:\Data\Excel\"
        .Title = "Select the folder"
        
        'Use the Show method to display the dialog box
        'and return the user's action.
        If .Show = -1 Then
            MsgBox .SelectedItems(1)
        End If
    End With
    
    'Clear the object variable from memory.
    Set FolderPicker = Nothing
End Sub
```

The code above creates a Folder Picker dialog box using the FileDialog object. The routine used the **InitialFileName** property to set the default starting directory.

When the **Show** method is called to display the dialog box, program execution pauses until the user dismisses the dialog box. Hence, we can determine if the user selected OK (-1) or Cancel (0) to dismiss the dialog box. If the user selects OK, a message box displays the file path.

At the end of the routine, the FolderPicker object variable is set to **Nothing** to ensure the FileDialog object is cleared from memory when the procedure ends.

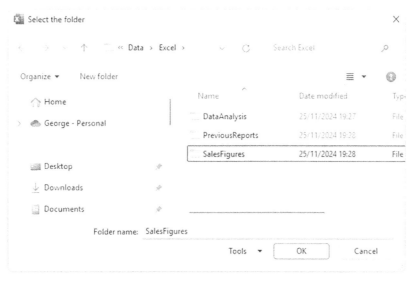

Figure 15-3: A Folder Picker dialog box allows you to return the directory path.

When you select a folder and click **OK**, the example displays the directory path in a message box.

Figure 15-4: The directory path returned from the Folder Picker dialog box.

Example 2

The following example creates a File Picker dialog box that can return several file names. The result is printed to the Immediate window:

```
Sub MyFilePicker()
    Dim FilePicker As FileDialog
    Dim SelectedFile As Variant

    'Create a FileDialog object as a File Picker dialog box.
    Set FilePicker = Application.FileDialog(msoFileDialogOpen)

    With FilePicker
        'Add filters for all files and text files.
        'Make text files the default filter.
        .Filters.Add "All files", "*.*"
        .Filters.Add "Text Files", "*.csv; *.txt", 1
        .Title = "Select file(s)"

        'Display the dialog box and check whether the user clicked OK.
        If .Show = -1 Then
            For Each SelectedFile In .SelectedItems
                Debug.Print SelectedFile
            Next SelectedFile
        End If
    End With

    'Clear the object variable from memory.
    Set FilePicker = Nothing
End Sub
```

Chapter 15: Using Built-In Dialog Boxes

The procedure above sets two filters for the File Picker dialog box using the **Add** method of the **Filters** property of the **FileDialog** object. The **Add** method has the following syntax where *expression* is a **FileDialog** object variable:

expression.Add (*Description*, *Extensions*, *Position*)

The procedure makes **Text Filters** the default filter by setting the **Position** argument of the **Add** method to 1.

A **For…Each** block loops through the **SelectedItems** collection of the FileDialog object and prints each item to the Immediate window using Debug.Print.

On executing the code, you'll get the following dialog box:

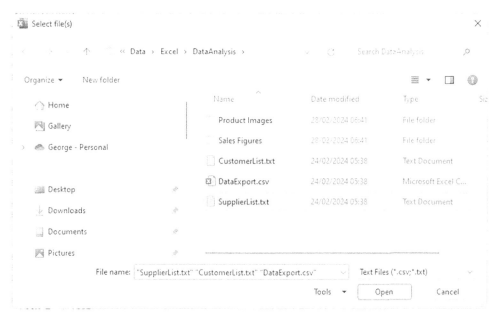

Figure 15-5: A File Picker dialog box allows you to return one or more file names.

When you select one or more files and click **Open**, the result is displayed in the Immediate window as shown below:

355

```
Immediate
C:\Data\Excel\DataAnalysis\CustomerList.txt
C:\Data\Excel\DataAnalysis\DataExport.csv
C:\Data\Excel\DataAnalysis\SupplierList.txt
```

Figure 15-6: The returned file names are displayed in the Immediate window.

Displaying Ribbon Dialog Boxes

You can use VBA to programmatically perform most actions in Excel that you could manually perform with commands on the ribbon. However, as your code executes the programmed actions, it does not display the built-in dialog boxes used to perform them manually. It would look really chaotic if different dialog boxes were opening and closing in a flash as your macro ran!

However, you may have scenarios where you want to display a ribbon command dialog box from code that allows users to manually perform an action. You can do this by using the **ExecuteMso** method of the **CommandBars** object.

Syntax

```
Application.CommandBars.ExecuteMso (idMso)
```

The **ExecuteMso** method executes the ribbon control specified in the **idMso** parameter. This method is useful for instances where Excel doesn't have an object model for a particular command. It works on built-in controls and dialog boxes.

The following code displays the **Format Cells** dialog box:

```
Application.CommandBars.ExecuteMso "FormatCellsDialog"
```

Chapter 15: Using Built-In Dialog Boxes

When the above code is executed, the Format Cells dialog box is displayed:

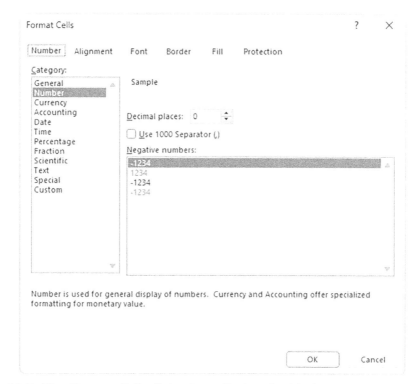

Figure 15-7: The Format Cells dialog box displayed with the ExecuteMso method.

Note that you can't transfer any setting selected in the dialog box to your code. Any actions performed by the user in the dialog box are directly applied to the active worksheet.

Excel will display an error message if you try executing a command in the wrong context using ExecuteMso. Excel's menu commands are context-dependent. Commands not applicable in certain contexts are greyed out (or disabled) on the ribbon. For example, the **Format Cells** dialog box is disabled when a chart is the active object. Consequently, Excel generates an error message if you try to display the Format Cells dialog box in code using this method when a chart is selected.

Excel Help does not provide a list of commands you can use as the argument for the idMso parameter. However, you can identify the name of a command you want to use by going to **Excel Options** > **Customize Ribbon**.

357

Mastering Excel VBA Programming

To open **Excel Options**, right-click anywhere on the ribbon and select **Customize the Ribbon**. In the list on the left, find and select the command you want to use. When you hover your mouse over the command, you'll get a tooltip that reveals the command's name in parentheses. In the case of the **Format Cells** dialog box, the argument we can use for the idMso parameter is **FormatCellsDialog**.

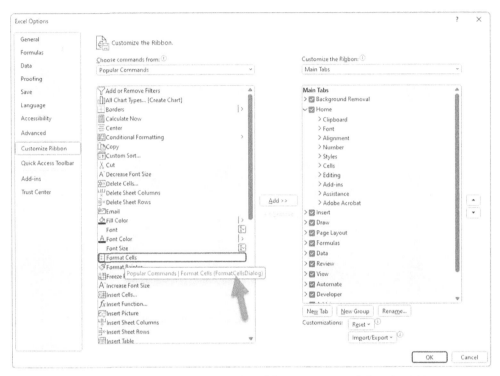

Figure 15-8: You can identify the name of a ribbon command for the idMso parameter by going to Excel Options > Customize Ribbon.

Chapter 16

Working with Excel Form Controls

In this chapter:

- Knowing the difference between form controls and UserForm controls.
- Using the List Box form control.
- Naming a form control.
- Using the Combo Box form control.
- Using the Spin Button form control.
- Using the Option Button form control.

You can add controls directly to an Excel worksheet to create an interactive user interface. For example, you can create a dropdown list in a cell to enable users to select values from the list. Excel Form controls are not part of the VBA language, as they can be used without writing code. However, some controls are useful for executing VBA procedures (or macros) from Excel's interface.

Introduction to Form Controls

Form controls are different from **UserForm** controls found in the VBA Toolbox. Form controls enable you to add automated functionality to your worksheet without writing VBA event procedures. Form controls do not have event procedures, but you can assign macros to run when a control is clicked. For example, you can assign a Sub procedure to a **Button** control that runs when users click it.

Form Controls can be found on the ribbon by selecting **Developer** > **Controls** > **Insert**, as shown in the image below:

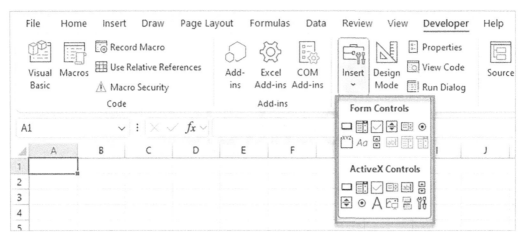

Figure 16-1: Form Controls in the Controls group on the Developer tab.

Naming a Form Control

When you create a Form control on your worksheet, Excel gives it a default name displayed in the **Name** box (on the left-hand side of the formula bar). Changing the name of a Form control is often unnecessary as they do not have event procedures for which you can write code. However, if you have several controls on a worksheet to keep track of, you can rename them.

To rename a Form control, right-click the control to put it in design mode, delete the default name in the Name box, type a new name, and press Enter.

Preparing the Data List

The sample data for the examples in this chapter can be found in the **FormControls_Solution.xlsm** workbook, which is included with the practice files for this book.

First, you need to create the data list to be used for the examples:

1. Create a new macro-enabled workbook and name it **FormControls.xlsm**.
2. In FormControls.xlsm, change the name of *Sheet1* to *Products*.
3. Copy and paste the data in the range A1:C20 from the *Products* sheet in FormControls_Solution.xlsm to the *Products* sheet in FormControls.xlsm. The data should look like the image below.

	A	B	C
1	**Product Name**	**Price**	**Qty In Stock**
2	Collection Belvoir Console Table	$413.00	9
3	Collection Bradley Riser Recline Fabric Chair	$519.00	6
4	Collection Martha Fabric Wingback Chair	$700.00	5
5	Collection New Bradley Manual Recliner Chair	$609.00	7
6	Collection New Malvern Console Table	$499.00	10
7	Cora Fabric Chair	$854.00	10
8	Fabric Chair	$348.00	5
9	Fabric Chair in a Box	$923.00	4
10	Fabric Chair in a Box - Denim Blue	$264.00	4
11	Fabric Tub Chair	$300.00	5
12	Fabric Wingback Chair	$247.00	9
13	Floral Fabric Tub Chair	$289.00	9
14	Habitat Oken Console Table	$786.00	10
15	Harley Fabric Cuddle Chair	$586.00	10
16	House Kent Oak Console Table	$859.00	10
17	Habitat Hyde Armchair	$898.00	5
18	Jesper Fabric Accent Chair - Yellow	$300.00	4
19	GFW Pettine Fabric Accent Chair - Blush Pink	$200.00	10
20	Aidapt Chelsfield Fabric Wingback Chair - Cream	$300.00	4
21			

< > **Products** | List Box | Combo box | Spin button | Option

Figure 16-2: The data list used for the examples in this chapter.

4. Select range A1:C20 and enter **ProductList** in the **Name** box (as shown in the image below). Naming the range enables you to use the name in formulas anywhere in the workbook without referencing the sheet name.

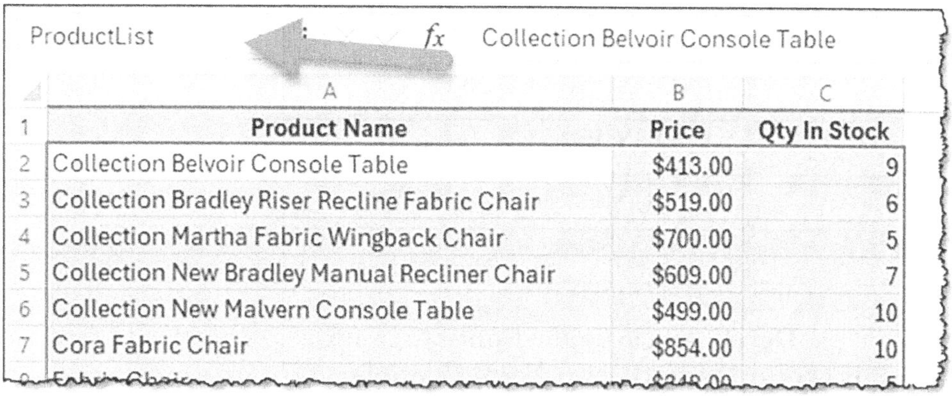

Chapter 16: Working with Excel Form Controls

	A	B	C
1	Product Name	Price	Qty In Stock
2	Collection Belvoir Console Table	$413.00	9
3	Collection Bradley Riser Recline Fabric Chair	$519.00	6
4	Collection Martha Fabric Wingback Chair	$700.00	5
5	Collection New Bradley Manual Recliner Chair	$609.00	7
6	Collection New Malvern Console Table	$499.00	10
7	Cora Fabric Chair	$854.00	10

ProductList — fx — Collection Belvoir Console Table

Figure 16-3: Naming the range enables you to use the name as an absolute reference.

ProductList is the data source used as the **Input range** for the Form controls covered in this chapter.

List Box Example

This example creates a list box that uses the range A2:A20 in **ProductList** as its input range. The index number of the selected item in the list box is used as an argument in formulas to retrieve items from different columns in ProductList.

Follow the steps below to add a list box to a worksheet:

1. Add a new worksheet to the workbook created in the previous section (FormControls.xlsm).

2. Enter the values in the table below in the new worksheet:

Cell	Value
A1	Product Name
B1	Price

363

C1	Qty In Stock
A2	=INDEX(ProductList,E1,1)
B2	=INDEX(ProductList,E1,2)
C2	=INDEX(ProductList,E1,3)
E1	1

3. On the **Developer** tab, in the **Controls** group, click **Insert**, and then select **List Box (Form Control)** under **Form Controls**.

4. Draw the list box on the worksheet, starting from cell A5 as its upper-left corner and about D12 as the lower-right corner.

> **Note** To resize the list box after initially drawing it, hover your mouse over one of the *sizing handles* (around its edges) until the pointer changes to a double-headed arrow, then drag to resize the control.

You can increase the width of column A to match the width of the list box, as the column size is independent of the controls on the worksheet.

5. Right-click the list box and select **Format Control**.

Figure 16-4: Opening the Format Control dialog box for the list box.

Chapter 16: Working with Excel Form Controls

6. In the **Format Control** dialog box, enter the following information:

   - In the input range box, enter **Products!A2:A20**.

   - In the **Cell link** box, enter **E1**.

     When an item is selected in the list box, the return value will be stored in cell E1. This value is an index number indicating the position of the selected item on the list. The INDEX formulas in cells A2, B2, and C2 use the value in E1 to return values from different columns in **ProductList**.

   - Under **Selection type**, ensure **Single** is selected.

     The **Multi** and **Extend** options are only useful when used with a macro that returns the values of the list. Also, the **3-D shading** setting is for adding a three-dimensional look to the list box.

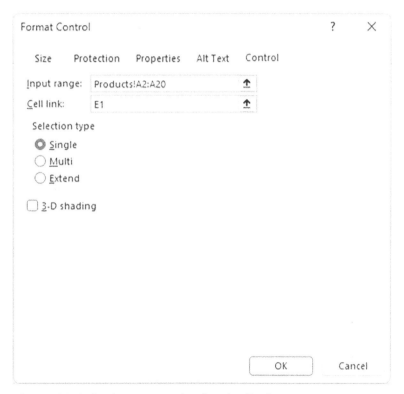

Figure 16-5: Setting properties for the list box.

7. Click **OK**.

365

The list box should now display the items from the range A2:A20 in the Products worksheet.

8. To activate the list box, click any cell on the worksheet. Excel exits the design mode of the list box, making it ready for use.

> **Note** You can right-click the list box to re-enter design mode at any point. When the list box is in design mode, it does not respond to clicks. To activate the list box, click any cell in the worksheet.

9. To test the list box, click an item on the list.

    - Cell **E1** is updated to a number representing the position of the selected item in the list box.

    - The INDEX formula in **A2** uses the value in E1 to retrieve the **product name** from range A2:A20 in the Products worksheet.

    - The formula in **B2** uses the value in E1 to retrieve and display the **price** of the selected item.

    - Finally, the formula in **C2** uses the value in E1 to retrieve the **quantity in stock** for the selected item.

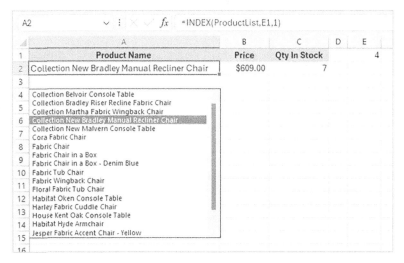

Figure 16-6: Setting properties for the list box.

Combo Box Example

This example creates a combo box Form control that uses the data list created previously, named **ProductList**, as its data source. The index number of the item selected in the combo box is used as an argument in formulas in the worksheet to retrieve and display items from different columns in ProductList.

Follow the steps below to add a combo box to a worksheet:

1. Add a new worksheet to the workbook used in the previous example (FormControls.xlsm).

2. Enter the values in the table below in the new worksheet:

Cell	**Value**
A1	Product Name
B1	Price
C1	Qty In Stock
A2	=INDEX(ProductList,E1,1)
B2	=INDEX(ProductList,E1,2)
C2	=INDEX(ProductList,E1,3)
E1	1

3. On the **Developer** tab, in the **Controls** group, click **Insert**, and then select **Combo Box (Form Control)** under **Form Controls**.

4. Draw the combo box on the worksheet in cells A4 to C4.

> **Note** To resize the combo box at any point, right-click the control to switch to design mode. Then, hover your mouse over one of its sizing handles until the pointer changes to a double-headed arrow, then drag to resize.

5. Increase the width of column A in the worksheet to match the width of the combo box so that it can fully display any name selected in the combo box. Resizing worksheet columns does not affect the size of Form controls on the worksheet.

6. Right-click the combo box and select **Format Control**.

7. In the **Format Control** dialog box, enter the following information:

    - In the input range box, enter **Products!A2:A20**.

    - In the **Cell link** box, enter **E1**.

        When an item is selected in the combo box, the return value is stored in cell E1. This value is an index number indicating the position of the selected item on the list. The INDEX formulas in cells A2, B2, and C2 use the value in E1 to return values from different columns in **ProductList**.

    - In the **Drop down lines** box, enter 10. This value specifies the number of items displayed in the dropdown list before you scroll to view the other items.

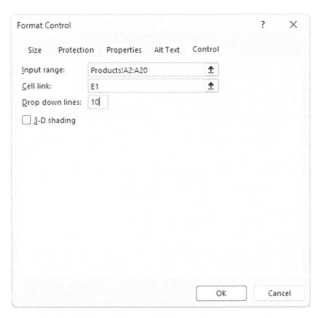

Figure 16-7: Setting properties for a combo box.

Chapter 16: Working with Excel Form Controls

8. Click **OK**.

9. To activate the combo box, click any cell on the worksheet. Excel exits the design mode of the combo box, making it ready for use.

> **Note** You can right-click the combo box to re-enter design mode at any point. When the combo box is in design mode, it doesn't respond to clicks.

10. Click the combo box to display the dropdown list, then select an item on the list.

    - Cell **E1** is updated to a number representing the position of the selected item in the combo box.

    - The INDEX formula in cell **A2** uses the number in E1 to retrieve the *product name* from range A2:A20 in the **Products** worksheet.

    - The formula in **B2** uses the number in E1 to retrieve the *price* of the selected item.

    - Finally, the formula in **C2** uses the number in E1 to retrieve the *quantity in stock* for the selected item.

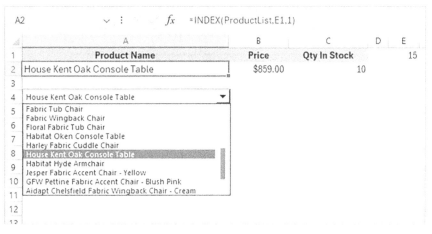

Figure 16-8: Using a combo box in Excel.

Spin Button Example

This example creates a **Spin Button** control that can increment or decrement a number in a cell. A spin button is useful as an input tool for worksheet entries within a defined range. For example, number of items, months, age, etc. In this example, the value derived from the spin button is used in INDEX formulas to retrieve items from different columns in a list.

Follow the steps below to add a spin button to a worksheet:

1. Add a new worksheet to the workbook used in the previous example, FormControls.xlsm.

2. Enter the values in the table below in the new worksheet:

Cell	Value
A1	Product Name
B1	Price
C1	Qty In Stock
A2	=INDEX(ProductList,E1,1)
B2	=INDEX(ProductList,E1,2)
C2	=INDEX(ProductList,E1,3)
E1	Record Index
E2	1

3. On the **Developer** tab, in the **Controls** group, click **Insert**, and then select **Spin Button (Form Control)** under **Form Controls**.

4. Draw the spin button on the worksheet in range A5:A6.

5. Increase the width of column A to about the width of four columns so that it can fully display any product names from ProductList. Resizing worksheet columns does not affect form controls on the worksheet.

Chapter 16: Working with Excel Form Controls

6. Right-click the spin button and select **Format Control**.

7. In the **Format Control** dialog box on the **Control** tab, enter the following information:

Setting	Value	Description
Current value	1	This value ensures the spin button's initial value points to the first item in the list.
Minimum value	1	Specifies the first item on the list, ensuring the spin button's top position is the first item in the list.
Maximum value	19	Specifies the maximum number of items in the list, ensuring the spin button doesn't go past the last item in the list.
Incremental change	1	This number specifies how much each click increments the current value.
Cell link	E2	Holds the current value of the spin button.
3-D shading	Checked	Gives the control a 3D look.

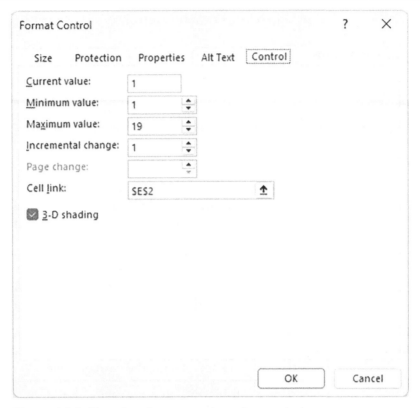

Figure 16-9: Entering format settings for a spin button.

8. Click **OK** to confirm your entries.

9. To activate the spin button, click any cell on the worksheet. Excel exits the design mode of the spin button, making it ready for use.

> **Note** To re-enter design mode at any point, right-click the control. When the spin button is in design mode, it doesn't respond to clicks.

10. Click the spin button up or down to change the value in cell E2.

    - The INDEX formula in cell A2 uses the number in E2 to retrieve the *product name* from range A2:A20 in the **Products** worksheet.

    - The formula in cell B2 uses the value in cell E2 to retrieve and display the *price* of the selected item.

- Finally, the formula in cell C2 uses the value in cell E2 to retrieve the *quantity in stock* for the selected item.

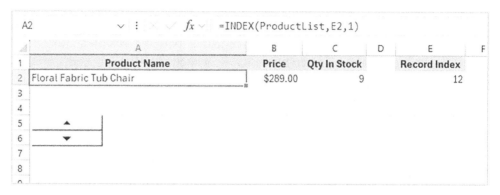

Figure 16-10: Using a spin button to scroll through a list.

Option Button Example

This example provides two option buttons that enable a user to change the style of a data table in Excel. The example involves recording two macros that are attached to the buttons. Each macro is executed when its associated button is clicked.

▶ Step 1: Create the Data Table

Follow the steps below to create the table for this example:

1. Add a new worksheet to the workbook used in the previous example, **FormControls.xlsm**.

2. Add data to the worksheet that looks like this table in range A1:D13:

Month	East	West	North
Jan	784	867	684
Feb	509	563	890
Mar	553	679	985
Apr	984	965	923
May	910	941	623
Jun	603	762	620
Jul	504	767	809
Aug	658	686	612
Sep	849	817	594
Oct	772	528	979
Nov	506	695	511
Dec	621	557	782

3. Convert the range to an Excel table.

Chapter 16: Working with Excel Form Controls

i. Select any cell in the list.
ii. On the Excel ribbon, select **Insert > Tables > Table**.

Figure 16-11: The Create Table dialog box.

iii. In the **Create Table** dialog box, ensure the range A1:A13 is selected, and then select **OK**.

4. Name the list. On the worksheet, select the range A2:A13. In the **Name** box, type "DataList", and then press Enter.

▶ **Step 2: Place Two Option Buttons in the Worksheet**

Follow the steps below to place option buttons in the worksheet:

1. Insert two **Option Button** controls in the worksheet in range F3:F5.

   On the **Developer** tab, in the **Controls** group, select **Insert > Option Button (Form Control)**.

2. Name the option buttons.

   Right-click the first option button to enter design mode. In the **Name** box of the worksheet, type in **optStyleOne** and press Enter. Using the same method, name the second option button **OptStyleTwo**.

3. Edit the text of the option buttons.

   Right-click optStyleOne, select **Edit Text** and then change its text to **Style One**. Using the same method, change the text of OptStyleTwo to **Style Two**.

4. Draw a **Group Box** control around the option buttons, as shown in the image below.

375

On the **Developer** tab, in the **Controls** group, select **Insert > Group Box (Form Control)**.

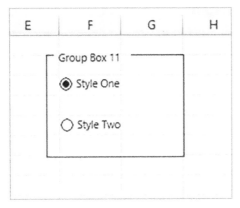

Figure 16-12: Adding option buttons to a worksheet.

5. Right-click the text of the group box, select **Edit Text** on the shortcut menu, and change the text to **Style Options**.

Your worksheet should look like the image below at this point:

	A	B	C	D	E	F	G	H
1	Month	East	West	North		Format Option		
2	Jan	784	866	684				
3	Feb	509	563	890		● Style One		
4	Mar	553	679	985				
5	Apr	984	965	923		○ Style Two		
6	May	910	941	623				
7	Jun	603	762	620				
8	Jul	504	767	809				
9	Aug	658	686	612				
10	Sep	849	817	594				
11	Oct	772	528	979				
12	Nov	506	695	511				
13	Dec	621	557	782				
14								

Figure 16-13: Using option buttons to select list styles.

Chapter 16: Working with Excel Form Controls

▶ **Step 3: Record Macros That Change the Table Style**

1. On the **Developer** tab, in the **Code** group, select **Record Macro**.

2. In the **Record Macro** dialog box, name the macro **StyleOne**.

3. In the **Store macro in** box, select **This Workbook**.

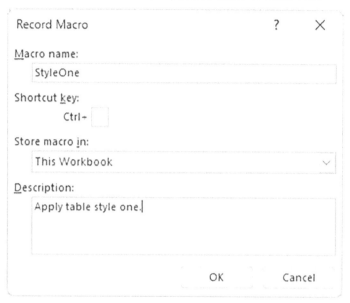

Figure 16-14: Recording a macro that will be used with an option button.

4. Click **OK**.

5. Perform the following actions to record the macro:

   i. Select the table added to the worksheet in Step 1 above.

   ii. On the **Table Design** tab, in the **Table Styles** group, click the **Quick Styles** dropdown and select a style for the table.

   For this example, StyleOne is the third item on the first row of the **Quick Styles** menu named *Table Style Light 2*.

   iii. On the **Developer** tab, select **Stop Recording**.

6. Repeat steps 1 to 5 above to record a second macro named **StyleTwo**. For StyleTwo, select the fifth item on the first row of the **Quick Styles** menu, named *Table Style Light 4*.

377

Excel generates the following macro for StyleOne:

```
Sub StyleOne()
'
' StyleOne Macro
' Style one to format list.
'
    Range("DataList[#All]").Select
    ActiveSheet.ListObjects("DataList").TableStyle = _
"TableStyleLight2"
    Range("A1").Select
End Sub
```

The following macro is generated for StyleTwo:

```
Sub StyleTwo()
'
' StyleTwo Macro
' Style two to format list.
'
  Range("DataList[#All]").Select
  ActiveSheet.ListObjects("DataList").TableStyle = _
"TableStyleLight4"
    Range("A1").Select
End Sub
```

▶ **Step 4: Add Code to the Option Buttons**

Follow the steps below to assign the recorded macros to the option buttons:

1. Right-click the option button named **optStyleOne**, and then select **Assign Macro**.

Chapter 16: Working with Excel Form Controls

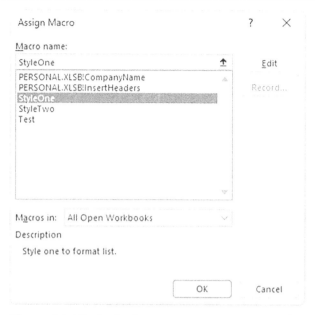

Figure 16-15: Assigning a macro to an option button.

2. In the **Assign Macro** dialog box, select the macro named **StyleOne** and click **OK**.

3. Carry out steps 1-2 above for the option button named **optStyleTwo** while selecting the macro named **StyleTwo**.

▶ **Step 5: Test the option buttons**

1. Click any cell in the worksheet to exit design mode and activate the option buttons.

2. Click the option buttons. The table style should change appropriately.

Note This is a lengthy example that has many steps. If you encounter an error when you click the option buttons, examine the code for the macros in the Visual Basic Editor and fix any issues. It is not unusual to encounter errors when you record a macro, but they are usually easy to identify and fix in the Visual Basic Editor.

379

Chapter 17

Accessing External Data with ADO

In this chapter:

- Working with data in VBA – an overview.
- Introducing ActiveX Data Objects (ADO).
- Retrieving data from a data source.
- Using the Connection and Recordset objects.
- Understanding the different recordset cursor types and lock types.
- Navigating through records in a recordset.
- Opening a recordset with an SQL query.
- Trapping and handling data access errors.

Chapter 17: Accessing External Data with ADO

In this chapter, you will learn how to programmatically connect to an external data source and retrieve data for your Excel application using ActiveX Data Objects (ADO). ADO enables you to connect to an external data source and retrieve just the data you need to work with. You can manipulate the data in Excel and save any changes to the external data source. ADO can connect to different types of external data sources. For example, your external data can be in a Microsoft Access database or a Microsoft SQL Server database.

Where to Store Data

Many applications you'll create will involve storing and managing data. You can store data in Excel or an external database if the data is too large for Excel. You may also need to work with existing data stored in other formats that you can change. OLE DB enables you to access data in different formats. The OLE DB architecture is described later in this chapter.

There are several options for data storage, but if you're working with Microsoft applications, your options are likely Excel, Access, or a database server like Microsoft SQL Server. In this chapter, you'll learn how to retrieve data from Access and SQL Server.

Storing Data in Excel

If you have a small amount of data to store and use with your application, Excel may be the best tool to store the data. When the data is local to the application, it's easier and faster to access and use. Excel is also the best place to store data that does not conform to a relational data structure, such as charts and other graphical data.

Excel is not the best tool for storing larger data sets, but it is one of the best tools for analyzing data, creating charts, and other formats. Hence, even with large data sets that cannot be stored in Excel, we need an easy method to access and use the data in Excel. You can access data in other file formats using OLE DB or ODBC connections and then use Excel's data analysis tools to work with the data.

Excel Versus Relational Databases

If you are building an application from scratch that stores data, you need to determine where the data will be stored. Since we're working with Excel, it may make sense to store the data in Excel worksheets, but as discussed previously, Excel is not always the best tool for storing data. Sometimes, developers store data in Excel when a relational database solution would have been better.

When deciding whether to use Excel or a relational database to store data for your project, consider the following questions:

- Do you need to store transactions?

    Relational databases are better for storing transactions. For example, do you have orders with several order lines? If so, it would be best to store the data in a relational database where orders and order lines can be stored in different linked tables to avoid data duplication.

- Do you anticipate an expansion that may include a lot more data in the future?

    If you anticipate an expansion of the system, the data could become too large and complex for Excel. In such a case, a relational database may be a better option. A relational database like Microsoft Access is more scalable. For example, Access has a 2 GB maximum file size limit, but you can work around the size limit by linking to tables in other Access databases, each of which can be as large as 2 GB. There are also no limits to how many records you can store in an Access table. Conversely, there is a limit to the number of rows you can create in Excel. Excel's data model's component can only go up to 700 MB before you begin to experience performance issues.

- Does your application need to archive data?

    Relational databases like Access or SQL Server are better for applications requiring data archiving. Excel might be more suitable if your application deletes data without archiving it. For example, if you import forex data from the Internet daily and discard the data at the end of the day, Excel might be more suitable.

- Do you need data validation on data entry?

    You can create UserForms in Excel to perform validation checks when entering data. However, extensive work is required to create something as effective as the built-in data validation features in Access. You can insert data validation and other constraints in a table design in Access to prevent users from entering invalid data.

You have several options if you store your data in a relational database. You can use Access, SQL Server Express, or SQL Server.

Tip: SQL Server Express is targeted for smaller-scale deployments and is suitable for desktop PC use. It is also free for commercial use.

Note: Relational database design is outside the scope of this book. If you want a comprehensive guide on creating an Access database, see my book, *Mastering Access 365*.

Working with Data

You can import external data directly into Excel or connect to the data programmatically. ADO enables you to retrieve data from an external data source and either import it into Excel or store it in memory for use in your application.

Manually Importing External Data

Occasionally, you may have data in a database file format with interoperability issues with Excel. Instead of grappling with difficult methods of connecting to the data from Excel, you could export the data to a compatible file format. Comma-separated values (CSV) files can easily be imported into Excel, Access, or SQL Server. Excel provides many features for manually importing data. The menu options enable you to import data from various sources, including text/CSV files, Access database, SQL Server, Web pages, ODBC, PDF, etc.

To manually import data into Excel, select **Data > Get & Transform > Get Data**.

Excel's performance can be significantly affected if a workbook contains too much data. If you have hundreds of thousands of records to work with, it would be better to keep the data in the external data source and only import the records you need to work with. Excel provides a powerful query tool called the Power Query Editor, which allows you to connect an external data source and retrieve only certain rows and columns by applying filters.

> **Note** An in-depth coverage of how to manually import external data is outside the scope of this book. However, if you need detailed instructions on importing data from different formats, including using the Power Query Editor, see my book *Mastering Excel 365*.

Using ActiveX Data Objects (ADO)

The best way to programmatically access external data in Excel is to use ADO. ADO is flexible and allows you to access ODBC and non-ODBC-compliant data sources.

With ADO, you can copy the data into the worksheet or store it in memory and perform different types of operations on the data, including viewing, adding, updating, and deleting records.

The rest of this chapter focuses on using ADO to retrieve data in an Excel application.

Overview of ADO

ActiveX Data Object (ADO) is the data access method used in most Office applications. ADO is the data access method for Microsoft Visual Basic 6.0, from which VBA was derived. So, naturally, it became the data access method for VBA. The ADO object model provides objects and collections that enable you to connect Excel to a data source, fetch and manipulate data, and disconnect from the data source when you're done.

Chapter 17: Accessing External Data with ADO

This section covers an overview of the ADO object model and OLE DB technology. OLE DB allows you to access different types of data stores using a standard approach.

Overview of OLE DB

Object Linking and Embedding Database (OLE DB) is an application programming interface (API) designed by Microsoft to access data from various sources in a standardized manner. OLE DB makes universal data access possible. Conversely, Open Database Connectivity (ODBC) is a system that allows you to connect to relational databases. ADO provides an interface between data consumers, such as Excel and OLE DB data.

At the abstract level, OLE DB has three types of components:

- Data Consumers
- Service Components
- Data Providers

The following illustration is an overview of the OLE DB architecture, showing how ADO fits into the structure:

385

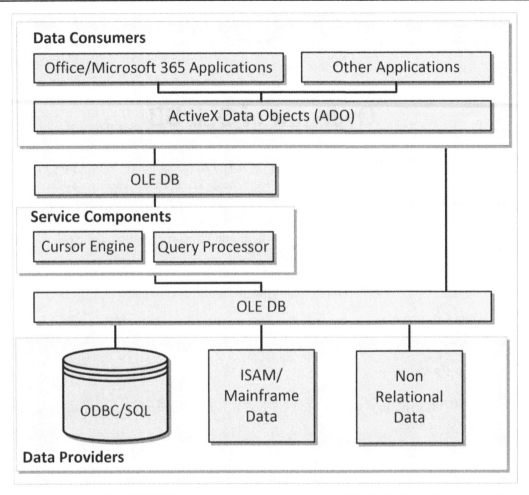

Figure 17-1: The OLE DB architecture showing how ADO fits into the hierarchy.

Data Consumers

Data consumers are applications that need to connect to data sources that provide an OLE DB interface. ADO is the data access method that provides the programming interface for connecting to OLE DB data. Hence, applications that use ADO for data access are OLE DB data consumers.

Service Components

A service provider does not store data but serves as a consumer and provider. A type of service provider called a service component processes and transports data between data consumers and data providers. These components include cursor engines and query processors.

OLE DB is organized into separate components so that data providers don't need the inherent ability to provide data in every way an ADO may want to access it. Service components allow ADO to access OLE DB data from providers that don't offer the handling of result sets or interpreting SQL queries.

Data Providers

Data providers are data sources like Microsoft Access, SQL Server, Oracle, ODBC data, or other types of file systems with data that other applications may need to access. Each data provider type must provide an OLE DB-compliant interface that data consumers or service components can access. A consistent interface ensures data consumers (applications) don't require different access methods for different data providers. Data consumers only need an OLE DB-compliant method (like ADO) to access various data sources.

The ADO Object Model

The ADO object hierarchy provides objects and collections that you can use to access all types of data.

The following image shows the ADO object model and how the objects and collections relate to each other:

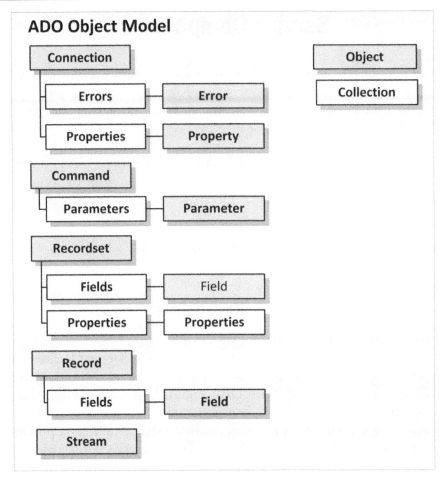

Figure 17-2: The ADO object model.

The three ADO objects you're most likely to use are the **Connection** object, the **Command** object, and the **Recordset** object.

The Connection Object

The highest object in the ADO object hierarchy is the **Connection** object. It establishes a connection between the application and a data source like an Access, SQL Server, or Oracle database.

The Recordset Object

The **Recordset** object is used to programmatically access the records returned from a database. You can use the Recordset object to navigate, edit, add, or delete records.

Recordset objects are made up of rows and columns, also called records and fields. You can move through a recordset one record at a time with the **MoveNext** and **MovePrevious** methods. You can also use the **Move**, **MoveFirst**, and **MoveLast** methods to move through a recordset. As you navigate a recordset, you can use the **BOF** (beginning-of-file) and **EOF** (end-of-file) properties to check that you don't move beyond the beginning or end of the **Recordset** object.

Setting a Reference to the ADO Library

Before using ADO in your workbook, you need to set a reference to the ADO object library.

Follow the steps below to set a reference to the ADO library:

1. Press Alt+F11 to switch to the Visual Basic Editor.
2. In the Project Explorer window, select the VBA project where you want to add ADO code.
3. On the Visual Basic Editor menu, select **Tools** > **References**.
4. In the **References** dialog box, scroll down and select **Microsoft ActiveX Data Objects 6.1 Library**, and select **OK**.

The Microsoft ActiveX Data Objects 6.1 Library is the latest ADO library at the time of this writing.

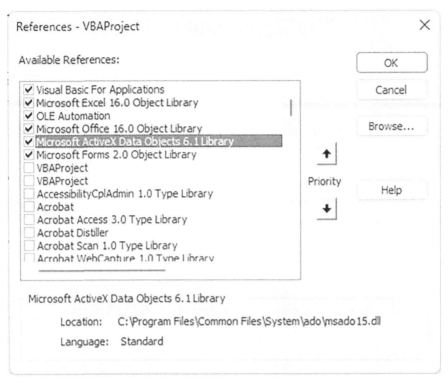

Figure 17-3: Setting a reference to the ADO Library.

Retrieving Data from a Data Source

In this section, we'll cover how to establish a connection to a data source, create a recordset, and navigate through its records. We'll also cover examples of referencing fields and data in recordsets.

Creating a Connection

One of the first things you must do to access data with ADO is to establish a connection to the data source with a **Connection** object. Establishing a connection involves setting properties of the Connection object, such as the data type and location, and then opening the connection. After creating the Connection object, you can use the connection to create one or more recordsets.

The illustration below shows the relationship between a recordset and a connection object:

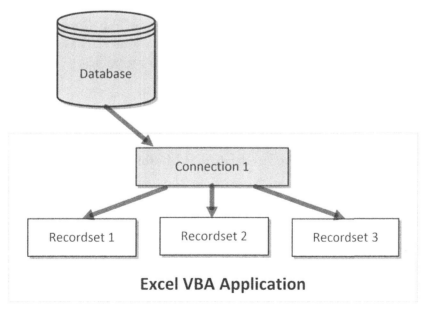

Figure 17-4: The relationship between a recordset and a connection object.

Declaring a Connection Object

To create a connection to a data source, you must first declare a Connection object in your code and then create a new instance of the object. We will be working with an Access database named **HighlandFurniture.accdb**.

> **Note** You can find the HighlandFurniture.accdb Access database with the practice files for Chapter 17.

In the example code below, the variable connHF is declared as a **Connection** data type. The next line then uses the **Set** statement to instantiate a new **Connection** object:

```
Dim connHF As ADODB.Connection
Set connHF = New ADODB.Connection
```

Setting Connection Properties

To establish a connection, you have to set properties of the **Connection** object that specify the information required to connect to the data source. These properties include the **Provider** and the **ConnectionString**, among other properties.

Property	Description
Provider	This property is the name of the OLE DB provider for the connection. For example, the current OLE DB provider for an Access database is **Microsoft.ACE.OLEDB.12.0**. The OLE DB provider for an SQL Server database is **SQLOLEDB**.
ConnectionString	Specifies the information required to connect to a data source, such as the provider, file path, userID, etc. The required connection string parameters can be different depending on the data source being accessed.

Chapter 17: Accessing External Data with ADO

For a comprehensive list of ADO Connection object properties, search for "Connection Object Properties, Methods, and Events" in VBA online Help.

The following example code sets the Provider property for the **connHF** connection to the OLE DB data provider used for Microsoft Access:

```
connHF.Provider = "Microsoft.ACE.OLEDB.12.0"
```

Opening the Connection

After specifying the data provider for your Connection object, use its **Open** method to open a connection to the data source by passing the database path in the *ConnectionString* parameter. The following example code opens a connection to the **HighlandFurniture.accdb**:

```
connHF.Open "C:\Data\AccessDBs\HighlandFurniture.accdb"
```

Alternatively, you can put all the connection information in the **ConnectionString** property, as shown below:

```
connHF.ConnectionString = "Provider=Microsoft.ACE.OLEDB.12.0;" & _
        "Data Source= C:\Data\AccessDBs\HighlandFurniture.accdb;" & _
        "Persist Security Info=False;"
```

If you provided all the connection information in the **ConnectionString** property, call the **Open** method with no arguments, as shown below:

```
connHF.Open
```

> **Note** If you have used ADO before, you may be familiar with the Jet database engine used with Microsoft Office applications. Jet does not work with 64-bit Office installations. Therefore, the Access Connectivity Engine (ACE), which supports both 32-bit and 64-bit architectures, has superseded Jet. The ACE Provider is installed by default with 64-bit versions of Microsoft 365.

Creating a Recordset

A **Recordset** object allows you to use a **Connection** object to retrieve data from a table or an SQL query in a data source. The Recordset object allows you to navigate the records and perform various actions to manipulate the data.

Similar to a Connection object, to create a Recordset object, you must first declare a variable as a Recordset type before instantiating a new Recordset object.

The following example code declares and creates a new instance of a Recordset object:

```
Dim rsCustomers As ADODB.Recordset
Set rsCustomers = New ADODB.Recordset
```

Note that the **Set** statements and **New** keyword are used to create a new instance of a Recordset object. If the rsCustomers variable previously contained a Recordset object, it is released when the new Recordset object is created.

After creating a new instance of a recordset, you use the **Open** method of the Recordset object to open it.

You need to provide the following Recordset object properties to open a recordset:

- **Source**: This string value specifies the subset of data to be returned from the connection. The string could be a table name, an SQL statement, a predefined query, or a stored procedure.
- **ActiveConnection**: This value determines the Connection object to be used to open the recordset, which would be the Connection object you created earlier in the procedure.

The example below opens the recordset by providing "tblCustomers" as the **Source** and connHF as the **ActiveConnection**:

```
rsCustomers.Open "tblCustomers", connHF
```

Opening a recordset based on external data could generate errors for different reasons. For example, the data source may not be at the specified location, it may have been moved, or the ConnectionString may contain errors. Therefore, including an error handling routine to data access code in a production application is important. The error handler allows you to trap and process the error, including providing information or instructions to the user before gracefully exiting the procedure. Error handling for data access code is covered later in this chapter.

Closing the Recordset and Connection

After opening and using a recordset in your code, you need to close the recordset and remove it from memory. A cleanup process ensures the recordset does not waste computer memory or keep one or more tables in the data source locked. To close a recordset, call the **Close** method of the Recordset object. Then, to remove it from memory, set the object to **Nothing**.

Likewise, after using a connection, close it using its **Close** method. Then, remove it from memory by setting it to **Nothing**.

The example code below shows how to close a Recordset object and a Connection object and remove them from memory:

```
rsCustomers.Close
connHF.Close
Set rsCustomers = Nothing
Set connHF = Nothing
```

Transferring records to a Worksheet

When retrieving data with ADO, it is often necessary to copy the data to a worksheet so that you can work with it. Suppose you want to create a PivotTable with the data returned from a recordset. You can't make the Recordset object the data source of the PivotTable in Excel. Instead, you must insert the data into a worksheet and then base the PivotTable on the worksheet.

You can use the **CopyFromRecordset** method of the Range object to copy the records from a Recordset object to your worksheet. The method inserts the contents of the recordset into the worksheet starting at the upper-left cell of the specified range.

Syntax:

expression.CopyFromRecordset(*Data, MaxRows, MaxColumns*)

The object qualifier *expression* represents a Range object.

Description of Parameters

Name	Description
Data	Required. Specifies the Recordset object to copy onto the worksheet.
MaxRows	Optional. Specifies the maximum number of rows to copy onto the worksheet. If this argument is omitted, all the records in the recordset are copied to the worksheet.
MaxColumns	Optional. Specifies the maximum number of columns to copy onto the worksheet. If this argument is omitted, all the columns in the recordset are copied to the worksheet.

Assuming the recordset you've created is named rsCustomers, you can use the following example code to copy all retrieved data to Sheet1 of the active workbook, starting from range A1:

```
Worksheets("Sheet1").Range("A1").CopyFromRecordset rsCustomers
```

The example in the next section demonstrates how to use the **CopyFromRecordset** method to copy data from an ADO recordset to an Excel worksheet.

Retrieving Microsoft Access Data with a Recordset

This example connects to the Highland Furniture Access database (HighlandFurniture.accdb) and creates a recordset based on the table tblCustomers. Then, the procedure copies the data onto Sheet1 of the active Excel workbook.

Chapter 17: Accessing External Data with ADO

> **Note** The **HighlandFurniture.accdb** Access database can be found in the folder for the practice files for Chapter 17.

Follow the steps below to create the procedure:

1. Create a new Excel Macro-Enabled Workbook and name it **ADOData.xlsm** or another name you choose.
2. Open the Visual Basic Editor (**Developer** > **Code** > **Visual Basic**).
3. In the Project Explorer window, select the VBA project for ADOData.xlsm (or the workbook you're using).
4. Right-click and select **Insert** > **Module** to insert a new module.
5. Insert the following code in the new module.

```
Sub AccessConnection()
    Dim connHF As ADODB.Connection
    Dim rsCustomers As ADODB.Recordset
    
    'Create a new instance of a Connection object
    Set connHF = New ADODB.Connection
    
    'Set the Provider for Microsoft Access
    connHF.Provider = "Microsoft.ACE.OLEDB.12.0"
    
    'Open a connection to the database
    connHF.Open "C:\Data\AccessDBs\HighlandFurniture.accdb"
    
    'Instantiate a new recordset object
    Set rsCustomers = New ADODB.Recordset
    
    'Open the tblCustomers table
    rsCustomers.Open "tblCustomers", connHF
    
    'Copy the records to Sheet1 in the active workbook
    With Worksheets("Sheet1")
        .Cells.ClearContents
        .Range("A1").CopyFromRecordset rsCustomers
    End With
    
    'Close the recordset and connection
    rsCustomers.Close
    connHF.Close
    Set rsCustomers = Nothing
```

```
        Set connHF = Nothing
End Sub
```

The code above performs the following actions:

- The first two lines in the procedure declare the variables for the Connection object and Recordset object.

- A new instance of a **Connection** object is created with the **Set** statement and the **New** keyword.

- The **Provider** property for the Connection object is set to **Microsoft.ACE.OLEDB.12.0** (the current OLE DB provider for Office applications).

- The connection is opened by specifying the Access file location in the **ConnectionString** parameter of the Connection object's **Open** method. Change this file path to the location of the database on your computer.

- The **Set** statement is used to instantiate a new Recordset object.

- The recordset is opened with the **Open** method, passing in "tblCustomers" as the **Source** parameter and connHF as the **ActiveConnection** parameter.

- With the recordset now open, we can use the data in our application. For this example, the returned records are copied to Sheet1 of the active workbook using the **CopyFromRecordset** method.

- Finally, the cleanup routine closes the **Recordset** and **Connection** objects and sets both variables to **Nothing**. The cleanup ensures the data is removed from memory and any lock on the source data is removed.

Returning Field Headers

To return field headers with a recordset, use the **Fields** collection of the **Recordset** object to return the **Name** property of each field. The following code is similar to the previous example. However, the code also returns the field headers by looping through the **Fields** collection of the recordset and inserting field names in the first row of the worksheet. The records start from the second row.

```
Sub ReturnFieldHeaders()
    'Set connection to a new Connection object
    Dim connHF As ADODB.Connection
    Dim rsCustomers As ADODB.Recordset
    Dim i As Long


    'Set connection to a new Connection object
    Set connHF = New ADODB.Connection

    'Set the Provider for Microsoft Access
    connHF.Provider = "Microsoft.ACE.OLEDB.12.0"

    'Open a connection to the database
    '**Change path for your database**
    connHF.Open "C:\Data\AccessDBs\HighlandFurniture.accdb"

    'Instantiate a new recordset object
    Set rsCustomers = New ADODB.Recordset

    'Open the tblCustomers table
    rsCustomers.Open "tblCustomers", connHF

    'Paste the recordset data in Sheet1
    With Worksheets("Sheet1")
        .Cells.ClearContents

        'Return the field headers for the recordset
        For i = 0 To rsCustomers.Fields.Count - 1
            .Range("A1").Offset(0, i).Value = _
                rsCustomers.Fields(i).Name
        Next i
        .Range("A2").CopyFromRecordset rsCustomers
    End With

    'Close the recordset and connection
    rsCustomers.Close
    connHF.Close
    Set rsCustomers = Nothing
    Set connHF = Nothing
End Sub
```

Additional Recordset Properties

You can use additional properties of the Recordset object to control the behavior of a recordset. This section describes the **CursorType** and **LockType** properties, which you can set when opening a recordset:

CursorType Property

The value specified for the **CursorType** property of the Recordset object determines how the recordset works. For example, a static cursor returns a static set of records that you can use to find data or generate reports. Changes by other users while you open the recordset will not be visible to you.

You can set the **CursorType** property before opening the recordset, or you can specify it in the *CursorType* parameter of the **Open** method when opening the recordset. If a cursor type is not specified, the default cursor type used by ADO is **adOpenForwardOnly**.

The following table lists the CursorType constants you can use to open a recordset:

CursorType	Value	Description
adOpenForwardOnly	0	Default. Similar to a static cursor, but you can only scroll forward through the recordset. You can't make changes. This is the default cursor if this property is omitted.
adOpenKeyset	1	Similar to a dynamic cursor. You can't see records added or removed, but you can see changed records.
adOpenDynamic	2	A dynamic cursor allows you to see changes to the records by other users. You can also change the records.
adOpenStatic	3	A static cursor retrieves a copy of the records. You can scroll forward and back but can't change the records. Useful for static reports.

LockType Property

The **LockType** property determines how records are locked as you work with them. This property is only required if you intend to update the data. You can omit this property for a read-only recordset, as ADO uses **adlockReadOnly** by default if a lock type is not provided.

Not all data providers support the lock types requested by ADO. If a provider does not support the requested LockType setting, it will use an equivalent type of locking that it supports.

The following table is a list of LockType constants you can use in ADO:

Constant	Value	Description
adLockUnspecified	-1	No lock type is specified. Used mainly for clones that inherit the lock type of the original recordset.
adLockReadOnly	1	Default. Records are read-only. You cannot change the data.
adLockPessimistic	2	Specifies a pessimistic lock, record by record. The record is locked as soon as editing begins and only released after the **Update** method is called.
adLockOptimistic	3	Specifies an optimistic lock, one record at a time. Records are only locked when an **Update** method is called.
adLockBatchOptimistic	4	Specifies an optimistic lock, which fetches a set of records at once, allowing you to change multiple records and then apply them in a batch. This lock type is required for batch updates.

To see a complete list of members of the Recordset object, search for "Recordset" in the Object Browser.

Accessing Data in Recordsets

When working with a recordset, you can reference the fields of each record programmatically in your code. Each Recordset object has a **Fields** collection representing the **Field** objects in a record or row of data.

The following example accesses the field called CompanyName in the rsCustomers recordset:

```
rsCustomers.Fields("CompanyName")
```

A faster way to access a field is to reference the field's name directly rather than through the Fields collection of the Recordset object. The code below uses a direct reference to access the CompanyName field of the rsCustomers recordset:

```
rsCustomers!CompanyName
```

To reference field names that include spaces using the direct reference method, enclose the field name in square brackets, as shown below:

```
rsCustomers![Company Name]
```

After retrieving records with a recordset, you can access the fields and display their values to the user. For instance, suppose that you have a UserForm in which you want to display data returned from a recordset. You can programmatically access the recordset fields and assign the values to text box controls on the UserForm. You have to repeat the process as the user scrolls through the recordset.

The example below populates two text boxes on a UserForm called CustomersForm with values from a recordset:

```
CustomersForm.FirstNameText.Text = rsCustomers!FirstName
CustomersForm.LastNameText.Text = rsCustomers!LastName
```

Navigating Records

In a recordset, only one record can be accessed at a time, called the *current record*. The first record is the current record by default when you open a recordset. When navigating through a recordset, a *record pointer* indicates which record is the current record in the recordset. A **Recordset** object has several methods and properties that allow you to move to specific records in the recordset. You can use five methods to navigate through a recordset: **MoveFirst**, **MoveLast**, **MovePrevious**, **MoveNext**, and **Move**.

The following illustration shows the various move methods and properties used to navigate through a recordset:

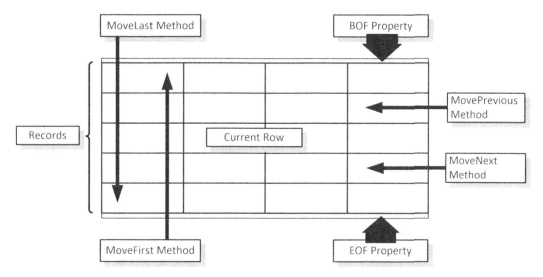

Figure 17-5: The different methods and properties used to navigate a recordset.

Using Move Methods

You can use move methods to navigate through a recordset sequentially or jump to specific records. The table below describes the various move methods and the actions they perform:

Method	What it does
Move	Moves the record pointer by a specified number of rows, which becomes the current record. You specify the number of rows to move the record pointer with the **NumRecords** parameter. A positive number moves forward, while a negative number moves backward.
MoveFirst	Moves the record pointer to the first record in the recordset. This record becomes the current record.
MoveLast	Moves the record pointer to the last record in the recordset. This record becomes the current record.
MoveNext	Moves the record pointer forward by one record in the recordset. This record becomes the current record. If the current record is the last one, MoveNext moves the pointer after the last record and sets the **EOF** property to True. Attempting to move forward past this point generates an error.
MovePrevious	Moves the record pointer one position backward towards the top of the recordset. This record becomes the current record. If the current record is the first in the recordset, MovePrevious moves the record pointer before the first record and sets the **BOF** property to True. An attempt to move backward past this point generates an error.

Note To move backward through a recordset, you must open it with a cursor type that supports backward movement. If you open a recordset without specifying a CursorType, ADO uses the default cursor **adOpenForwardOnly**, which doesn't support moving backward.

You can use move methods to create navigation buttons on a UserForm that displays records from a recordset. The navigation buttons enable the user to scroll through the recordset and work the records on the UserForm.

The following example code uses the Click event of a button to move to the next record in the rsCustomers recordset:

Chapter 17: Accessing External Data with ADO

```
Private Sub NextButton_Click()
    rsCustomers.MoveNext
    PopulateControls
End Sub
```

The PopulateControls procedure in the example above is used to repopulate the controls on the UserForm each time the current record is changed.

The code below uses the Click event of a button to move to the previous record in a recordset and then repopulates the controls in the dialog box:

```
Private Sub PreviousButton_Click()
    rsCustomers.MovePrevious
    PopulateControls
End Sub
```

BOF and EOF Properties

You use the **BOF** (beginning-of-file) and **EOF** (end-of-file) properties to ensure you don't move beyond the limits of a recordset when navigating through it with move methods. You can also use BOF and EOF properties to check whether a Recordset object has any records.

When you open a recordset, the current record defaults to the first record (if the recordset has records), while the BOF and EOF properties are set to False. As you move through the recordset, if the record pointer goes before the first record, the BOF property is set to True. Likewise, the EOF property is set to True when the record pointer goes after the last record. Thus, you can use these properties to determine when you're at the beginning or end of the recordset.

The following code ensures the button named PreviousButton never goes beyond the first record of the rsCustomers recordset when clicked:

```
Private Sub PreviousButton_Click()
    ' Move to the previous record
    rsCustomers.MovePrevious

    'If the current record position is at the beginning of the file
    ' set it to the first record.
```

```
    If rsCustomers.BOF Then
        rsCustomers.MoveFirst
    End If
End Sub
```

In the code example above, when the user clicks the button, the record pointer moves to the previous record in the recordset. The routine then checks whether the record pointer is before the first record. If it is (i.e., BOF is set to True), the record pointer is then set to the first record in the recordset using the MoveFirst method. Checking the BOF property ensures that the procedure never tries to move beyond the beginning of the recordset. The EOF property returns True if the record pointer is at a position after the last record. The BOF and EOF properties are set to True if the recordset returns no records.

In the code example below, the button named **NextButton** can be used to navigate to the next record in the rsCustomers recordset:

```
Private Sub NextButton_Click()
    'Move to the next record
    rsCustomers.MoveNext

    'Populate the controls with the new values
    If Not rsCustomers.EOF Then
        PopulateControls
    End If

    'Check to see if the record pointer
    'moved beyond the last record
    If rsCustomers.EOF Then
        rsCustomers.MoveLast
    End If
End Sub
```

In the example above, the user cannot move beyond the last record because the MoveLast method sets the current record to the last record whenever EOF is True.

Looping Through All Records

You can loop through the records in a recordset with one of VBA's looping structures. The following code loops through all records in the rsCustomers recordset using a **Do...Loop** statement and prints the values in the CompanyName field to the Immediate Window:

```
'loop through records
Do Until rsCustomers.EOF
   Debug.Print rsCustomers!CompanyName
   rsCustomers.MoveNext
Loop
```

Filtering Records

You can use the **Filter** property to filter a recordset and limit the returned records. The full recordset is still available in memory, but only those that meet the filter's criteria are displayed as part of the recordset.

The following code filters the recordset to only show customers located in CA (California):

```
rsCustomers.Filter = "State= 'CA'"
```

Removing a Filter

To remove the filter applied to a recordset, set the **Filter** property of the Recordset object to the **adFilterNone** constant. The following line of code removes any filter applied to the rsCustomers recordset and makes all records available:

```
rsCustomers.Filter = adFilterNone
```

Practice: Navigating a Recordset on a UserForm

In this practice, you'll connect to the **HighlandFurniture.accdb** Access database and open a recordset based on the tblSuppliers table. You'll then create a UserForm, which can be used to display and scroll through the records in the recordset.

The solution for this practice is in the **Ch17_ADO.xlsm** workbook, which is included with the practice files for Chapter 17.

You need to first create the UserForm to view the records. The completed UserForm should look like the image below:

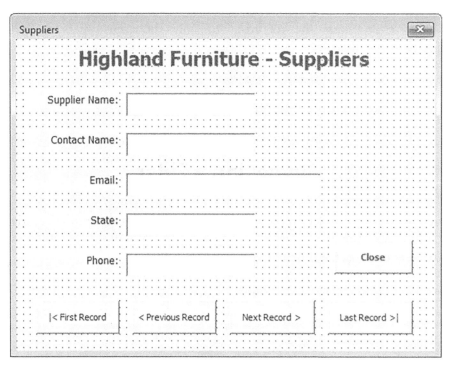

Figure 17-6: A UserForm to view records returned by a recordset.

Step1: Create a new UserForm

Follow the steps below to create a new UserForm:

1. Create a new macro-enabled workbook and name it **ADOData.xlsm** or another name you choose.
2. On the Excel ribbon, select **Developer** > **Code** > **Visual Basic** to open the Visual Basic Editor.
3. In the Project Explorer window of the Visual Basic Editor, select the VBA project for ADOData.xlsm (or the workbook you're using).
4. Right-click the VBA project and select **Insert** > **UserForm**.

   The Visual Basic Editor adds a new UserForm to the **Forms** folder in the project.
5. In the Properties window, set the **Name** property of the UserForm to **frmSuppliers**.
6. Set the **Caption** property of the UserForm to **Suppliers.**

Step 2: Add controls to the UserForm

1. Using the information in the table below, add controls to the UserForm:

Control	Name	Caption
TextBox	TextSupplierName	
TextBox	TextContactName	
TextBox	TextEmail	
TextBox	TextState	
TextBox	TextPhone	
CommandButton	FirstButton	|< First Record
CommandButton	PreviousButton	< Previous Record
CommandButton	NextButton	Next Record >

| CommandButton | LastButton | Last Record >\| |
| CommandButton | CloseButton | Close |

2. Set the **Cancel** property of **CancelButton** to **True**.
3. Add **Label** controls to the UserForm to label each text box. Also, add a header title to the dialog box, as shown in the image of the completed UserForm at the beginning of this example.
4. Change the **Caption** property of each label so that it appropriately identifies the control it is labeling. The names of the labels do not need to be changed from the default names. See the UserForm image at the beginning of this example for how the labels are captioned.

Step 3: Enter the Code to Load the Data

For this example, we need to add code to the following event procedures:

UserForm event	What the code does
UserForm_Initialize	Creates the Connection object and Recordset object. The routine then populates the text boxes on the dialog box with the values from the recordset.
UserForm_Terminate	Closes the Connection and Recordset objects and removes them from memory.
FirstButton_Click	A navigation button that moves to the first record in the recordset.
PreviousButton_Click	Moves to the previous record in the recordset.
NextButton_Click	Moves to the next record in the recordset.
LastButton_Click	Moves to the last record in the recordset.
CloseButton_Click	Closes the dialog box.

Follow the steps below to create the required procedures:

Chapter 17: Accessing External Data with ADO

1. Declare the variables.

    Open the code window for the **frmSuppliers** UserForm. In the Declarations section, under Option Explicit, enter the following code:

    ```
    'Declare the connection and recordset objects at UserForm
    level
    Dim connHF As ADODB.Connection
    Dim rsSuppliers As ADODB.Recordset
    ```

    It is necessary to declare the variables for the Connection object and Recordset object in the Declarations section of the UserForm to ensure these objects are available to all event procedures in the UserForm.

2. In the code window, select the **Initialize** event in the **Procedure** box. Enter the following code so that the event procedure looks like the code below. Please change the connection string to the location where you stored the HighlandFurniture.accdb file on your computer.

    ```
    Private Sub UserForm_Initialize()
        'Set connection to a new Connection object
        Set connHF = New ADODB.Connection

        'Set the Provider for Microsoft Access
        connHF.Provider = "Microsoft.ACE.OLEDB.12.0"

        'Open a connection to the database
        '**Change the connection string to your db location**
        connHF.Open "C:\Data\AccessDBs\HighlandFurniture.accdb"

        'Instantiate a new recordset object
        Set rsSuppliers = New ADODB.Recordset

        'Open the tblCustomers table
        rsSuppliers.Open "tblSuppliers", connHF, adOpenDynamic

        'Call procedure that assigns the values to text boxes
        PopulateControls
    End Sub
    ```

    The Initialize event automatically runs when the UserForm is displayed. Thus, any code that prepares the UserForm for use when it is first opened should be placed in the Initialize event procedure of the UserForm.

The code above creates a Connection object, which is then connected to the **HighlandFurniture.accdb** Access database. A recordset to the **tblSuppliers** table is then opened using the connection.

3. Create a Sub procedure in the UserForm's Code window named **PopulateControls** that looks like the code below:

```
Sub PopulateControls()
    'Assign values from the current record
    'to text boxes on the UserForm
    With FrmSuppliers
        .TextSupplierName.Text = rsSuppliers!SupplierName
        .TextContactName.Text = rsSuppliers!ContactName
        .TextEmail.Text = rsSuppliers!Email
        .TextCity.Text = rsSuppliers!City
        .TextPhone.Text = rsSuppliers!Phone
    End With
End Sub
```

The text boxes on the UserForm need to be populated each time the current record changes. This procedure assigns values from the current record to the text box controls. Different buttons on the UserForm can change the position of the current record. So, placing these assignments in a separate procedure that can be called from different event procedures is important. This approach avoids code duplication.

4. Enter the following code for the **UserForm_Terminate** event:

```
Private Sub UserForm_Terminate()
    'Close the connection and recordset
    rsSuppliers.Close
    connHF.Close
    Set rsSuppliers = Nothing
    Set connHF = Nothing
End Sub
```

This code ensures that when the UserForm is closed, the Connection and Recordset objects are closed and removed from memory. The **Terminate** event runs whichever way the UserForm is closed. For example, the user could click the Close button we added or the Close (x) button on the title bar to close the dialog box.

Chapter 17: Accessing External Data with ADO

5. Enter the following code for the **FirstButton_Click** event:

```
Private Sub FirstButton_Click()
    'Move to the first record in the recordset
    rsSuppliers.MoveFirst
    PopulateControls
End Sub
```

The above code moves to the first record of the recordset and displays it on the UserForm by calling the PopulateControls procedure.

6. Enter the following code for the **LastButton_Click** event:

```
Private Sub LastButton_Click()
    'Move to the last record in the recordset
    rsSuppliers.MoveLast
    PopulateControls
End Sub
```

The above code moves to the last record of the recordset and displays it on the UserForm by calling the PopulateControls procedure.

7. Insert the following code in the **NextButton_Click** event:

```
Private Sub NextButton_Click()
    'Move to the next record
    rsSuppliers.MoveNext

    'Populate the controls with the new current record
    If Not rsSuppliers.EOF Then
        PopulateControls
    End If

    'Did the record pointer move past the last record?
    If rsSuppliers.EOF Then
        rsSuppliers.MoveLast
        MsgBox "This is the last record.", vbExclamation
    End If
End Sub
```

When the user clicks the **Next Record** button, the procedure does the following:

- Moves the record pointer to the next record in the recordset.

413

- Ensures the EOF property is **False** before calling the PopulateControls procedure. Checking the EOF property ensures the routine doesn't try to access a record after the last one.

- If the EOF property is **True**, the record pointer is moved to the last record in the recordset. The user is then informed that they're at the last record.

8. Insert the following code in the **PreviousButton_Click** event:

```
Private Sub PreviousButton_Click()
    ' Move to the previous record
    rsSuppliers.MovePrevious

    If Not rsSuppliers.BOF Then
        PopulateControls
    End If

    'If the BOF property is True, move to the first record
    If rsSuppliers.BOF Then
        rsSuppliers.MoveFirst
        MsgBox "This is the first record.", vbExclamation
    End If
End Sub
```

When the user clicks the **Previous Record** button, the procedure does the following:

- Moves the record pointer to the previous record in the recordset.

- Ensures the BOF property is not **True** before calling the PopulateControls procedure. Checking the BOF property ensures the code doesn't try to access a record before the first.

- If the BOF property is **True**, the record pointer is moved to the first record in the recordset. The user is then informed that they're at the first record.

Chapter 17: Accessing External Data with ADO

Step 4: Testing the UserForm

1. Run the UserForm from inside the Visual Basic Explorer.

   Excel displays the **Suppliers** dialog box with the first record in the recordset.

   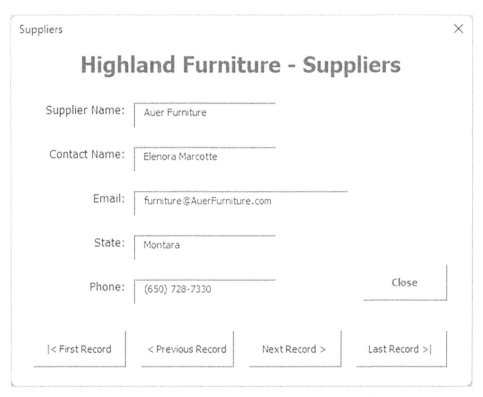

   Figure 17-7: Navigating through the Access records returned by a recordset.

2. Test the navigation buttons on the dialog box by clicking them to navigate through the recordset.

3. Click the **Close** button to close the dialog box.

415

> **Note** Even though the practice above used a dynamic recordset (adOpenDynamic), the UserForm does not support updating records in the recordset. The text boxes on the UserForm are not bound to the fields of the underlying recordset.

Building a Query

In this section, you'll learn how to write SQL statements and use SQL queries to create ADO recordsets. Previously, we covered how to open and navigate through a recordset based on a whole table. However, working with a subset of records based on a query is usually more efficient. You can use an SQL query to return only the records required rather than all the records in a table.

Overview of SQL

SQL (Structured Query Language) is a database query language that has been around for a long time and has evolved into one of the most widely used languages to query and modify data in a database. With an SQL query, you can retrieve a selection of records from a table based on criteria specified in your SQL statement. An SQL statement defines an SQL command like SELECT, UPDATE, or DELETE. SQL statements may also include clauses like WHERE and ORDER BY. SQL statements are typically used to retrieve or amend data, but you can also use SQL statements to modify the structure of the database. You can use SQL statements to retrieve data from several tables by joining tables in your SQL expression.

The benefits of using SQL are more evident when working across a network. In such a scenario, ADO transmits a subset of records across the network instead of a whole table, making it faster.

The following SQL statement returns only one field from the tblCustomers table:

```
SELECT CompanyName FROM tblCustomers
```

Different data source providers may require slightly different SQL syntax. For example, an SQL statement written for a Microsoft Access database may not work for an SQL Server database. Dates are formatted differently in Access compared to SQL Server. Review the SQL documentation for a data provider for syntax variances before writing SQL statements to retrieve data from that source. The SQL statements used in this section are valid for Microsoft Access.

Selecting Records with SQL

The SELECT statement in SQL selects specific fields from one or more database tables. A SELECT statement can include WHERE and ORDER BY clauses that you can use to filter and order the returned records.

Syntax:

SELECT *fieldlist*
FROM *table_name*
[WHERE *selectcriteria*]
[ORDER BY *field1* [ASC | DESC][, *field2* [ASC | DESC]][, ...]]]

The table below explains the different parts of the syntax of a SELECT statement:

Part	Description
fieldlist	The name of one or more fields to be returned by the query, along with any aliases used as field names.
FROM *table_name*	This clause specifies one or more tables or predefined queries containing the fields to be returned.
WHERE *selectcriteria*	Optional. You can use this clause to provide criteria that define which records to return from the table(s) listed in the FROM clause.
ORDER BY *field1*, *field2*	Optional. The ORDER BY clause can sort the returned records based on one or more fields. You can sort in ascending (ASC) or descending (DESC) order.

Using SELECT

In a SELECT statement, you can use the asterisk (*) to select all fields in a table. The following SELECT statement selects all fields from the tblCustomers table:

```
SELECT * FROM tblCustomers
```

To return only some fields, specify the names of the fields in the field list. For instance, to select the FirstName and LastName fields from the tblCustomers table, use the following SELECT statement:

```
SELECT FirstName, LastName FROM tblCustomers
```

To select records from multiple tables, list the names in the table list separated by a comma. For example, the SELECT statement below retrieves all fields from the tblSuppliers and the tblProducts tables:

```
SELECT * FROM tblSupplier, tblProducts
```

To select particular fields from multiple tables, list the names in the field list, separated by a comma. For example, the following SELECT statement retrieves the SupplierName and ProductName fields from the tblProducts and tblSuppliers tables:

```
SELECT tblSuppliers.SupplierName, tblProducts.ProductName
FROM tblProducts, tblSuppliers
```

Using the WHERE Clause

Use the WHERE clause to limit the records selected from the data source. The following statement retrieves all fields of customers that live in New York:

```
SELECT * FROM tblCustomers WHERE City = 'New York'
```

The SQL statement above uses single quotes in the WHERE clause criteria because *City* is a text field. To filter the data using a date field, enclose the date in number signs (#).

For example, the statement below retrieves all records in which the order date is after 01/01/2025:

```
SELECT * FROM tblOrders WHERE OrderDate > #01/01/2025#
```

Using Logical Operators with the WHERE Clause

You can use several SQL logical operators with the WHERE clause to refine your search criteria further.

LIKE Operator

You can use the LIKE operator with wildcards instead of exact values. The following example retrieves all records where the last name starts with the letter "A":

```
SELECT * FROM tblCustomers WHERE LastName LIKE 'A%'
```

BETWEEN Operator

Use the BETWEEN operator to return a selection of records between two values, as shown in the SQL statement below:

```
SELECT * FROM tblOrders
WHERE OrderDate BETWEEN #01/01/2025# AND #07/01/2025#
```

Note the use of the number signs (#) surrounding the dates.

IN Operator

Use the IN operator to return all records within a given selection. The SQL statement below returns all records from the selected states:

```
SELECT * FROM tblCustomers WHERE State IN ('CA', 'NY', 'UT')
```

Using the ORDER BY Clause

Use the ORDER BY clause to sort a recordset in ascending or descending order. The ASC option specifies ascending order, while DESC specifies descending order. The example below retrieves all records from the tblCustomers table and sorts them in ascending order using the CompanyName field:

```
SELECT * FROM tblCustomers ORDER BY CompanyName ASC
```

Tip: If you are retrieving data from an Access database, you can create the required SQL statement using the graphical query interface in Access. Then, copy the SQL statement and use it in your VBA code.

Opening a Recordset with an SQL Query

To open a recordset with an SQL statement, you can pass the SQL statement as the **Source** argument of the **Open** method, as shown in the example below:

```
rsCustomers.Open "SELECT * FROM tblCustomers", connHF
```

If your SQL statement is long, you can assign it to a string variable and use the variable as the **Source** argument of the **Open** method. This improves the readability of your code.

The following code assigns the SQL statement to a string variable before the variable is used to Open the recordset:

```
SQLText = "SELECT * FROM tblCustomers"
rs.Open SQLText, connHF
```

When concatenating an SQL statement broken into several lines, ensure you add a space to the end of each line, other than the last line, so that words are properly spaced. The following code shows an SQL statement broken into several lines to make it more readable:

```
SQLText = "SELECT CompanyName, FirstName, LastName " & _
```

```
            "FROM tblCustomers " & _
            "WHERE State IN ('CA', 'NY', 'UT')"
```

In a SELECT statement, you can also reference values in text boxes, combo boxes, list boxes, and other controls on a UserForm. The following SQL statement uses the value from a text box named **TextCompanyName** on a UserForm as the criteria for the WHERE clause:

```
SQLText = "SELECT * FROM tblCustomers " & _
          "WHERE CompanyName = '" & TextCompanyName.Value & "'"
```

Note that the value retrieved from the text box is enclosed in single quotes because it is a text field. You don't need single quotes for a numerical field.

The following example is a complete procedure where a recordset is opened with an SQL SELECT statement:

```
Sub SQLQueryConnection()
    Dim connHF As ADODB.Connection
    Dim rs As ADODB.Recordset
    Dim SQLText As String

    'Set connection to a new Connection object
    Set connHF = New ADODB.Connection

    'Set the Provider for Microsoft Access
    connHF.Provider = "Microsoft.ACE.OLEDB.12.0"

    'Open a connection to the Highland Furniture database
    connHF.Open "C:\Data\AccessDBs\HighlandFurniture.accdb"

    'Instantiate a new recordset object
    Set rs = New ADODB.Recordset

    'Define the SQL statement
    SQLText = "SELECT * FROM tblCustomers " & _
              "ORDER BY CompanyName ASC"

    'Open the recordset
     rs.Open SQLText, connHF

    'Copy and paste records in Sheet1 of the active workbook
    With Worksheets("Sheet1")
        .Cells.ClearContents
        .Range("A1").CopyFromRecordset rs
    End With
```

```
    'Close the recordset and connection
    rs.Close
    connHF.Close
    Set rs = Nothing
    Set connHF = Nothing
End Sub
```

In the code above, the SQL statement was assigned to a variable named *SQLText*. *SQLText* is used as an argument for the **Open** method. The procedure then copies the retrieved records to **Sheet1** in the active workbook, as shown below.

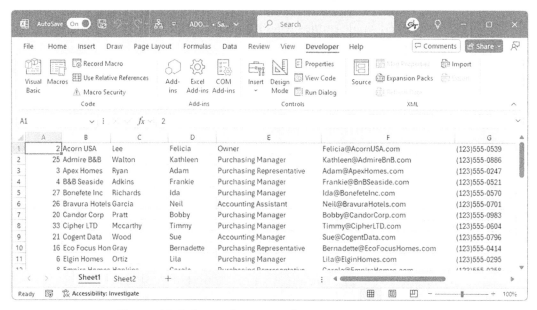

Figure 17-8: Records returned using an SQL query.

Handling Data Access Errors

Data access errors can be trapped and processed in a similar way to other types of errors in VBA. Enable an error trap with the **On Error** statement. Then, create an error-handling routine to handle any encountered errors. The **Err** object contains information on any generated errors. If you use inline error handling instead of an error trap to handle errors, always use the **Clear** method to clear the errors and reset the **Err** object before proceeding with code execution. For more details on the **Err** object and how to create an error handling routine, see Chapter 9.

The following example code uses an error handler routine to trap and process any error encountered when connecting to an Access database. In the event of an error, the code also ensures a cleanup operation is performed to close any open connections and recordsets before the procedure ends.

The following code contains a deliberate error in the FROM clause:

```
Sub ADOErrorHandler()
    Dim connHF As ADODB.Connection
    Dim rs As ADODB.Recordset
    Dim SQLText As String
    Dim ADOErr As Error

   On Error GoTo Err_Handler

    'Create a new instance of a Connection object
    Set connHF = New ADODB.Connection

    'Set the Provider for Microsoft Access
    connHF.Provider = "Microsoft.ACE.OLEDB.12.0"

    'Open a connection to the Highland Furniture database
    connHF.Open "C:\Data\AccessDBs\HighlandFurniture.accdb"

    'Instantiate a new recordset object
    Set rs = New ADODB.Recordset

    '***Deliberate error***
    'The table "Customers" does not exist.
    'It should be "tblCustomers"
    SQLText = "SELECT * FROM Customers " & _
            "ORDER BY CompanyName ASC"
```

```vba
        'Open the recordset
         rs.Open SQLText, connHF

        'Copy and paste records in the active worksheet
        With Worksheets("Sheet1")
            .Cells.ClearContents
            .Range("A1").CopyFromRecordset rs
        End With
Cleanup:
        'Close the recordset and connection
        If Not (rs Is Nothing) Then
            If (rs.State And adStateOpen) = adStateOpen Then
                rs.Close
            End If
            Set rs = Nothing
        End If
        If Not (connHF Is Nothing) Then
            If (connHF.State And adStateOpen) = adStateOpen Then
                connHF.Close
            End If
            Set connHF = Nothing
        End If
        Exit Sub

Err_Handler:
    MsgBox "Error number: " & Err.Number & vbNewLine & _
            Err.Description, vbCritical, "Error"
    GoTo Cleanup
End Sub
```

The example code above connects to the HighlandFurniture.accdb Access database.

There is a deliberate error in the FROM clause of the SQL statement. A table named **Customers** doesn't exist in the database. Attempting to open the recordset with a non-existent table will generate an error.

The **On Error** statement at the top of the procedure enables the error handler. At the bottom of the procedure, an error handling code that informs the user of the error number and description is added under the line label **Err_Handler**.

After handling the error, the routine uses a **GoTo** statement to move program execution to the *Cleanup* line label, where cleanup actions are performed. The cleanup operation checks whether the Connection object and the Recordset object were initialized and opened before the error occurred. If these objects are open, they're closed and removed from memory before an **Exit Sub** statement is used to exit the procedure.

If no error occurs during the execution of the procedure, program execution carries on normally through to the cleanup routine. After the cleanup, an **Exit Sub** statement exits the procedure before reaching the error handler.

Retrieving SQL Server Data

This example covers retrieving data from an SQL Server database and copying the data to an Excel worksheet. First, the procedure connects to an SQL Server database named **HighlandFurniture**. Then, the procedure creates a recordset based on an SQL query and copies the returned records to Sheet1 in the active Excel workbook.

The procedure also contains an error handler. Including an error handler when connecting to a remote computer is good practice, as errors can occur for many reasons. Your error handler should provide a meaningful message to the user, including helpful instructions on what to do next, if necessary, before cleanly exiting the procedure.

You need access to an SQL Server database to run the following example. You can create the HighlandFurniture database in SQL Server and export **tblCustomers** from the **HighlandFurniture.accdb** Access database to the SQL Server database. HighlandFurniture.accdb is included with the practice files for this chapter.

Alternatively, you can test this example with another test database on an SQL Server to which you have access. In such a case, change the **ConnectionString** to point to your SQL Server database. To change the ConnectionString, change the **Server** and **Database** properties. You may need to provide a username and password if you're using **Standard Security** rather than a **Trusted Connection**. Check with your database administrator for the required connection string if your SQL Server uses Standard Security.

In your VBA project, insert the following code in an existing module or a new module:

```
Sub SQLSeverConnection()
    Dim connHF As ADODB.Connection
    Dim rs As ADODB.Recordset
    Dim SQLText As String
```

```vba
    Dim ConnText As String
    
    'Enable the error handler
    On Error GoTo Err_Handler
    
    'Create a new Connection object
    Set connHF = New ADODB.Connection
    
    'Define connection string for SQL Server DB
    ConnText = "Server=WINDT;" & _
               "Database=HighlandFurniture;" & _
               "Trusted_Connection=yes;"
    
    'Open the connection
    With connHF
        .Provider = "MSOLEDBSQL"
        .ConnectionString = ConnText
        .Open
    End With
    
    'Instantiate a new Recordset object
    Set rs = New ADODB.Recordset
    
    'Define the SQL statement
    SQLText = "SELECT CustomerID, LastName, FirstName " & _
              "FROM tblCustomers"
    
    'Open the recordset
     rs.Open SQLText, connHF
    
    'Copy the records to Sheet1 in the active workbook
    With Worksheets("Sheet1")
        .Cells.ClearContents
        .Range("A1").CopyFromRecordset rs
    End With

Cleanup:
    'Close the recordset and connection if open
    If Not (rs Is Nothing) Then
        If (rs.State And adStateOpen) = adStateOpen Then
            rs.Close
        End If
        Set rs = Nothing
    End If
    If Not (connHF Is Nothing) Then
        If (connHF.State And adStateOpen) = adStateOpen Then
            connHF.Close
        End If
```

```
        Set connHF = Nothing
    End If
    Exit Sub

Err_Handler:
    MsgBox "Error number: " & Err.Number & vbNewLine & _
           Err.Description, vbCritical, "Error"
    GoTo Cleanup
End Sub
```

In the code above, the Connection object uses the OLE DB provider for SQL Server, MSOLEDBSQL. The ConnectionString provides the other connection properties, such as the server's name, database name, and security method. The SQL statement selects three fields, CustomerID, LastName, and FirstName, from the tblCustomers table.

Chapter 18

Creating Charts

In this chapter:

- An overview of using charts to visually represent data in Excel.
- Using the macro recorder to generate the VBA code.
- Using the AddChart2 method to create a chart from scratch.
- Adding, removing, and editing individual chart elements in code.
- Applying chart layouts and formatting in code.

As charts often present an easier way to understand data, you can use them to create visual representations of your data. Charts can show trends that may not be apparent when the data is viewed as numbers. A visual representation often creates more of an impact on your audience.

Before delving into writing code to create Excel charts, we'll create a chart manually while recording the VBA code with the macro recorder. The macro recorder is a great tool for generating the required syntax for tasks you want to perform in code. You can examine the generated code and use the information when writing your code. You'll also learn how to create a chart from scratch programmatically.

Chart Basics

When you create a chart, you can embed it in an existing worksheet or place it on a separate sheet. With both methods, the chart is linked to the source data on which it is based. Any change to the source data will be reflected in the chart.

Embedded Charts

An embedded chart is inserted in a worksheet, usually on the same worksheet that holds the chart's source data. An embedded chart lets you view or print the chart and its source data together.

Chart Sheets

A chart sheet is a standalone sheet that holds a chart but not its source data. A chart sheet can be used to create charts that are more suitable for presentation or printing. You can print a chart sheet on a page without showing its source data.

Changing Your Default Chart Type

If you mostly use one chart type, you can set it as your default chart type in Excel. VBA will use the default chart type if you don't explicitly specify it when creating a chart programmatically.

You can change/set your default chart type in Excel by doing the following:

1. On the ribbon, select **Chart Design** > **Change Chart Type** > **All Charts**.

    Excel opens the **Change Chart Type** dialog box.

2. On the **All Charts** tab, select the chart you want to set as the default.

3. At the top of the **All Charts** tab, right-click the selected option and select **Set as Default Chart**.

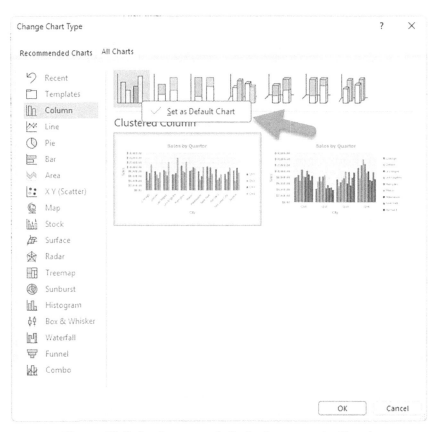

Figure 18-7: Setting your default chart type in Excel.

Manually Creating a Chart

Before writing code to create a chart, it is a good idea to create a few charts manually while recording your actions with the macro recorder. This gives you code that you can reference for tips as you write code from scratch to create a chart.

The **Charts** group on the **Insert** tab has several commands to create different types of charts in Excel. You can select a chart type, for example, the **Insert Column or Bar Chart** button, to display a list of chart options available for that chart type.

Alternatively, you can select the **Recommended Charts** button to open the **Insert Chart** dialog box that shows a list of all the chart types you can create in Excel.

The solutions for the examples in this chapter can be found in the **Ch18_CreatingCharts.xlsm** workbook that comes with the practice files for this book.

▶ **Step 1 - Create a chart from the Insert Chart dialog:**

1. Create a new macro-enabled workbook named **Charts.xlsm**.

2. Copy the data from the range A3:E14 in *Sheet1* from **Ch18_CreatingCharts.xlsm** to *Sheet1* in your new workbook.

   Note You can create your own sample data to work through this example if you don't want to use the sample data from the practice file.

3. On the **Developer** tab, in the **Code** group, select **Record Macro**.

4. In the **Record Macro** dialog box, name the macro **CreateSalesChart** and store the macro in the current workbook (This Workbook).

Mastering Excel VBA Programming

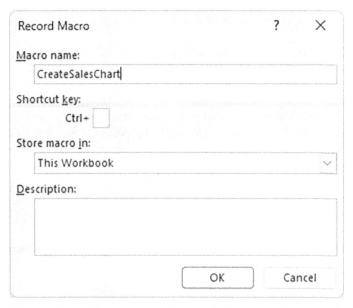

Figure 18-1: The Record Macro dialog box. To record the steps when manually creating a chart.

5. Select the range of data for the chart. For this example, it is A3:E14 (as shown in the image below).

	A	B	C	D	E
1	Sales by quarter				
2					
3	City	Qtr1	Qtr2	Qtr3	Qtr4
4	Chicago	$8,087.00	$4,380.00	$7,507.00	$11,236.00
5	Denver	$8,254.00	$6,851.00	$5,333.00	$7,853.00
6	Las Vegas	$8,911.00	$8,373.00	$6,573.00	$12,140.00
7	Los Angeles	$7,016.00	$6,833.00	$7,493.00	$13,984.00
8	Memphis	$10,672.00	$8,465.00	$7,887.00	$12,427.00
9	Miami	$8,466.00	$8,888.00	$9,979.00	$9,682.00
10	Milwaukee	$8,222.00	$4,641.00	$6,198.00	$10,112.00
11	New York	$10,312.00	$5,578.00	$9,938.00	$7,312.00
12	Portland	$9,077.00	$4,679.00	$5,544.00	$7,064.00
13	Salt Lake City	$7,182.00	$4,905.00	$8,087.00	$9,796.00
14	Seattle	$8,619.00	$4,062.00	$9,692.00	$7,568.00
15					
16					

Figure 18-2: The range of data to use for the chart.

Chapter 18: Creating Charts

6. On the **Insert** tab, select **Recommended Charts**.

   Excel displays the **Insert Chart** dialog box.

   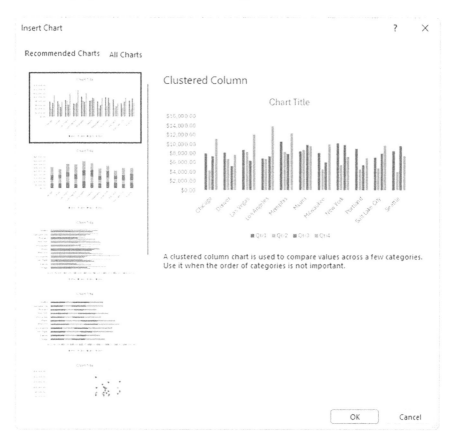

   Figure 18-3: Selecting a Clustered Column chart.

7. On the **Insert Chart** dialog box, select the **Clustered Column** chart and select **OK**.

   Excel creates a floating chart in the same worksheet as your data.

8. Reposition the chart on the worksheet by clicking any blank area in the chart to select it and then drag it so that it is adjacent to the data as shown below:

433

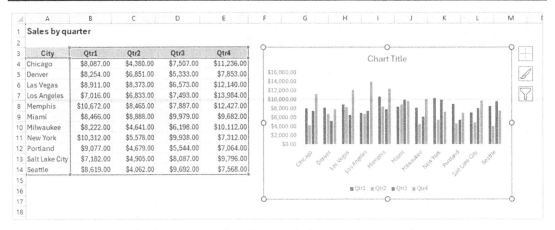

Figure 18-4: A chart inserted in the worksheet next to the data.

▶ **Step 2 - Format the chart:**

1. Select a predefined chart layout.

   On the ribbon, select **Chart Design** > **Quick Layout** > **Layout 9**.

   Layout 9 creates axis titles and moves the legend to the right of the chart.

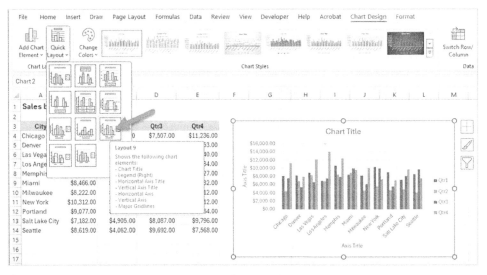

Figure 18-5: Selecting a quick layout for the chart.

Chapter 18: Creating Charts

2. Change the labels on the chart:

    i. Click the **Chart Title** label to select it and change its text to **Sales by Quarter**.

    > **Note** You can also select elements on the chart using the **Chart Elements** dropdown list in the **Current Selection** group on the **Format** tab. The Format tab is displayed when the chart is selected.

    ii. Select the vertical axis label and change the text to **Sales**.

    iii. Select the horizontal axis label and change the text to **City**.

3. Format the plot area:

    i. On the **Format** tab, in the **Current Selection** group, select **Plot Area** in the **Chart Elements** box.

    Excel selects the plot area of the chart.

    ii. On the **Format** tab, in the **Current Selection** group, select **Format Selection**.

    Excel displays the **Format Plot Area** panel on the right of the window.

    iii. In the **Format Plot Area** panel, under **Fill**, select **Solid Fill**.

    iv. Under **Color**, select **Light Gray** from the color palette (the third color on the first row of colors).

4. On the **Developer** tab, click **Stop Recording** to stop the macro recorder.

The finished chart should look like the following image:

Mastering Excel VBA Programming

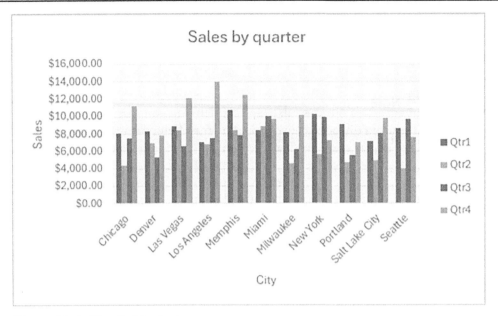

Figure 18-6: The finished chart.

▶ **Step 3 - View the code for the recorded macro:**

1. In the Visual Basic Editor, open the code window for Module1 (or the module where the macro code was stored).

2. Review the code generated by the Macro Recorder.

    The code should be in the Sub procedure named **CreateSalesChart** (or the name you entered for the macro name).

3. Save the macro by clicking the **Save** button on the Visual Basic Editor toolbar.

The code to create the chart that is generated by the macro recorder is shown below:

```
Sub CreateSalesChart()
'
' CreateSalesChart Macro
'
    Range("A3:E14").Select
    ActiveSheet.Shapes.AddChart2(201, xlColumnClustered).Select
    ActiveChart.SetSourceData Source:=Range("Sheet1!$A$3:$E$14")
    ActiveSheet.Shapes("Chart 4").IncrementLeft 9.75
    ActiveSheet.Shapes("Chart 4").IncrementTop -54.75
    ActiveChart.ApplyLayout (9)
    ActiveChart.ChartTitle.Select
    ActiveChart.ChartTitle.Text = "Sales by quarter"
```

```
        Selection.Format.TextFrame2.TextRange.Characters.Text = "Sales
by quarter"
        With Selection.Format.TextFrame2.TextRange.Characters(1,
16).ParagraphFormat
            .TextDirection = msoTextDirectionLeftToRight
            .Alignment = msoAlignCenter
        End With
        With Selection.Format.TextFrame2.TextRange.Characters(1,
16).Font
            .BaselineOffset = 0
            .Bold = msoFalse
            .NameComplexScript = "+mn-cs"
            .NameFarEast = "+mn-ea"
            .Fill.Visible = msoTrue
            .Fill.ForeColor.RGB = RGB(89, 89, 89)
            .Fill.Transparency = 0
            .Fill.Solid
            .Size = 14
            .Italic = msoFalse
            .Kerning = 12
            .Name = "+mn-lt"
            .UnderlineStyle = msoNoUnderline
            .Spacing = 0
            .Strike = msoNoStrike
        End With
        ActiveChart.ChartArea.Select
        ActiveChart.Axes(xlCategory).AxisTitle.Select
        ActiveChart.Axes(xlCategory, xlPrimary).AxisTitle.Text = "City"
        Selection.Format.TextFrame2.TextRange.Characters.Text = "City"
        With Selection.Format.TextFrame2.TextRange.Characters(1,
4).ParagraphFormat
            .TextDirection = msoTextDirectionLeftToRight
            .Alignment = msoAlignCenter
        End With
        With Selection.Format.TextFrame2.TextRange.Characters(1, 4).Font
            .BaselineOffset = 0
            .Bold = msoFalse
            .NameComplexScript = "+mn-cs"
            .NameFarEast = "+mn-ea"
            .Fill.Visible = msoTrue
            .Fill.ForeColor.RGB = RGB(89, 89, 89)
            .Fill.Transparency = 0
            .Fill.Solid
            .Size = 10
            .Italic = msoFalse
            .Kerning = 12
            .Name = "+mn-lt"
            .UnderlineStyle = msoNoUnderline
```

```
            .Strike = msoNoStrike
    End With
    ActiveChart.ChartArea.Select
    ActiveChart.Axes(xlValue).AxisTitle.Select
    ActiveChart.Axes(xlValue, xlPrimary).AxisTitle.Text = "Sales"
    Selection.Format.TextFrame2.TextRange.Characters.Text = "Sales"
    With Selection.Format.TextFrame2.TextRange.Characters(1,
5).ParagraphFormat
        .TextDirection = msoTextDirectionLeftToRight
        .Alignment = msoAlignCenter
    End With
    With Selection.Format.TextFrame2.TextRange.Characters(1, 5).Font
        .BaselineOffset = 0
        .Bold = msoFalse
        .NameComplexScript = "+mn-cs"
        .NameFarEast = "+mn-ea"
        .Fill.Visible = msoTrue
        .Fill.ForeColor.RGB = RGB(89, 89, 89)
        .Fill.Transparency = 0
        .Fill.Solid
        .Size = 10
        .Italic = msoFalse
        .Kerning = 12
        .Name = "+mn-lt"
        .UnderlineStyle = msoNoUnderline
        .Strike = msoNoStrike
    End With
    ActiveChart.ChartArea.Select
    ActiveChart.PlotArea.Select
    With Selection.Format.Fill
        .Visible = msoTrue
        .ForeColor.ObjectThemeColor = msoThemeColorBackground2
        .ForeColor.TintAndShade = 0
        .ForeColor.Brightness = 0
        .Solid
    End With
    Application.CommandBars("Format Object").Visible = False
End Sub
```

In the next section, you'll write code to create the same chart.

Creating a Chart Programmatically from Scratch

You can write code to create a chart and perform any action you can manually perform with commands on the Excel ribbon.

Using the AddChart2 method

To add a chart to an Excel worksheet, use the **AddChart2** method of the **Shape** object. **AddChart2** lets you specify the chart's style, type, location, and size.

Syntax:

expression.AddChart2 (*Style, XlChartType, Left, Top, Width, Height, NewLayout*)

The *expression* qualifier represents a **Shape** object.

Description of Parameters

All arguments are optional. Using **AddChart2** with no arguments creates a chart using your default chart type.

Name	Description
Style	Specifies the chart style. Each chart type can have one or more styles. To use the default style for the chart type specified in the XlChartType argument, enter -1.
XlChartType	Specifies the chart type. You can specify an enumerated name or its associated value here. For the full list of chart types, search for "XlChartType enumeration (Excel)" in VBA help.
Left	The position of the left edge of the chart in points. Font sizes are usually measured in points.
Top	The position of the top edge of the chart in points.

Width	The width of the chart in points.
Height	The height of the chart in points.
NewLayout	When set to True, this argument applies dynamic formatting rules to the chart. For example, the method will omit a legend for a single series chart.

Example

The example below creates a chart based on the same data list you placed in the Charts.xlsm workbook for the previous example. Copy the data to *Sheet2* of the Charts.xlsm workbook for this example.

	A	B	C	D	E
1	**Sales by quarter**				
2					
3	City	Qtr1	Qtr2	Qtr3	Qtr4
4	Chicago	$8,087.00	$4,380.00	$7,507.00	$11,236.00
5	Denver	$8,254.00	$6,851.00	$5,333.00	$7,853.00
6	Las Vegas	$8,911.00	$8,373.00	$6,573.00	$12,140.00
7	Los Angeles	$7,016.00	$6,833.00	$7,493.00	$13,984.00
8	Memphis	$10,672.00	$8,465.00	$7,887.00	$12,427.00
9	Miami	$8,466.00	$8,888.00	$9,979.00	$9,682.00
10	Milwaukee	$8,222.00	$4,641.00	$6,198.00	$10,112.00
11	New York	$10,312.00	$5,578.00	$9,938.00	$7,312.00
12	Portland	$9,077.00	$4,679.00	$5,544.00	$7,064.00
13	Salt Lake City	$7,182.00	$4,905.00	$8,087.00	$9,796.00
14	Seattle	$8,619.00	$4,062.00	$9,692.00	$7,568.00

Figure 18-8: The data source for the chart in this example.

In the Visual Basic Editor, create a new module in the VBA project for the Charts.xlsm workbook and enter the following code:

```
Sub CreateChart()
    Dim NewChart As Chart
    
    ActiveSheet.Range("A3:E14").Select
    Set NewChart = ActiveSheet.Shapes.AddChart2(Style:=201, _
        XlChartType:=xlColumnClustered, _
        Left:=Range("G3").Left, _
        Top:=Range("G3").Top, _
        Width:=Range("G3:N16").Width, _
        Height:=Range("G3:N16").Height).Chart
End Sub
```

When you run the code above, it creates a chart using the data in range A3:E14 of the active worksheet and places the chart in range G3:N16. The image below shows the resulting chart:

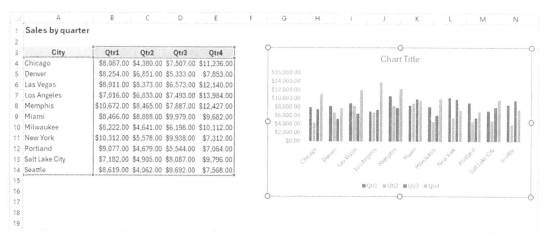

Figure 18-9: The resulting chart generated by the code above.

Using Direct Referencing

The macro recorded in the previous section selects ranges and objects before performing actions on them. In your code, use direct object referencing instead of selections. Selecting ranges before manipulating them can significantly slow down code execution. Direct referencing is one of the reasons why written code can be more efficient than code generated by the macro recorder.

For example, instead of using the following:

`Range("A3:E14").Select`

Use direct referencing like this:

`SalesChart.SetSourceData Source:=ActiveSheet.Range("A3:E14")`

Identifying Chart Styles

Each chart type has one or more styles. The style number used in the previous code example is 201, which is the default style number for a **Clustered Column** chart.

To identify the number for the chart style you want to create programmatically, do the following:

1. Create a chart manually in Excel.

2. Select the chart and apply a style from **Chart Design > Chart Styles** (shown in the image below).

Figure 18-10: Selecting a chart style to identify its number for the *Style* argument of the AddChart2 method.

3. Keep the chart selected in Excel. Then, switch to the Visual Basic Editor by pressing Alt+F11.

4. Display the Immediate window by selecting **View > Immediate Window** (or press Ctrl+G).

5. In the Immediate window, enter **?ActiveChart.ChartStyle** and press Enter. The returned value is the style number for the selected chart.

```
Immediate
  ?ActiveChart.ChartStyle
   203
```

Figure 18-10: Using the Immediate window to identify the number of the currently selected chart style.

6. Use this number for the *Style* argument of the **AddChart2** method in your VBA code.

Referencing a new Chart Object

If we ignore the arguments of the AddChart2 method for now, the following code creates a new blank chart object:

```
Dim SalesChart As Chart
Set SalesChart = ActiveSheet.Shapes.AddChart2().Chart
```

After creating a new **Chart** object using the above code, use its **SetSourceData** method to specify its source data, as shown below:

```
SalesChart.SetSourceData Source:=ActiveSheet.Range("A3:E14")
```

Referencing an Existing Chart

It can be tricky to reference an existing embedded chart by name because Excel appends a suffix number to the name of each new chart. The suffix is incremented for each new chart, for example, Chart 1, Chart 2, Chart 3, etc. During a session, if the user created and deleted several charts before arriving at the final one, the name of the last chart could be difficult to determine. The last chart could be Chart 5, Chart 8, or Chart 20, depending on how many charts were created during the session, even if only one chart remains in the worksheet.

Hence, to reference an embedded chart, you can use the **ChartObjects** collection to return the chart object by specifying its index number. If there is only one chart on the worksheet, its index number would be 1.

The following code sets a reference to an existing chart on Sheet2 and updates its title:

```
Dim MyChart As Chart
Set MyChart = Sheets("Sheet2").ChartObjects(1).Chart
MyChart.ChartTitle.Caption = "My Chart Title"
```

To refer to a chart on its own sheet named *Chart1* (which is different from a worksheet), use the following code:

```
Dim MyChart As Chart
Set MyChart = Sheets("Chart1")
MyChart.ChartTitle.Caption = "My Chart Title"
```

Setting Individual Chart Characteristics

After creating a chart in VBA and assigning it to a chart object variable, you can use the variable to access properties and methods of the **Chart** object to add, remove, reposition, or format individual elements of the chart. You can also change the chart's style, type, and source data.

Specifying the Size and Position of a Chart

You can specify the position and size of the chart in points or by using cell references. The *CreateChart* procedure created earlier in this chapter used cell references for the *Left*, *Top*, *Width*, and *Height* arguments to determine the placement and size of the chart on the worksheet. You don't have to try to determine the exact points to use if cell references would suffice.

Applying a Chart Layout

To create a chart with axis titles, you can programmatically add the elements individually or select a predefined chart layout with axis titles. In the previous section, we recorded a macro while creating a chart that used *Layout 9*. When you examine the macro, you'll see that Excel applied Layout 9 to the chart with the following code:

```
ActiveChart.ApplyLayout (9)
```

Hence, in our code example, we can apply Layout 9 to the chart with the following code:

```
SalesChart.ApplyLayout (9)
```

Layout 9 adds titles to the x and y axes, displays the legend on the right of the chart, and places the chart title at the top.

Using the SetElement Method

You can use the **SetElement** method of the Chart object to add, remove, or manipulate chart elements. SetElement takes a single argument, which is an **MsoChartElementType** enumerated constant.

Syntax

expression.SetElement (*Element*)

expression is a variable representing a **Chart** object.

MsoChartElementType constants

The table below lists some common constants used with the **SetElement** method.

Name	Value	Description
msoElementChartTitleAboveChart	2	Show the chart title above chart.
msoElementChartTitleNone	0	Remove the chart title.
msoElementPrimaryCategoryAxisTitleHorizontal	305	Show the x-axis title horizontally.
msoElementPrimaryCategoryAxisTitleNone	300	Remove x-axis title.
msoElementPrimaryValueAxisTitleRotated	303	Show rotated y-axis title.
msoElementPrimaryValueAxisNone	352	Remove y-axis title.
msoElementLegendRight	101	Show legend on the right.
msoElementLegendBottom	104	Show legend at the bottom.
msoElementLegendNone	100	Remove the legend.

For the full list of constants, search for "MsoChartElementType enumeration (Office)" using your favorite internet search engine.

Editing the Chat Title

To change the chart title, use the following code:

```
SalesChart.ChartTitle.Caption = "Sales by Quarter"
```

You can also use the following code to change the title of the active chart:

```
ActiveChart.ChartTitle.Caption = "Sales by Quarter"
```

The examples above work if your chart already has a title. If the chart doesn't have a title, or you're not sure if it does at runtime, you can use the following code to ensure it has a title before changing its caption:

```
SalesChart.SetElement (msoElementChartTitleAboveChart)
```

You can also change the formatting of the title with the following code, which changes the font, size, and color of the title:

```
With SalesChart.ChartTitle.Format.TextFrame2.TextRange.Font
        .Name = "Aptos ExtraBold"
        .Fill.ForeColor.ObjectThemeColor = msoThemeColorAccent4
        .Size = 14
End With
```

To get other theme colors, search for "MsoThemeColorIndex Enum" in VBA Help.

Individually Adding Axis Titles

You can change the axis titles in the same way as the chart title. You can use the SetElement method to add axis titles to the chart individually if you have not done so by applying a predefined layout.

Add an axis title to the x-axis, also known as **Category Axis**:

```
SalesChart.SetElement (msoElementPrimaryCategoryAxisTitleHorizontal)
```

The following code adds the y-axis title, also known as **Value Axis**:

```
SalesChart.SetElement (msoElementPrimaryValueAxisTitleRotated)
```

To change the text and format, use the Caption and Format properties, respectively. The following example code changes the text of the x and y axes of the chart:

```
With SalesChart
    .Axes(xlCategory, xlPrimary).AxisTitle.Caption = "City"
    .Axes(xlValue, xlPrimary).AxisTitle.Caption = "Sales"
End With
```

Formatting the Plot Area

To format the plot area, we can examine the macro recorded earlier in this section to see the code generated by Excel. When we copy and adapt the code for our example, it looks like this:

```
With SalesChart.PlotArea.Format.Fill
    .Visible = msoTrue
    .ForeColor.ObjectThemeColor = msoThemeColorBackground2
    .Solid
End With
```

Putting It All Together

The following code combines the individual lines of code covered in the preceding sections into a procedure that programmatically creates a chart similar to the one we manually created earlier in this chapter. You can examine the code below and compare it to the code generated by the macro recorder.

```
Sub CreateFormattedChart()
    'Formatted chart based on the data in Sheet2
    
    Dim SalesChart As Chart
```

```
    'Create a blank chart object.
    Set SalesChart = ActiveSheet.Shapes.AddChart2(Style:=201, _
        XlChartType:=xlColumnClustered, _
        Left:=Range("G3").Left, _
        Top:=Range("G3").Top, _
        Width:=Range("G3:N16").Width, _
        Height:=Range("G3:N16").Height).Chart

    'Specify the source data, layout, and labels.
    With SalesChart
        .SetSourceData Source:=ActiveSheet.Range("A3:E14")
        .ApplyLayout (9)
        .ChartTitle.Caption = "Sales by Quarter"
        .Axes(xlCategory, xlPrimary).AxisTitle.Caption = "City"
        .Axes(xlValue, xlPrimary).AxisTitle.Caption = "Sales"
    End With

    'Format the chart title.
    With SalesChart.ChartTitle.Format.TextFrame2.TextRange.Font
        .Name = "Aptos ExtraBold"
        .Fill.ForeColor.ObjectThemeColor = msoThemeColorAccent4
        .Size = 14
    End With

    'Format the plot area.
    With SalesChart.PlotArea.Format.Fill
        .Visible = msoTrue
        .ForeColor.ObjectThemeColor = msoThemeColorBackground2
        .Solid
    End With
End Sub
```

The above code produces the following chart:

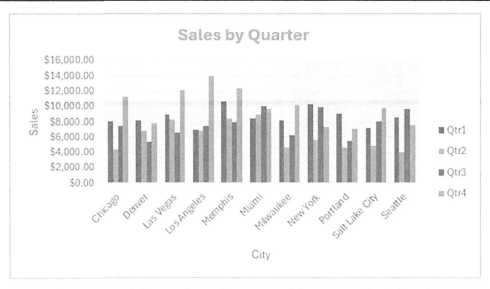

Figure 18-11: The resultant chart created from scratch with code.

Chapter 19

Creating PivotTables

In this chapter:

- An overview of dynamically summarizing Excel data with pivot tables.
- Preparing the source data for the pivot table.
- Using the macro recorder to generate the VBA code.
- Creating a pivot table with VBA from scratch.
- Adding fields to pivot table areas.
- Formatting a pivot table.
- Grouping pivot table data.

An Excel PivotTable is a powerful tool that enables you to create dynamic tables that summarize large amounts of data in different views without changing the original data. In this chapter, you'll learn how to build a PivotTable manually while recording the actions with the macro recorder and then create it programmatically from scratch.

PivotTable Basics

The source data for a PivotTable can be a list in Excel, another PivotTable, or data from an external database like Microsoft Access. A PivotTable is placed on a worksheet. Once created, you can manipulate the PivotTable to dynamically change the view of the data.

The sample data and code for the examples in this chapter can be found in the **Ch19_PivotTables.xlsm** worksheet available with the practice files for Chapter 19

Preparing Your Data

Some preparation is required to get a data list ready for a PivotTable. The source data used for a PivotTable needs to be organized as a list or converted to an Excel table (this is recommended, although not essential).

A few steps to prepare the source data for a PivotTable:

1. The data should have column headings in a single row at the top.
2. Remove any temporary totals or summaries that are not part of the core data.
3. The data cannot have empty rows. So, delete any empty rows.
4. Remove any extraneous data surrounding the list.
5. You may also want to convert the range to an Excel table (but this is optional).

Chapter 19: Creating PivotTables

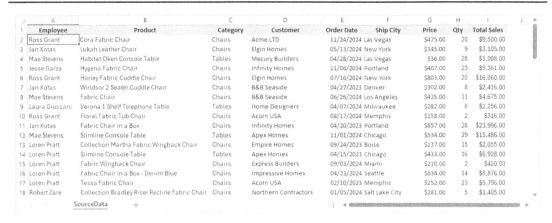

Figure 19-1: The data source used for the pivot tables created in this chapter.

Once the data has been prepared, it is ready for a PivotTable.

Creating a PivotTable Manually

▶ **Step 1: Create the Pivot Table**

Follow the steps below to create a PivotTable:

1. Create a new macro-enabled workbook.

2. Copy the *SourceData* worksheet from **Ch19_PivotTables.xlsm** to your new workbook.

3. On the Excel status bar, click the **Record Macro** button (it is the button next to **Ready** on the left of the status bar).

4. In the **Record Macro** dialog box, name the macro **CreatePT01** and store the macro in the current workbook (This Workbook).

453

Mastering Excel VBA Programming

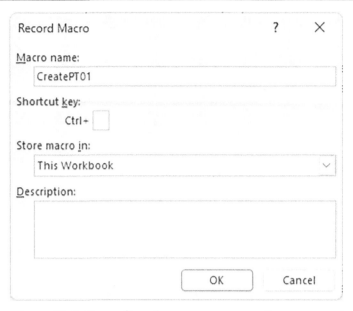

Figure 19-2: Recording the steps to manually create a pivot table.

5. Select **OK** to start recording the macro.
6. Select any cell in the data range, and then select **Insert > Tables > PivotTable**. Excel displays the **PivotTable from table or range** dialog box.

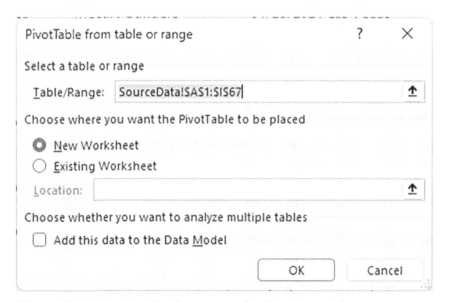

Figure 19-3: Selecting the data source for the pivot tables.

Chapter 19: Creating PivotTables

7. **Select the table or range**: Excel will attempt to identify the table or range you want to use for your PivotTable and insert the reference in the **Table/Range** box. If this is inaccurate, manually select the range by clicking the Expand Dialog button (up arrow) on the **Table/Range** box.

8. Select where you want to place the PivotTable. The default location is in a new worksheet. Having your PivotTable on a separate worksheet from your source data is best. Therefore, select the **New Worksheet** option if it's not already selected.

9. Click **OK**.

Excel creates a new worksheet with a PivotTable placeholder in the worksheet area and the PivotTable Fields pane on the right side of the window.

Figure 19-4: A PivotTable placeholder.

On the Excel user interface, the PivotTable Fields pane has four areas where you can place fields:

- **Filters**: The fields added here act as filters at the top of the report that enable you to display values in the PivotTable based on different criteria.

455

- **Columns**: The fields added here become column headings in the PivotTable.
- **Rows**: The fields in this area become row headings of the PivotTable.
- **Values**: These fields are aggregated as numeric values in the PivotTable.

To add a field to your PivotTable, select the checkbox next to the field name in the PivotTable Fields pane. When you select fields, they are added to their default areas. Non-numeric fields are added to the **Rows** area. Date and time fields are added to the **Columns** area. Numeric fields are added to the **Values** area.

You can also drag fields from the list to one of the four areas. You can drag a field from one area to another. To remove a field from an area, click the dropdown arrow on the field and select **Remove Field**. You can also clear the checkbox for the field in the fields list or drag it out of the box and drop it back on the fields list.

▶ **Step 2: Specify the Fields**

For this example, we want a summary of our data that shows the total spent by each customer per item category.

To add fields to the PivotTable placeholder generated in the previous step, follow the steps below:

1. In the PivotTable Fields pane, select the **Customer** field on the list to add it to the **Rows** box. The PivotTable will also be updated with the list of customers as row headings.
2. Drag the **Category** field to the **Columns** box.
3. In the fields list, select **Order Total**. Excel should automatically add it to the **Values** box.

   The PivotTable will now be updated to look like the image below:

Row Labels	Beds	Chairs	Sofas	Tables	Grand Total
Acme LTD	2390	13226			15616
Acorn USA		6112		7180	13292
Apex Homes			4731	33082	37813
B&B Seaside		24933	1400	24064	50397
Elgin Homes	3066	43636	2000	10868	59570
Empire Homes		2055	5190	7300	14545
Express Builders		420		10584	11004
Home Designers		38934	5400	13388	57722
Impressive Homes		8876		5899	14775
Infinity Homes	5542	43277	4200	42335	95354
Mecury Builders	2560	16752		1008	20320
Northern Contractors		1405	6460	596	8461
Orion Spaces	4684	4806			9490
Grand Total	18242	204432	29381	156304	408359

Figure 19-5: The resultant PivotTable showing the sales for each category per customer.

4. On the Excel status bar, select the **Stop Recording** button to stop the macro recorder.

▶ **Step 3 - View the recorded macro:**

1. In the Visual Basic Editor, open the code window for Module1 (or the module in which the code was stored).

2. Review the code generated by the Macro Recorder.

   The code should be in the Sub procedure named **CreatePT01** (or the name you entered for the macro name).

3. Save the macro by clicking the **Save** button on the Visual Basic Editor toolbar.

In the next section, we'll create this pivot table programmatically. You can use the recorded macro to help identify some of the commands required to create the PivotTable from code.

Creating a PivotTable Programmatically

To create a PivotTable using VBA, you first need to create a **PivotCache** object to describe the input area of the data. The following code creates a Range object that references the source data and then creates the PivotCache object that we'll use to create the PivotTable:

```
Dim DataRange As Range
Dim PTable As PivotTable
Dim PTCache As PivotCache

'Define source data
Set DataRange = Worksheets("SourceData").Range("A1").CurrentRegion

'Create the pivot cache
Set PTCache = ActiveWorkbook.PivotCaches.Create( _
    SourceType:=xlDatabase, _
    SourceData:=DataRange)
```

Using the CreatePivotTable Method

To define a PivotTable, use the **CreatePivotTable** method of the **PivotCache** object. This method has four parameters, but only *TableDestination* is required. The other parameters are optional. *TableName* allows you to name the PivotTable. To learn more about the CreatePivotTable method, search for "CreatePivotTable method (Excel)" in VBA Help.

Syntax:

expression.CreatePivotTable (*TableDestination, TableName, ReadData, DefaultVersion*)

expression represents a **PivotCache** object.

Chapter 19: Creating PivotTables

The code segment below creates a new worksheet in the active workbook. Then, it uses the **CreatePivotTable** method to create a blank PivotTable (also known as a placeholder) based on the pivot cache created earlier.

```
'Add a new worksheet to hold the pivot table.
Worksheets.Add

'Create the pivot table from the pivot cache.
Set PTable = PTCache.CreatePivotTable( _
          TableDestination:=Range("A1"))
```

The **TableDestination** parameter lets you specify where to place the pivot table in the worksheet.

The image below shows the pivot table areas to be populated with fields:

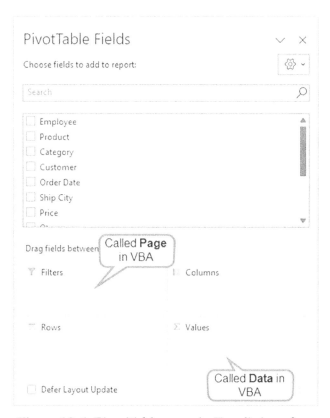

Figure 19-6: PivotTable areas in Excel's interface.

459

> **Note** VBA still uses the old names for some PivotTable areas to maintain compatibility with older versions of Excel. In versions before Excel 2010, the field areas of a PivotTable were **Page**, **Column**, **Row**, and **Data**. In the current version of Excel, the four areas of a PivotTable are Filters, Columns, Rows, and Values. VBA syntax still uses the old terms for these areas: **Page**, **Column**, **Row**, and **Data**.

Adding Fields to PivotTable Areas

The **AddFields** method of the **PivotTable** object enables you to specify one or more fields for the Rows, Columns, or Filters areas of a PivotTable. Defining data fields for the PivotTable Data (Values) area is slightly tricker as you need to set a few properties of the **PivotField** object for each data field to add.

Specifying Column and Row Fields

You can use the following parameters of the **AddFields** method to define the fields of your pivot table:

- The **RowFields** parameter allows you to define fields for the Rows area of the PivotTable Fields list.
- The **ColumnFields** parameter allows you to define fields for the Columns area.
- The **PageFields** parameter lets you specify fields for the Filters area.

The following code adds two fields to the Rows area and one field in the Columns area of the PivotTable created earlier:

```
'Specify row and column fields.
 PTable.AddFields RowFields:=Array("Ship City", "Customer"), _
                  ColumnFields:="Category"
```

In the code above, note that the **Array** function was used to specify two values for the **Rowfields** parameter. The **ColumnFields** parameter only has one value in our example, so it did not require using the Array function.

Specifying Data Fields

A data field goes in the PivotTable's **Data** area (referred to as Values on Excel's interface). To add a data field to the PivotTable, set the **Orientation** property of the **PivotField** object to **xlDataField**. The Orientation property sets the position of the field in the referenced PivotTable, such as xlDataField or xlColumnField.

Use the **Function** property to specify the aggregate function for the data field. For example, **xlSum** sums the values while **xlCount** counts the values.

The **Position** property specifies the position of the field in the PivotTable if you added more than one data field. Use 1 for the first field, 2 for the second field, and so on.

You may also prefer to name your data field because Excel provides a default name like *Sum of Total Sales*, which can be confusing. You can use the **Name** property to specify a more fitting name.

> **Note** You can't reuse a name already in your PivotTable fields list. However, add a trailing space to use a similar name. For example, "Total Sales" = "Total Sales ".

The following code defines the *Total Sales* field as a data field, and the aggregate function specified is **xlSum** (as we want to sum the values):

```
With PTable.PivotFields("Total Sales")
     .Orientation = xlDataField
     .Function = xlSum
     .Position = 1
     .NumberFormat = "#,##0"
     .Name = "Total Sales "
End With
```

Note The example above uses **xlSum** because we're summing the data field. However, other PivotTable scenarios may require a different aggregate function. There are 11 functions available, including xlSum, xlCount, xlAverage, xlStdDev, xlMin, and xlMax. Of all the functions, only xlCount works with a text field. Use xlCount to count the records in the pivot table.

Putting It All Together

The following listing shows the complete code to generate the PivotTable:

```
Sub CreatePivot01()
    Dim DataRange As Range
    Dim PTable As PivotTable
    Dim PTCache As PivotCache

    'Define source data.
    Set DataRange = Worksheets("SourceData").Range("A1").CurrentRegion

    'Create the pivot cache.
    Set PTCache = ActiveWorkbook.PivotCaches.Create( _
        SourceType:=xlDatabase, _
        SourceData:=DataRange)

    'Add a new worksheet to hold the pivot table.
    Worksheets.Add

    'Create the pivot table from the pivot cache.
    Set PTable = PTCache.CreatePivotTable( _
        TableDestination:=Range("A1"))

    'Specify row and column fields.
    PTable.AddFields RowFields:=Array("Ship City", "Customer"), _
                    ColumnFields:="Category"

    'Specify the data (or value) field
    With PTable.PivotFields("Total Sales")
        .Orientation = xlDataField
        .Function = xlSum
        .Position = 1
```

```
        .NumberFormat = "#,##0"
        .Name = "Total Sales "
    End With
End Sub
```

The code above generates the PivotTable shown in the image below:

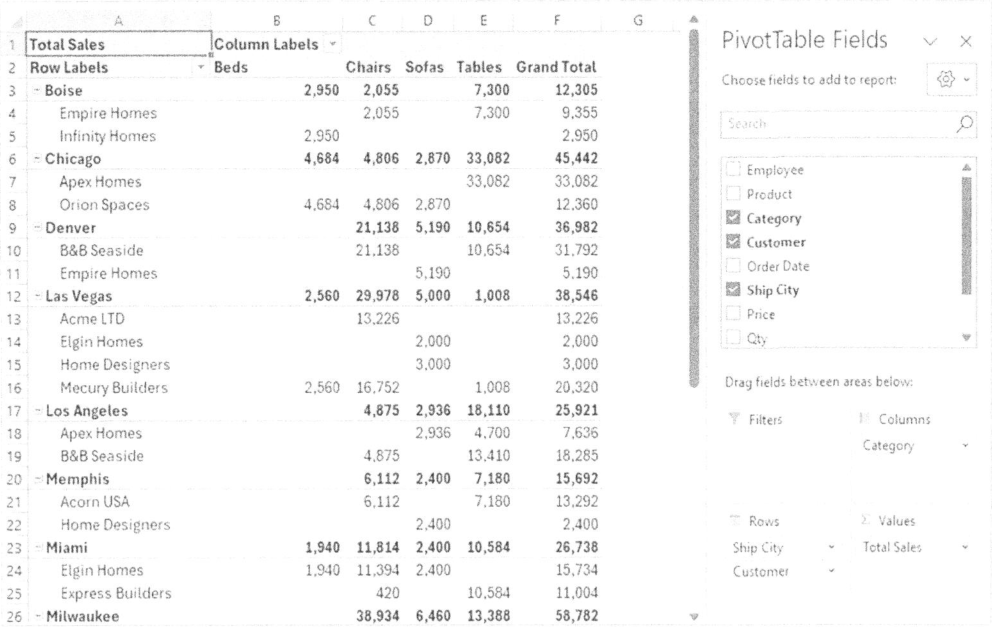

Total Sales	Column Labels				
Row Labels	Beds	Chairs	Sofas	Tables	Grand Total
Boise	2,950	2,055		7,300	12,305
Empire Homes		2,055		7,300	9,355
Infinity Homes	2,950				2,950
Chicago	4,684	4,806	2,870	33,082	45,442
Apex Homes				33,082	33,082
Orion Spaces	4,684	4,806	2,870		12,360
Denver		21,138	5,190	10,654	36,982
B&B Seaside		21,138		10,654	31,792
Empire Homes			5,190		5,190
Las Vegas	2,560	29,978	5,000	1,008	38,546
Acme LTD		13,226			13,226
Elgin Homes			2,000		2,000
Home Designers			3,000		3,000
Mecury Builders	2,560	16,752		1,008	20,320
Los Angeles		4,875	2,936	18,110	25,921
Apex Homes			2,936	4,700	7,636
B&B Seaside		4,875		13,410	18,285
Memphis		6,112	2,400	7,180	15,692
Acorn USA		6,112		7,180	13,292
Home Designers			2,400		2,400
Miami	1,940	11,814	2,400	10,584	26,738
Elgin Homes	1,940	11,394	2,400		15,734
Express Builders		420		10,584	11,004
Milwaukee		38,934	6,460	13,388	58,782

Figure 19-7: The resultant pivot table generated by the code above.

Formatting a PivotTable

After creating a PivotTable, you can manually format and set many properties using commands on the **PivotTable Analyze** and **Design** tabs. You can also perform these actions in VBA. In this section, you'll learn how to apply styles, remove totals, replace blank cells with zeros, and display the pivot table in a tabular format.

Applying PivotTable Styles

Excel uses the default table style settings on your computer for your PivotTable. You can set a different style programmatically by specifying one of the styles found on the Excel ribbon: **Design** tab > **PivotTable Styles** group (when a PivotTable is active).

The following code applies banded rows and the "Pivot Style Medium 9" style:

```
PTable.ShowTableStyleRowStripes = True
PTable.TableStyle2 = "PivotStyleMedium9"
```

You can identify the name of the style you want from Excel's interface. Go to **Design** tab > **PivotTable Styles** group. Hover your mouse over a style on the list to see a pop-up of its name (as shown in the image below). Use the portion of the name after the comma in your code without spaces.

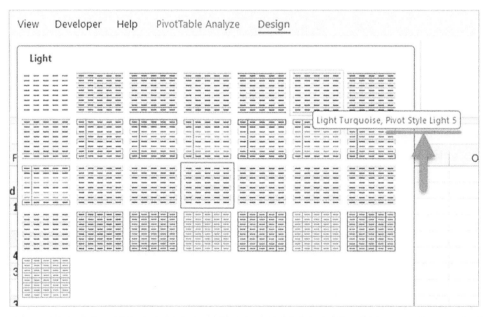

Figure 19-8: Identifying the name of a pivot table style. In this case, the name is PivotStyleLight5.

Removing Grand Totals

To use the data from the PivotTable for charts or other analysis reports, you could remove the grand totals and subtotals. You can also split any grouped data in the leftmost column into their own columns.

The code below removes the grand totals on the right and bottom of the pivot table:

```
With PTable
    .ColumnGrand = False
    .RowGrand = False
    .RepeatAllLabels xlRepeatLabels
End With
```

Removing Subtotals

The best way to remove all subtotals relating to a field is to set the **Subtotals** property of the **PivotField** object to False. We also want to display the pivot table in tabular form to ensure each field is displayed in a separate column, as shown in the code below:

```
PTable.PivotFields("Ship City").Subtotals(1) = False
```

The **Subtotals** property comprises a collection of index numbers representing each aggregate function. Setting an index to False removes its related subtotal. Setting index 1 (Automatic) to False removes all subtotals for that field.

Next, we want to display the pivot table in tabular form to ensure each field is displayed in a separate column. The code below shows the pivot table in tabular form:

```
PTable.RowAxisLayout xlTabularRow
```

Replacing Blank Values

The **PivotTable Options** dialog box, accessed from the **PivotTable Analyze** tab, allows you to set empty cells in the pivot table to 0 (zero). You can also do this programmatically by setting the **NullString** property of the PivotTable object to "0", as shown in the code below:

```
PTable.NullString = "0"
```

Excel enters a numerical zero in each empty cell even though you have to set the property to a text zero. Setting empty cells to zero is based on individual requirements, of course. It may not be necessary for all situations.

Putting It All Together

The following is the complete procedure used to generate and format the PivotTable as described above:

```
Sub PivotTableFormatting()
    Dim DataRange As Range
    Dim PTable As PivotTable
    Dim PTCache As PivotCache

    'Define source data.
    Set DataRange = 
Worksheets("SourceData").Range("A1").CurrentRegion

    'Create the pivot cache.
    Set PTCache = ActiveWorkbook.PivotCaches.Create( _
        SourceType:=xlDatabase, _
        SourceData:=DataRange)

    'Add a new worksheet to hold the pivot table.
    Worksheets.Add

    'Create the pivot table from the pivot cache.
    Set PTable = PTCache.CreatePivotTable( _
        TableDestination:=Range("A1"))
```

Chapter 19: Creating PivotTables

```vb
    'Specify row and column fields.
    PTable.AddFields RowFields:=Array("Ship City", "Customer"), _
                    ColumnFields:="Category"

    'Specify the data (or value) field
    With PTable.PivotFields("Total Sales")
        .Orientation = xlDataField
        .Function = xlSum
        .Position = 1
        .NumberFormat = "#,##0"
        .Name = "Total Sales "
    End With

    'Select a style for the pivot table
    PTable.ShowTableStyleRowStripes = True
    PTable.TableStyle2 = "PivotStyleMedium9"

    'Remove totals
    With PTable
        .ColumnGrand = False
        .RowGrand = False
        .RepeatAllLabels xlRepeatLabels
    End With
    PTable.PivotFields("Ship City").Subtotals(1) = False

    'Display table in tabular form
    PTable.RowAxisLayout xlTabularRow

    'Populate empty cells with 0
    PTable.NullString = "0"
End Sub
```

The code above generates the following PivotTable:

	A	B	C	D	E	F	G
1	Total Sales		Category				
2	Ship City	Customer	Beds	Chairs	Sofas	Tables	
3	⊟Boise	Empire Homes	0	2,055	0	7,300	
4	Boise	Infinity Homes	2,950	0	0	0	
5	⊟Chicago	Apex Homes	0	0	0	33,082	
6	Chicago	Orion Spaces	4,684	4,806	2,870	0	
7	⊟Denver	B&B Seaside	0	21,138	0	10,654	
8	Denver	Empire Homes	0	0	5,190	0	
9	⊟Las Vegas	Acme LTD	0	13,226	0	0	
10	Las Vegas	Elgin Homes	0	0	2,000	0	
11	Las Vegas	Home Designers	0	0	3,000	0	
12	Las Vegas	Mecury Builders	2,560	16,752	0	1,008	
13	⊟Los Angeles	Apex Homes	0	0	2,936	4,700	
14	Los Angeles	B&B Seaside	0	4,875	0	13,410	
15	⊟Memphis	Acorn USA	0	6,112	0	7,180	
16	Memphis	Home Designers	0	0	2,400	0	
17	⊟Miami	Elgin Homes	1,940	11,394	2,400	0	
18	Miami	Express Builders	0	420	0	10,584	

Figure 19-9: The pivot table generated from the code above.

Grouping PivotTable Data

Most pivot tables are grouped by date. The **PivotTable Fields** pane in Excel allows you to group date fields into periods like years, quarters, and months. Put the relevant date field in the **Rows** area to show periods as row headings. Likewise, put the relevant date field in the **Columns** area to show the periods as column headings.

You can also programmatically group PivotTable data into periods. The **Group** method of the **Range** object allows you to group a range of data. For a numeric or date-based grouping, apply the **Group** method to a single cell in the data range you want to group.

Syntax for the Group method:

expression.Group (*Start, End, By, Periods*)

The qualifier *expression* represents a **Range** object.

All parameters are optional, but the main parameter you'll use is *Periods*, which is an array of Boolean values that define the different grouping periods, as shown in the table below:

Array element	Period
1	Seconds
2	Minutes
3	Hours
4	Days
5	Months
6	Quarters
7	Years

To group the data by a period, set the corresponding element in the array to **True** and all others to **False**. The following code groups the dates in the specified range by quarters and years:

```
'Group dates by Quarters and Years
'The values in the array represent:
'(Seconds, Minutes, Hours, Days, Months, Quarters, Years)
Range("A3").Group _
    Periods:=Array(False, False, False, False, False, True, True)
```

The code above passes an array of Boolean values to the *Periods* parameter with Quarters and Years set to True. Then, the **Group** method is applied to Range ("A3") because the dates to be grouped start from cell A3. This range should be on the same column and two rows below the range specified for the *TableDestination* parameter in the **CreatePivotTable** method.

Example: Grouping Data by Date

In this example, we want to group the data shown earlier in this chapter by **Order Date**. We want the order date in the first column so that the data can be viewed by years and quarters.

The following code creates a PivotTable where the Order Date is grouped by years and quarters:

```
Sub PivotTableByDate()
    Dim DataRange As Range
    Dim PTable As PivotTable
    Dim PTCache As PivotCache

    'Define source data.
    Set DataRange = _
Worksheets("SourceData").Range("A1").CurrentRegion

    'Create the pivot cache.
    Set PTCache = ActiveWorkbook.PivotCaches.Create( _
        SourceType:=xlDatabase, _
        SourceData:=DataRange)

    'Add a new worksheet to hold the pivot table
    Worksheets.Add

    'Create the pivot table from the pivot cache
    Set PTable = PTCache.CreatePivotTable( _
        TableDestination:=Range("A1"))

    'Specify row and column fields.
    PTable.AddFields RowFields:=Array("Order Date"), _
                     ColumnFields:="Category"

    'Specify the data (or value) field.
    With PTable.PivotFields("Total Sales")
        .Orientation = xlDataField
        .Function = xlSum
        .Position = 1
        .NumberFormat = "#,##0"
        .Name = "Total Sales "
    End With

    'Group dates by Quarters and Years
    'The values in the array represent:
```

```
        '(Seconds, Minutes, Hours, Days, Months, Quarters, Years)
        Range("A3").Group _
            Periods:=Array(False, False, False, False, False, True, True)

End Sub
```

The code above creates the PivotTable shown in the image below:

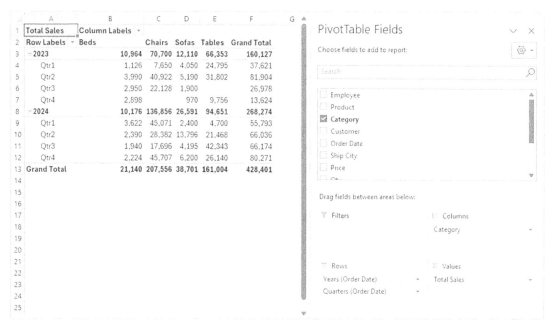

Figure 19-10: A pivot table grouped by years and quarters.

Chapter 20

User-Defined Functions and Add-ins

In this chapter:
- Creating a user-defined function.
- Adding a description to a user-defined function.
- Using a user-defined function in Excel.
- Introducing Excel add-ins.
- Converting a workbook to an add-in.
- Converting a user-defined function to an add-in.

Out of the box, Excel comes with a vast array of built-in worksheet functions, but its developers cannot anticipate every type of calculation a user may need. Therefore, Excel allows you to create a custom function (also known as a user-defined function or UDF) in VBA for any type of calculation. Excel add-ins enable you to package your functions and other applications as features you can add to Excel's interface and distribute to users. In this chapter, you'll learn how to create a custom function and convert it to an add-in to distribute to users.

Working with User-Defined Functions

Have you ever had to create formulas that require multiple levels of nested functions and/or several conditional statements? You can create reusable custom functions for complex calculations without built-in Excel functions.

Some benefits of custom functions include:

- You don't need to run a custom function like other procedures. They can be used directly in worksheets.

- You can create solutions for more complex calculations. VBA offers more versatility than Excel formulas.

- It's easier to understand and follow complex calculations involving several logical decisions in code than in formulas. Excel formulas can become cumbersome and difficult to follow if they have too many nested formulas and logical branches.

> **Note** This chapter uses the terms *custom function*, *user-defined function*, and *UDF* interchangeably.

Where to store the UDF

- **Personal Macro Workbook**: If you intend to use a custom function in different workbooks on the same computer, storing it in the Personal Macro Workbook (PERSONAL.XLSB) is best. You don't need to unhide the workbook to enter code in its VBA project file in the Visual Basic Editor. The functions stored in the Personal Macro Workbook are available to all workbooks on the computer.

- **Excel Macro-Enabled Workbook (.xlsm)**: If you intend to use the custom function in one workbook only, you can store it in the Personal Macro Workbook or a macro-enabled workbook.

- **Excel Macro-Enabled Workbook (.xlsm) or Add-in**: If you intend to distribute the custom function to users of other computers, store it in a macro-enabled workbook. This file can be converted to an add-in if necessary.

Creating a UDF

Before delving into creating a custom function, we need to review a few key aspects of Function procedures:

- A function can have between 0 and 255 arguments.

- You can't create custom functions with the macro recorder. They must be written manually in VBA.

- A Function procedure returns a value. If you need a procedure that runs several code instructions without returning a value, use a Sub procedure.

- You can use a Function procedure in two ways once created:
    i. Use it to calculate and return a value within another procedure.
    ii. Use it directly in a worksheet formula.

- A Function procedure used in a worksheet formula returns a value or an array. It can't be used to change worksheet objects like font, formatting, colors, etc. Use a Sub procedure if you want to change worksheet objects.

- The name of your custom function cannot duplicate any of the built-in function names in Excel, such as SUM, COUNT, AVERAGE, etc.

- You must list any arguments in parentheses and in the order in which they are processed.

Custom Function Example

Suppose we want to create a formula that calculates the bonus to be paid periodically to estate agents based on a graduated scale. The bonus paid to each agent is based on the number of rentals sold and the revenue generated for the period.

Chapter 20: User-Defined Functions and Add-ins

The solution would require several conditional statements that you can achieve with built-in Excel functions, but it can be done more cleanly in VBA. The function should perform this calculation automatically when the user provides the input values as arguments in Excel.

The sample data and code for the examples in this chapter are contained in the **Bonus_Solution.xlsm** workbook, which is included with the practice files for Chapter 20.

Bonus levels

The table below shows the graduated scale used to calculate the bonus to be paid:

Number of rentals sold	Bonus (%)
1	1.5%
2 - 4	2%
5 - 9	3%
10 or more	4%

The data model below summarises the number of rentals sold and the revenue generated by each agent.

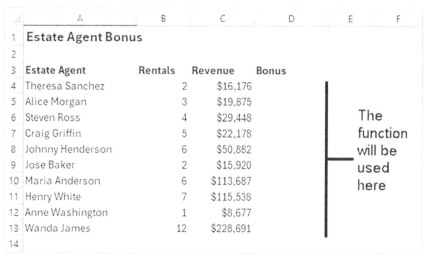

Figure 20-1: The table where the custom function will be used.

Using our graduated bonus scale, we need to calculate the bonus that needs to be paid to each estate agent in the range D4:D13. A custom function comes in handy for a scenario like this.

After defining the problem, we have a better idea of the kind of function required for the solution. The function will take in two arguments (the number of rentals sold and the revenue generated) and then return the calculated bonus:

Bonus(Rentals, Revenue)

Follow the steps below to create the function:

1. **Create a new module where your custom function will be defined.**

   Create a new macro-enabled workbook named **Bonus.xlsm**. For this example, we'll store the custom function in a separate macro-enabled workbook rather than the Personal Macro Workbook.

   Switch to the Visual Basic Editor by selecting the **Visual Basic** command button on the **Developer** tab (or press Alt+F11).

   In the Project Explorer window, right-click **VBAProject (Bonus.xlsm)** (or the VBA project for your workbook) and select **Insert > Module**.

   Excel opens the new module in the Code window.

2. **Write the code that calculates and returns the bonus.**

   The function's name is *Bonus,* and the arguments are *Rentals* and *Revenue.* This example uses a **Select Case** statement to test for and select the correct option. Enter the following code in the new module:

```
Function Bonus(Rentals, Revenue)
    Select Case Rentals
        Case Is = 1
            Bonus = Revenue * 0.015
        Case 2 To 4
            Bonus = Revenue * 0.02
        Case 5 To 9
            Bonus = Revenue * 0.035
        Case Is >= 10
```

```
            Bonus = Revenue * 0.04
    End Select
End Function
```

The Select Case statement tests *Rentals* (which is the number of rentals sold that will be passed in as an argument) against the different cases. When a test returns true, the Case block related to the test is executed. The result is assigned to *Bonus* as the return value of the function.

Once a return value is assigned to the function's name, the program exits the function and returns the value.

3. **Save your custom function.**

   On the Visual Basic Editor menu bar, select **File** > **Save** (or click the **Save** button on the Standard toolbar).

4. **Test your new custom function.**

   Switch back to Excel by clicking the **View Microsoft Excel** button on the Standard toolbar.

   In cell D4, enter the following formula:

   =Bonus(B4,C4)

   The formula returns a bonus that is 2% of the revenue, as shown in the image below. Copy the formula down to the other cells under the **Bonus** column using the fill handle of the cell to calculate the bonus for the other agents.

	A	B	C	D	E
1	**Estate Agent Bonus**				
2					
3	Estate Agent	Rentals	Revenue	Bonus	
4	Theresa Sanchez	2	$16,176	$323.52	
5	Alice Morgan	3	$19,875	$397.50	
6	Steven Ross	4	$29,448	$588.96	
7	Craig Griffin	5	$22,178	$776.23	
8	Johnny Henderson	6	$50,882	$1,780.87	
9	Jose Baker	2	$15,920	$318.40	
10	Maria Anderson	6	$113,687	$3,979.05	
11	Henry White	7	$115,538	$4,043.83	
12	Anne Washington	1	$8,677	$130.16	
13	Wanda James	12	$228,691	$9,147.64	
14					

Cell D4 contains: =Bonus(B4,C4)

Figure 20-2: The custom function calculates the bonus in the range D4:D13.

Adding a Description to a UDF

After creating the custom function, you can add a description that will be displayed in the **Insert Function** and **Function Arguments** dialog boxes. Although not essential, adding a description helps users understand what the function does.

Follow the steps below to add a description to your custom function:

1. Open the workbook containing the custom function (if the function was stored in the Personal Macro Workbook, any open workbook will do).

2. On the ribbon, select **Developer** > **Code** > **Macros** (or press Alt+F8).

    Excel displays the **Macro** dialog box.

3. In the **Macro Name** box, enter the name of your custom function.

    The function is not listed in the list of macros, so you must enter the name.

Chapter 20: User-Defined Functions and Add-ins

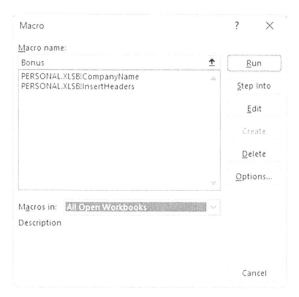

Figure 20-3: Enter the name of your custom function and select Options.

4. Select the **Options** button.

   Excel displays the **Macro Options** dialog box.

5. In the **Description** box, enter a description for the custom function.

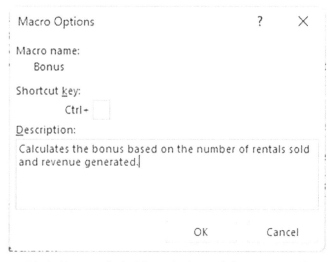

Figure 20-4: Enter a brief description of the custom function.

479

6. Select **OK** to confirm the entry.
7. Select **Cancel** to dismiss the Macro dialog box,

Viewing the user-defined function in the **Insert Function** dialog box now shows a description of the function (as shown in the image below).

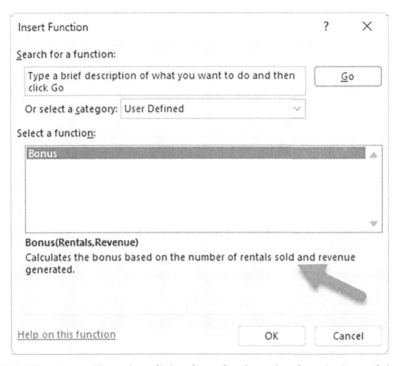

Figure 20-5: The Insert Function dialog box displays the description of the custom function.

Entering a UDF with the Insert Function dialog box

Use the **Insert Function** dialog box to view custom functions available in all open workbooks (including the Personal Macro Workbook).

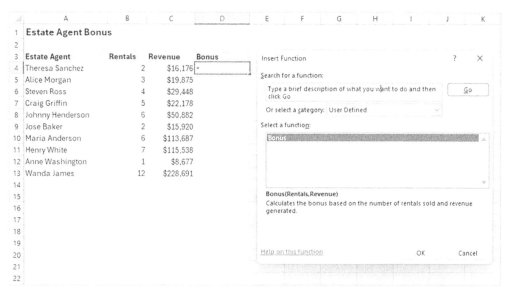

Figure 20-6: Entering the custom function using the Insert Function dialog box.

To use a custom function from the **Insert Function** dialog box, do the following:

1. On your worksheet, select the cell in which you want to enter the formula.

2. On the ribbon, select **Formulas > Function Library > Insert Function**.

   Excel opens the **Insert Function** dialog box.

3. In the Insert Function dialog box, select **User Defined** in the category box, and then select the **OK** button to open the **Function Arguments** dialog box.

4. Enter the arguments and select **OK**.

Mastering Excel VBA Programming

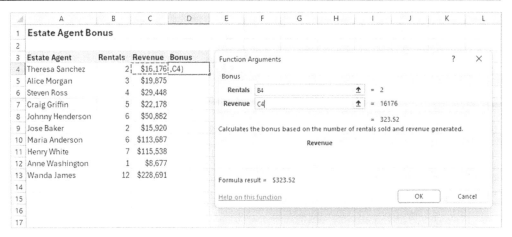

Figure 20-7: Entering arguments for the custom function.

The **Function Arguments** dialog box allows you to enter the arguments by selecting the cells on the worksheet.

5. Copy the formula by selecting the first cell's fill handle and dragging it down to the other cells in the column.

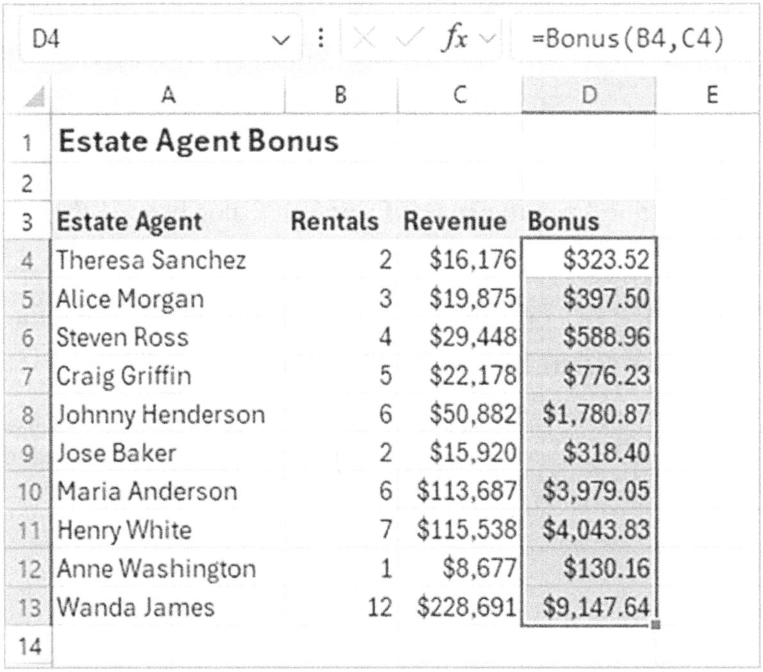

Figure 20-8: Fill the formula down to the other cells.

482

With that, you have successfully created and tested a custom function to perform a bespoke calculation.

Creating Excel Add-Ins

One great feature Excel provides is the ability to create add-ins. Excel add-ins enable you to package your VBA procedures as features that can be distributed to users and added to Excel.

Overview of Add-ins

An Excel add-in is used to provide custom functionality that enhances Excel. For example, you can convert a custom function, UserForm, or other macros that automate tasks into add-ins that you can distribute to users. After the user installs your add-in, the feature becomes available in Excel and loads automatically every time Excel is opened. A well-designed add-in would blend into Excel's interface and appear as part of the program.

Excel has built-in add-ins like the Analysis ToolPak, Euro Currency Tools, and Solver. You can also get Excel add-ins from third-party software suppliers.

Here are a few points to note about an Excel add-in file:

- Excel add-ins are saved with an XLAM file extension.
- The **IsAddin** property of the workbook is set to True.
- A workbook saved as an add-in isn't part of the Workbooks collection. Instead, it is part of the **AddIns** collection.
- Code in an installed add-in can still run even if macros are disallowed on the PC.
- A macro-enabled workbook must be open to make a custom function stored inside it available to other workbooks on the PC. Converting the macro-enabled workbook to an add-in and installing it on a PC makes the custom function available to all workbooks.

- An add-in is hidden by default. Users can't unhide it by selecting **View** > **Window** > **Unhide**.

Converting a Workbook to an Add-in

You can convert any Excel workbook to an add-in, but not all workbooks are suitable for conversion. Add-ins are always hidden, so you can't display data or charts stored in the add-in file. However, you can display UserForms and execute VBA procedures in the add-in. Hence, a workbook with no VBA procedures isn't ideal for conversion to an add-in.

You can add data to an add-in file to be used by your application, but you can't select cells in the file. Excel does not save add-ins automatically. Users can't see the add-in, and Excel won't prompt them to save it when exiting the application. If you need to save changes to the add-in at runtime, use the **Save** method of the **Worksheet** object.

To save any changes made to an add-in at runtime, you can add the following code to the **BeforeClose** event of the add-in file:

```
ThisWorkbook.Save
```

Follow the general steps below to convert a standard Excel workbook to an add-in file:

Step 1: Prepare your application for conversion to an Add-in:

1. Ensure your add-in has supporting code that allows any Sub procedures and UserForms to be executed from Excel. Function procedures can be run directly from Excel.

2. You may want to specify a shortcut key or add custom buttons to the ribbon or Quick Access Toolbar to run your application (see Chapter 2).

3. Test your application by running it and ensuring everything works as expected.

Chapter 20: User-Defined Functions and Add-ins

Step 2: Protect your application with a password (optional):

When deploying an add-in to users, you may want to set a password to protect your VBA application from being viewed and modified by others. This step is optional, depending on your requirements.

Follow the steps below to protect your VBA project with a password:

1. Switch to the Visual Basic Editor by pressing Alt+F11.

2. In the Project Explorer window, select the VBAProject for your workbook.

3. On the menu, select **Tools** > **VBAProject Properties** and select the **Protection** tab.

4. Select the **Lock project for viewing** checkbox and enter a password (twice).

5. Select **OK**.

Step 3: Save the workbook with an XLAM file extension:

1. Switch back to Excel by selecting **View Microsoft Excel** on the Standard toolbar (or press Alt+F11).

2. In Excel, select **File** > **Info** > **Show All Properties**.

    Excel expands the list under **Properties** on the right panel.

3. Enter a descriptive title for the add-in file in the **Title** property and a short description for the **Comments** property.

4. On the left pane, click **Save As**. Then, click **Browse to** display the **Save As** dialog box.

5. In the **Save as type** box, select **Excel Add-in (*.xlam)** from the dropdown list.

6. Specify the folder where you want to store the add-in. Excel defaults to the **AddIns** folder, but you can choose any folder.

7. Click **Save**.

Excel saves a copy of your workbook as an add-in (XLAM file) to the specified folder. The original workbook remains open.

After creating the add-in, you can install it in Excel using the **Add-ins** dialog box. This process is covered in the next section.

Converting a UDF to an Add-in

Previously, in this chapter, we created a custom function named **Bonus** that requires two arguments: *Rentals* and *Revenue*. It is great to be able to create custom functions for bespoke calculations, but there are some limitations.

Some issues with using custom functions:

- If stored in a macro-enabled workbook, the function can't be used in other workbooks on the PC unless the macro-enabled workbook is open.

- Even if you open the host workbook, the formulas using the function in other workbooks stop working whenever it closes. Thus, storing a custom function in a macro-enabled workbook is not ideal if the function needs to be used in different workbooks.

- You could store the function in the Personal Macro Workbook, which Excel opens as a hidden file by default. However, a slight snag is that Excel adds the PERSONAL.XLSB prefix to the function name when it is used. For instance, the *Bonus* function becomes *PERSONAL.XLSB!Bonus*. This prefix can make formulas difficult to read, especially if the function is used several times in a formula.

- The Personal Macro Workbook can only be used on one computer. So, you can't share custom functions stored in it with users on other computers.

A solution to the abovementioned issues is to convert the workbook containing the custom function to an Excel add-in. After the conversion and installation of the add-in, the custom function can be used in any workbook on the PC. Using an add-in also means the file name prefix is not required when using the custom function in formulas.

In the following steps, you'll save **Bonus.xlsm** as an add-in and install it on the PC.

> **Note:** You can skip Step 1 if you do not intend to password-protect your VBA project from unauthorized access.

Step 1: Protect the project file from unauthorized access (optional):

1. Open **Bonus.xlsm** (or the workbook containing your custom function).

2. Switch to the Visual Basic Editor by pressing Alt+F11.

3. In the Project Explorer window, right-click **VBAProject (Bonus.xlsm)** (or the project you're using), and select **VBAProject Properties** from the menu.

   Excel opens the **VBAProject – Project Properties** dialog box.

4. On the **Protection** tab, select the **Lock project for viewing** checkbox, and enter a password twice.

   Locking the project ensures that only authorized users can view and change it using the password.

   > **Important:** The Visual Basic Editor will challenge you to provide the password to the VBA project after the workbook has been closed and reopened. Thus, it is important that you enter a password that you can remember. Even better, write down the password and store it in a safe place for easy retrieval if needed. If you forget the password, Excel does not provide any tools to enable you to access the project.

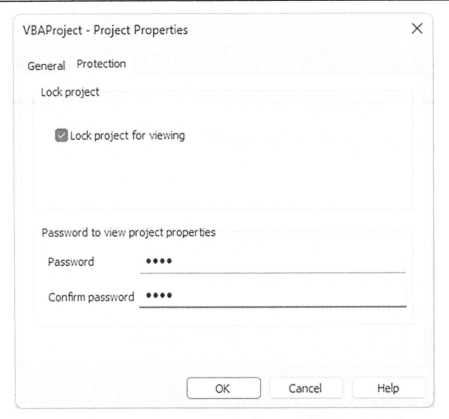

Figure 20-9: Password-protecting a VBA project before conversion to an add-in.

5. Click **OK** to apply the password and close the dialog box.

6. **Save your changes**. On the Visual Basic Editor toolbar, click the **Save** button.

Return to Excel to configure the add-in.

Step 2: Save Bonus.xlsm as an Add-in file.

Before saving the file as an add-in, we need to specify a title that will be displayed as the add-in name in Excel Options. We can also add comments that briefly describe what the function does.

Follow the steps below to save the workbook as an add-in:

Chapter 20: User-Defined Functions and Add-ins

1. Switch to Excel by clicking the **View Microsoft Excel** button on the Visual Basic Editor toolbar.

2. On the ribbon, select **File > Info > Show All Properties**. Excel expands the list under **Properties** on the right panel.

3. Enter "Bonus Add-in" for the **Title** property and "Calculates agent bonus" for the **Comments** property.

4. On the left panel, select **Save As** (or **Save a Copy** if the file is on OneDrive).

5. Click **More options** to open the **Save As** dialog box.

6. Select the folder where you want to save the file, and in the **File name** box, enter *Bonus Add-in*. Excel defaults to the **AddIns** folder, but you can choose any folder.

7. In the **Save as type** list, select **Excel Add-in (*.xlam)**.

8. Click **Save**.

Step 3: Activate the add-in in Excel Options.

After creating the add-in, you must install it on the PC to make its features available in Excel. Follow the steps below to enable the add-in:

1. In Excel, select **File > Options > Add-ins** to open the Add-ins pane of Excel Options.

2. In the **Manage** box, select **Excel Add-ins** and click **Go**.

   Excel opens the **Add-ins** dialog box.

3. Click **Browse**.

4. Navigate to the folder containing your add-in and select it.

5. Excel displays the add-in as one of the items on the list. Select the add-in (if it's not already selected) and click **OK**.

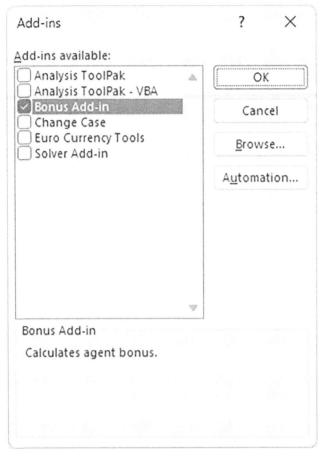

Figure 20-10: Using the Add-ins dialog box to enable the add-in, which includes it as a feature in Excel.

The add-in is now activated on the computer.

Step 4: Test the add-in.

Using the custom function in a new workbook:

1. Close **Bonus.xlsm** (or the original workbook containing your custom function).

2. Create a new standard Excel workbook (XLSX) or use an existing standard workbook.

3. Copy and paste the test data from *Sheet1* in the **Bonus_Solution.xlsm** practice file into your workbook (as shown in the image below).

4. Use the **Bonus** custom function by selecting the cell where you want the result and then entering the function in the formula bar. For example: =Bonus(B4,C4)

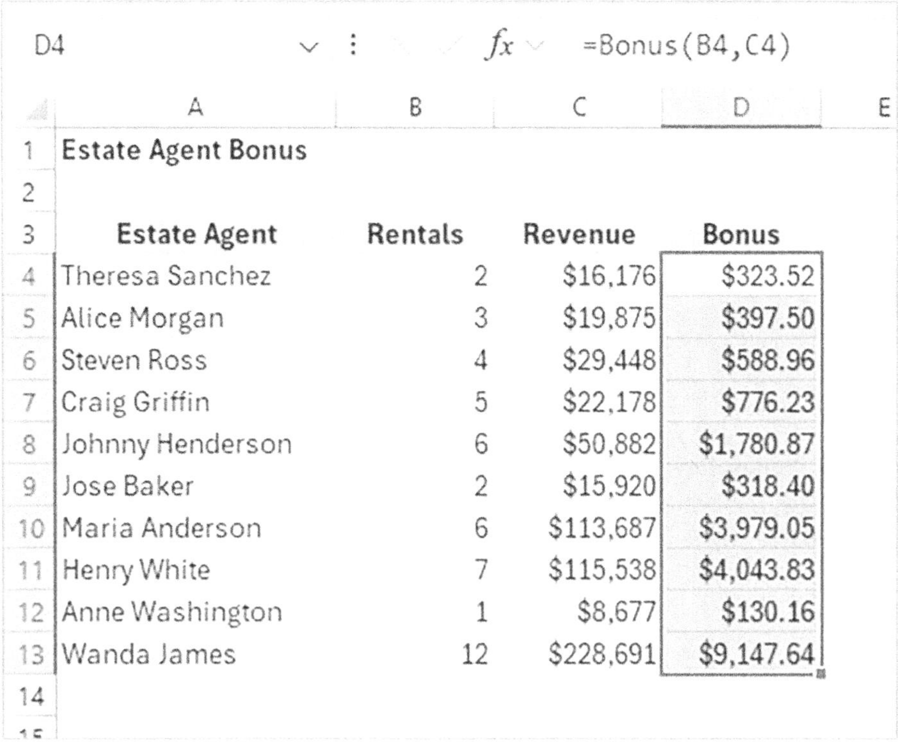

	A	B	C	D
1	Estate Agent Bonus			
2				
3	Estate Agent	Rentals	Revenue	Bonus
4	Theresa Sanchez	2	$16,176	$323.52
5	Alice Morgan	3	$19,875	$397.50
6	Steven Ross	4	$29,448	$588.96
7	Craig Griffin	5	$22,178	$776.23
8	Johnny Henderson	6	$50,882	$1,780.87
9	Jose Baker	2	$15,920	$318.40
10	Maria Anderson	6	$113,687	$3,979.05
11	Henry White	7	$115,538	$4,043.83
12	Anne Washington	1	$8,677	$130.16
13	Wanda James	12	$228,691	$9,147.64

Figure 20-11: The custom function installed by the add-in is available for use like any of the built-in Excel functions.

Your user-defined function is also listed without a prefix under **Insert Function** > **User Defined**.

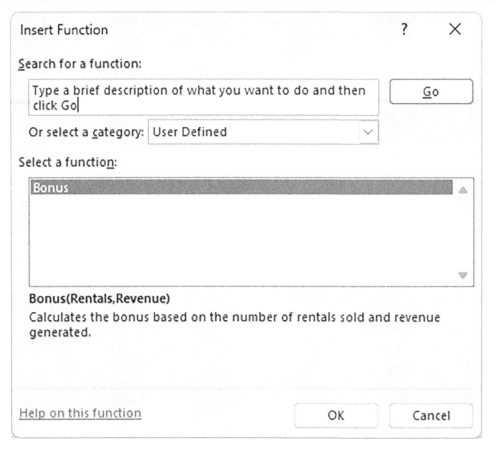

Figure 20-12: The custom function from the add-in can be inserted using the Insert Function dialog box.

More Help

Thank you for buying and reading this book. If you have any questions or comments, please feel free to contact me at support@excelbytes.com.

For more help with Excel VBA, you can visit Microsoft's online help for Excel VBA and search for a topic:

https://learn.microsoft.com/en-us/office/vba/api/overview/excel

Appendix

Code Window General Use Keys

The following keyboard shortcuts are for the Windows operating system. If you are using a Mac, please substitute the Mac equivalent.

Keyboard shortcut	Does this
F1	Shows context-sensitive Help.
F2	Displays the Object Browser.
F5	Runs a procedure or UserForm
F8	Runs code one line at a time.
Shift+F8	Runs code one procedure at a time.
F9	Toggles a breakpoint on or off.

Ctrl+Shift+F9	Clears all breakpoints.
Ctrl+Break	Stops code execution. Use when your application is in an infinite loop.
Home	Moves the cursor to the beginning of a line.
End	Moves the cursor to the end of a line.
Alt+F5	Runs the error handler when an application has halted because of a handled error.
Alt+F8	Steps into the error handler when an application has halted because of a handled error.
Ctrl+J	Displays list of members.
Ctrl+Shift+J	Displays list of constants.
Ctrl+I	Shows Auto Quick Info.
Ctrl+Shift+I	Shows Parameter Info.
Ctrl+Spacebar	Completes Word.

Index

A

A1 reference style, 259
A1 Referencing Style, 260
Absolute reference, 260
absolute references, 36
Activate
 UserForm, 314
Activate event, 225, 234
Activate method, 232
ActiveSheet, 213
ActiveSheet property, 213, 231
ActiveWorkbook, 213, 217
ActiveX Data Object (ADO), 384
Add method
 Named ranges, 273
 Workbook object, 230
 Workbooks collection, 217, 237
AddChart2 method, 439, 443
AddComment method, 205
AddFields method, 460
add-in, 486
add-ins, 483
AddIns collection, 483
Add-ins dialog box, 486, 489
Address property, 264
ADO object library, 389
ADO object model, 387

AfterUpdate event, 319
Application object, 198, 200, 212
arithmetic operators, 108
Array function, 121, 135, 136, 461
Arrays, 124
Assign Macro, 49
Assign Macro dialog box, 48
Auto Data Tips, 85
Auto Indent, 85
Auto List Members, 84, 210
Auto Quick Info, 84
Auto Syntax Check, 84
AutoFill feature, 266
AutoFill method, 266
AutoFit method, 204, 258

B

BackColor property, 285
BeforeClose event, 226, 484
BeforePrint event, 226
BETWEEN operator, 419
BOF property, 405, 414
Bookmarks, 78
Break mode, 165
Breakpoint, 166
Button control, 360

Index

C

Calculate event, 235
Call keyword, 141
Call Stack, 179, 180
Camel case, 95
Cancel property
    CommandButton, 313
Caption property, 285
    UserForm, 331
CCur, 121
Cells property, 242, 253
Change event, 235
Chart object, 444
ChartObjects collection, 444
Class modules, 64
Clear method, 204, 423
Close method
    Workbook object, 219
CloseMode argument, 315
Clustered Column chart, 442
Code Colors, 86
Code window, 62, 67, 84
Code windows, 71
Columns property, 242
combo box, 367
ComboBox control, 304
CommandBars object, 356
CommandButton control, 303
Comment Block, 82
Comments
    Code window, 81
Comparison operators, 109
Connection object, 391, 392
ConnectionString, 392, 393
Const statement, 106
Constants, 106, 107
ControlSource
    Frame, 308
    ListBox, 307
CopyFromRecordset method, 395
Count property, 238
CountA, 335
CountBlank, 213
CreatePivotTable method, 458, 459, 469
CSV files, 347
CurDir, 121
Currency number format, 253
Currency style, 258
CurrentRegion property, 245

CursorType constants, 400
CursorType property, 400
custom function, 486
custom functions, 473
custom group
    ribbon, 44
Customize dialog box, 89

D

Data consumers, 386
data types, 93
Data validation, 341
Date data type, 105
Date function, 121
DateAdd, 121
DateDiff, 121
DateSerial, 121
Day function, 121
Deactivate
    UserForm, 314
Deactivate event, 225, 235
Debug menu, 164
Debug object, 172
Debug toolbar, 89, 164, 169
Debug.Print, 170, 172, 317
Declarations section, 84, 96, 97
Default property
    CommandButton, 313
Delete method
    Worksheets collection, 233
Description property, 188
Developer tab, 28
Dim statement, 96, 103, 104
Direct referencing, 442
DisplayAlerts property, 233
Do...Loop, 152, 406
Do...While, 153
docked window, 88
Docking, 88
Drag-And-Drop Editing, 85
Draw tab, 48
dynamic array, 132
Dynamic Arrays, 263

E

Else clause, 150
ElseIf clause, 150

497

End Function, 73, 143
End Sub, 73
End Sub statement, 139
EOF property, 405, 414
Err object, 188, 191, 423
Err.Clear, 188
Err.Number, 189, 190
Err.Raise, 193
Err.Source, 188, 193
event procedure, 147
Excel Macro-Enabled template, 34
Excel Macro-Enabled Template (*.xltm), 32
Excel object model, 198, 199
Excel Options, 28, 29, 45
ExecuteMso, 357
ExecuteMso method, 225, 356
Exit Do, 153, 154
Exit For, 156
Exit Function statement, 144
Exit Sub statement, 140
Explicit variable declaration, 97

F

Fields collection, 398, 402
File Picker dialog box, 354, 355
FileDialog object, 352, 353, 355
Filter property, 407
Find dialog box, 74
fixed-length string, 105
fixed-size array, 125
Folder Picker dialog box, 352
FolderPicker object, 353
Font property, 285
For Each...Next, 158, 161
For...Each, 160
For...Next, 155, 156, 157
ForeColor property, 285
Form Control, 49
Form controls, 360
Format Cells dialog box, 256, 356
Format Control dialog box
    Form Controls, 51
Format function, 121
Format menu, 295
FormatCurrency, 121
FormatDateTime, 121
FormatPercent, 121
Formula property, 263
Formula2 property, 263

Formula2R1C1 property, 263, 270
Frame control, 309
Full Module View, 71
Function Arguments dialog box, 482
Function keyword, 73
Function procedure, 143
Function procedures, 138, 144

G

general procedures, 138
General tab
    VBA Options, 87
GetOpenFilename, 347
GetOpenFilename method, 346, 348, 349
GetSaveAsFilename method, 350
GoTo statement, 424
Group method, 468, 469

H

Height property, 285

I

Icons, 48
idMso parameter, 356, 357, 358
If statement, 149
If...Then...Else, 149
Immediate window, 170, 171
IN operator, 419
indenting
    Code window, 80
InitialFileName property, 353
Initialize, 314
Initialize event, 316, 411
    UserForm, 315
input box, 277, 278, 279
InputBox function, 118, 119
Insert Chart dialog box, 431, 433
Insert Function dialog, 481
Insert Function dialog box, 480
Insert Functions dialog box, 145
InStr, 121
IntelliSense, 84, 159, 211, 282
IsAddin property, 483
IsArray, 121
IsDate, 121
IsEmpty, 122

Index

IsError, 122
IsMissing, 122
IsNull, 122
IsNumeric, 120, 122, 183

K

keyboard shortcuts, 494

L

Label control, 300
LBound, 122, 127
LCase, 122
Left, 122
Len, 122
LIKE operator, 419
line-continuation character, 82
list box, 363
ListBox control, 306
ListIndex property
    ComboBox, 316
ListStyle
    ListBox, 307
Local Variables, 102
Locals window, 174
LockType constants, 401
LockType property, 401
Logic errors, 164
Logical operators, 109
LTrim, 122

M

Macro dialog box, 40
macro recorder, 35, 36, 37, 39
Macro Recorder, 436, 457
Macro security, 52
Macro Security, 51
Macro Settings, 52, 53
macro-enabled template, 31
Macro-Enabled Workbook, 30, 43
Margin Indicator Bar, 166, 168
Microsoft Access, 19, 24, 198, 381, 382, 387, 393, 396, 397, 399, 411, 417, 421, 423, 452
Mid, 122
modules
    Renaming, 65
Modules, 64

Month
    function, 122
MonthName function, 238
Move, 403, 404
Move method
    Worksheets collection, 232
MoveFirst, 403, 404
MoveLast, 403, 404
MoveNext, 403, 404
MovePrevious, 403, 404
MsgBox function, 112, 113, 115
MsoChartElementType, 445, 446
MSOLEDBSQL, 427
MultiSelect
    ListBox, 307

N

Name box, 360
Name object, 273, 274
Name property, 461
    Recordset object, 398
    UserForm, 284
    UserForm control, 292
    Worksheet, 231
Named ranges, 271
Names collection, 273, 274
Naming conventions, 95
Naming Rules, 94
New keyword, 394
NewSheet event, 227
Now
    function, 122
NullString property, 466
NumberFormat property, 253, 256

O

Object box, 69, 318
Object Browser, 77, 197, 208, 209, 210
ODBC, 381
Office Scripts, 20
Offset, 248, 253
Offset property, 246, 247
OLE DB, 381, 385, 387
On Error GoTo, 191
On Error Resume Next, 190
On Error statement, 184, 423, 424
Open dialog, 346

499

Open event, 223
Open method, 394
    Connection object, 393
operators, 108
Option Base 1, 127
option button, 374
Option Explicit, 84, 97, 99
OptionButton, 308
OptionButton control, 307
OptionButton controls, 311
Options dialog box, 83
ORDER BY clause, 420
Orientation property, 461

P

Pascal case, 95
Path property, 219
PathSeparator property, 219
Personal Macro Workbook, 30, 31, 32, 38, 473
PERSONAL.XLSB, 30, 31, 32, 38, 41, 42, 45, 47, 50, 63, 64, 72, 473, 486
Pictures, 48
PivotCache, 458
PivotCache object, 458
PivotTable, 452, 453, 455, 464, 465
PivotTable object, 460
PivotTable Styles, 464
Position property, 461
Preserve keyword, 133
Print statement, 171
Private statement, 103
Procedure box, 70, 318
Procedure Separator, 85
Procedure View, 71
Project Explorer, 62, 63, 64
Project Explorer window, 63
Properties window, 62, 283, 284, 291
Protection tab, 487
Provider, 392
Public keyword, 107
Public statement, 103, 107
Public variables, 103

Q

QueryClose
    UserForm, 314
QueryClose event, 315

Quick Access Toolbar, 47, 325, 326

R

R1C1 reference style, 259
R1C1 referencing style, 261, 262, 263
Raise method, 191, 193
Range object, 201, 241, 255
Range property, 243
Recommended Charts, 431
Record Macro button, 35
Recordset object, 389, 394, 402, 403
ReDim statement, 132, 133
References dialog box, 197
relative reference, 36
Relative reference, 259
Relative References, 37
Replace
    function, 122
Replace dialog box, 76
Require Variable Declaration, 84, 99
Resize, 248, 253
Resize property, 247
Resume Next, 186, 188
Resume statement, 185, 186, 187
Right
    function, 122
Rows property, 242, 253
RowSource
    ListBox, 307
RowSource property
    ComboBox, 305
    ListBox, 306
RTrim, 122
Run Sub/UserForm, 74
Runtime errors, 163, 182

S

Save method, 484
SaveAs dialog box, 351
SaveAs method, 218
SaveCopyAs, 218
Scope of Variables, 102
Select Case, 151, 476
SELECT statement, 417, 421
Selection property, 213, 244
Set statement, 217, 392
Set statements, 394

Index

SetElement method, 445, 446, 447
SetSourceData method, 443
Shape object., 439
Shapes, 48
Show method, 338
    FileDialog, 352, 353
    UserForm, 281
ShowModal property, 282
Source property, 188
Spin Button control, 370
Split
    Code window, 70
    function, 123
SQL (Structured Query Language), 416
SQL Server, 19, 24, 381, 382, 387, 392, 417, 425, 426, 427
SQL Server Express, 383
Standard modules, 64
Standard Security, 425
Standard toolbar, 61, 89
Static statement, 104
static variables, 104
Step Into, 169, 170
Step Out, 169
Step Over, 169
Stop statement, 166, 168
String
    function, 123
string variables, 105
Style property, 258
Sub keyword, 73, 139
Sub procedure, 139, 141
Sub procedures, 72, 138
Subtotals property, 465
Syntax errors, 163

T

Tab Order, 297
Tab Width, 85
TabIndex property, 298
TabStop property, 298
Terminate
    UserForm, 314
Terminate event, 412
TextBox control, 302
ThisWorkbook, 64, 213
ThisWorkbook object, 223, 224
ThisWorkbook property, 217
three-dimensional array, 131

Timer
    function, 123
TimeSerial
    function, 123
To keyword, 155
toolbox, 288
Toolbox, 286
Trim, 122
Trust Center, 52, 53, 54
Trusted Connection, 425
trusted location, 56
Trusted Locations, 54, 55
two-dimensional array, 129, 130
TypeName
    function, 123
TypeName function, 244
TypeScript, 20

U

UBound, 123, 127
UCase, 123
UDF, 473
undock a window, 88
Unload statement, 282, 336
Use Relative References, 36
user-defined function, 472
UserForm, 277, 280, 281, 310, 329, 408
UserForm toolbar, 89
UserForm_Initialize, 336
UserForms, 24, 64

V

Value, 307
Value property, 262
variable-length string, 105
Variables, 93
    Explicit declaration, 96
    Implicit declaration, 96
Variant data type, 96
vbCrLf, 118
vbNewLine, 118
Visual Basic Editor, 41, 60, 61, 65

W

watch expression, 179
Watch expression, 176

Watch Expression, 176
Watch window, 175
Weekday
    function, 123
WHERE clause, 418, 421
Width property, 285
WindowActivate event, 225
With statement, 202, 206, 293
Workbook object, 216
Workbook_Open event, 224
Workbooks collection, 216
WorksheetFunction, 204, 335
WorksheetFunction property, 212

Worksheets collection, 231

X

xlColumnField, 461
xlDataField, 461
xlSum, 461

Y

Year
    function, 123

About the Author

Nathan George is a computer science graduate with several years of experience in the IT services industry in different roles, which included Excel VBA programming, Access development, Excel training, and providing end-user support to Excel power users. One of his main interests is using computers to automate tasks and increase productivity. As an author, he has written several technical and non-technical books.

Leave a Review

If you found this book helpful, I would be very grateful if you can spend just 5 minutes leaving a customer review. You can go to the link below to leave a customer review.

https://www.excelbytes.com/excel-vba-review/

Thank you very much!

Other Books by Author

Take Your Excel Skills to the Next Level!

Mastering Excel 365 is your all-in-one guide to Excel. This guide contains everything you need to know to master the basics of Excel for Microsoft 365 and a selection of advanced topics relevant to real-world productivity tasks.

This guide has been designed as a resource for you whether you're an Excel beginner or a power user. You will learn how to use specific features and in what context to use them.

Available at Amazon:

https://www.amazon.com/dp/1915476119

Visit our website for more:

https://www.excelbytes.com/excel-books

Mastering Access 365

An Easy Guide to Building Efficient Databases for Managing Your Data

Has your data become too large and complex for Excel?

If so, then Access may just be the tool you need. Whether you're new to Access or looking to refresh your skills on this popular database application, you'll find everything you need to create efficient and flexible database solutions for your data in this book.

Mastering Access 365 offers straightforward step-by-step explanations using real-world examples.

This book comes with downloadable sample databases for hands-on learning.

For more info visit:

https://www.excelbytes.com/access-book/